D1492031

The publishers wish to thank the following for their assistance:

MAKE-UP SECTION
Linda Meredith School of Make-up
60, Church Road, Leyton, London, E10

Cosmetics:
Yves St Laurent
Florrie Roberts
Fashion Fair Cosmetics
Redken
Jerome Alexander
Stagelight
Charles of The Ritz
Clinique
Elizabeth Arden

Accessories, clothes etc:
Alexandre de Paris (make-up brushes)
Liberated Lady
Quasimodo Ltd
Pineapple Dance Studio
Hat Shop, Covent Garden

HAIR CARE SECTION
Hair artists:
Pat Spires and Trevor Walker of Sizzerin Hot

Make-up:
Kim Walker

Hair care products:
Wella Great Britain

Baby care products:
Boots Ltd

Wigs and electrical equipment:
The House of Carmen

Hair ornaments:
Madesils, London
Morris Masterclass International, London

Clothes design:
Kate Anthony – long, white silk jacket
Penny Warner – black jacket with check collar
Sarah Windsor – blue and white spotted sweater
Fred Spur of Whispers in the Ear – white crushed silk top with collar
No? Yes! – premier coat in pink

SKIN CARE SECTION
Garments supplied by:
Benetton
'Next' Clothes
Laura Ashley
Fenwicks
Dickins and Jones

Jewellery supplied by:
Adrien Mann
Dickins and Jones

Photography by Peter Barry and Peter Pugh-Cook
Designed by Philip Clucas
Produced by Ted Smart and David Gibbon

CLB 1516
Published in Great Britain 1985 by Colour Library Books Ltd.

Guildford, Surrey, England.
Display and text filmsetting by Acesetters Ltd.
Printed and bound by AGSA in Barcelona, Spain.

ISBN 0 86283 392 2
Dep. Leg. B-32.693-85

THE COMPLETE BEAUTY BOOK

Make-Up by Linda Meredith
pages 4 -128
Skin Care by Celia Hunter
pages 132- 256
Hair Care by Pat Spires
pages 260-384

COLOUR LIBRARY BOOKS

Make-Up Contents

Introduction
page 6

Cosmetics and Textures
pages 8-27

Tools of the Trade
pages 28-35

Preparation of the Skin
pages 36-43

Day Make-Up
pages 44-59

Evening Make-Up
pages 60-73

Colour in Make-Up
pages 74-85

Disco and Elaborate Evening
pages 86-93

Fashion Make-Up
pages 94-101

Model Make-Up
pages 102-111

Make-Up for Coloured Skin
pages 112-119

Questions and Answers
pages 120-128

Introduction

Many different looks are achieved through skilled use of make-up and clever, informed choice of the many cosmetics and textures available to us today.

The aim of this book is to take the 'science' out of the 'art' of make-up, because it is an area that has become unnecessarily complicated. The book teaches you the valuable basic make-up skills in a logical, step-by-step way and explains the reasons behind the methods. The techniques, colour application and choice of cosmetics described within are straightforward, professional and effective. There is simply no need to complicate them. You will find that some of the techniques go against what is generally accepted in the make-up world. This is because these new ideas have been tried and tested and found to be simpler and, in many cases, more effective than the established ones.

Once you have mastered the basic skills of make-up you can have the fun of experimenting with new ideas, or simply perfecting the style which you feel is right for you. In either case this book provides the solid groundwork necessary, and there are plenty of photographs and tips throughout to spark the imagination.

Cosmetics and Textures

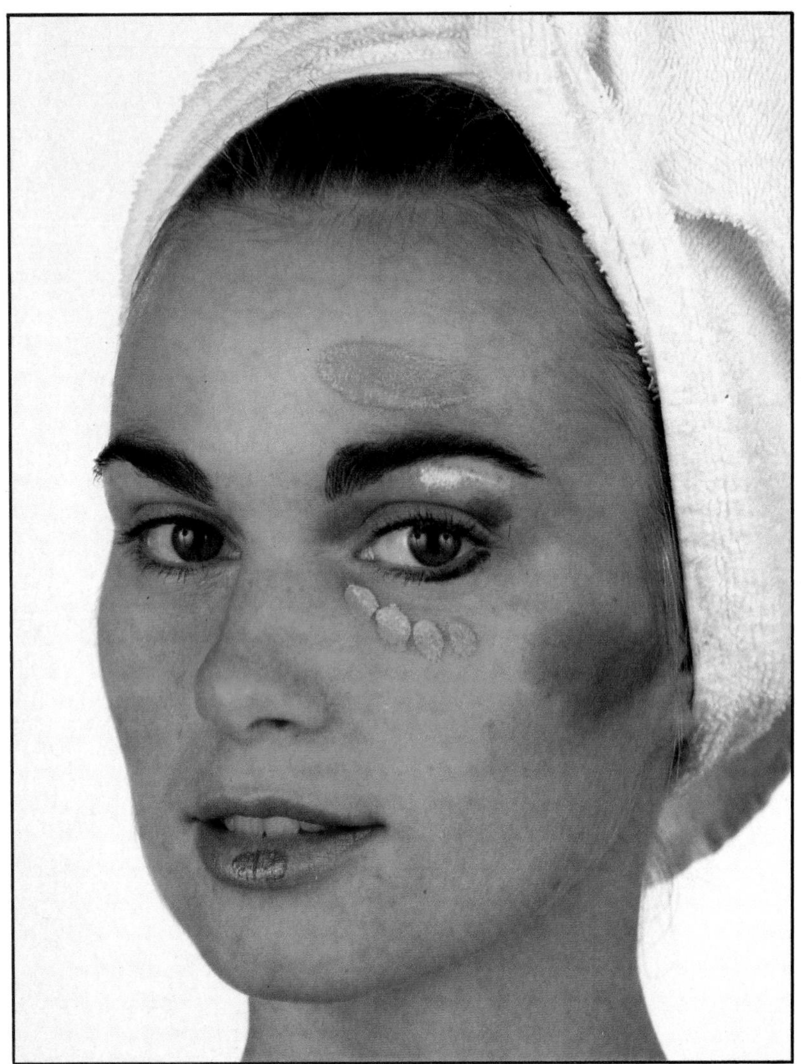

(Above) showing some of the many different cosmetics available. Shown are lipstick, foundation, blusher, contour, highlighter (on brow) and eye shadows.

Each cosmetic item (i.e. foundation, face powder, blusher, eye shadow, etc.) offers a choice of textures which could include liquid, cream, block, gel, powder, cream powder and so on. These textures dictate the end result of a make-up. And to highlight the dramatic effect that changes in the formulations of textures have on the finished 'product' we can draw a parallel between two identical make-ups. Look at the photograph of the heavily pan-sticked, dark-eyed ghost face of the sixties and compare it to the modern equivalent. The same dark-eyed, pale-faced look is there, but because of refined textures of cosmetics the result is altogether softer, more subtle and feminine.

Today there is a bewildering choice of cosmetics and textures, and this chapter identifies the different types and explains the purpose and effect of each. You will then be able confidently to select the right combination of products for yourself.

Foundation This is used to give the skin an even tone. To 'neutralise' red cheeks, broken veins and freckles. It is essential on the majority of skins if make-up is to look really effective.

Foundation also provides the base for all other make-up. It makes their application easier and provides a surface to which they can adhere.

Never think in terms of colour with foundation but in terms of Light, Medium and Dark. Remember, its main purpose is to even out natural skin tone and *not* to change the colour of the skin.

Textures Foundation is available in either liquid, cream or solid form. The majority of these are oil-based, ideally for use on dry, normal or combination skin, but they are also used extensively on oily skin. Water-based foundations are specifically for oily skins but have only relatively recently become available.

Liquids are the 'finest' and therefore 'lightest' of the three textures. They allow the normal skin tone to glow through and so give a smooth but natural look. Concealers can be used underneath to hide blemishes, dark circles under the eyes, etc. Liquid foundation should always be used for a day make-up unless your skin has a problem with widespread blemishes which dictate the need for extra cover. In which case...

Creams are 'heavier' than liquids and so

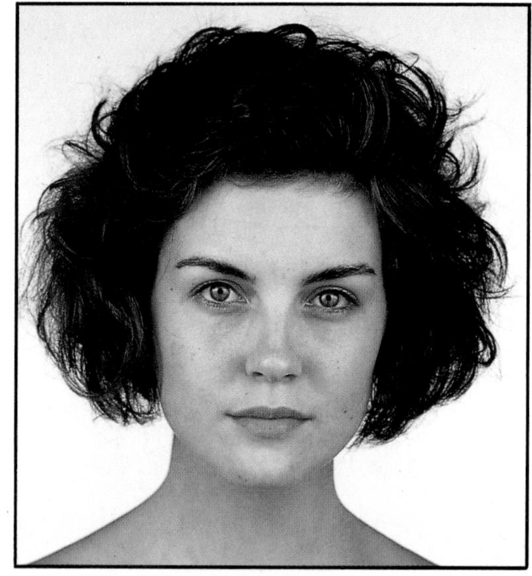

Even at a distance quite mild imperfections ruin the even skin tone effect essential to a perfect make-up look (right)

for 'normal' make-up as it is excessively heavy and obvious; it is therefore not mentioned again in this book.

'Tools' you need. Dot liquid and cream foundation with an eye shadow shading brush and blend with a sponge.

Tinted Gels and Tinted Moisturisers These are not classed as foundations as they do not give any coverage. However, they are acceptable as a base for make-up if used on a fairly even skin tone. They can be successful in giving skin a healthy glow or a tanned look. Loose or Block Powder can be applied on top.

'Tools' you need. Apply with fingers.

Face Powder The main purpose of face powder is to 'set' the foundation which would otherwise, within two to three hours, slide off the skin. It also gives staying power to lipstick, and prevents cream blusher and cream eye shadow from creasing. Face powder is the essential finishing touch to all good make-up.

Except for special effect, face powder is not used to add colour to the face. Those powders that are coloured today contain a tint which makes them light in texture, unlike the very heavy powders of yesteryear which contained a pigment.

Translucent powder is the most

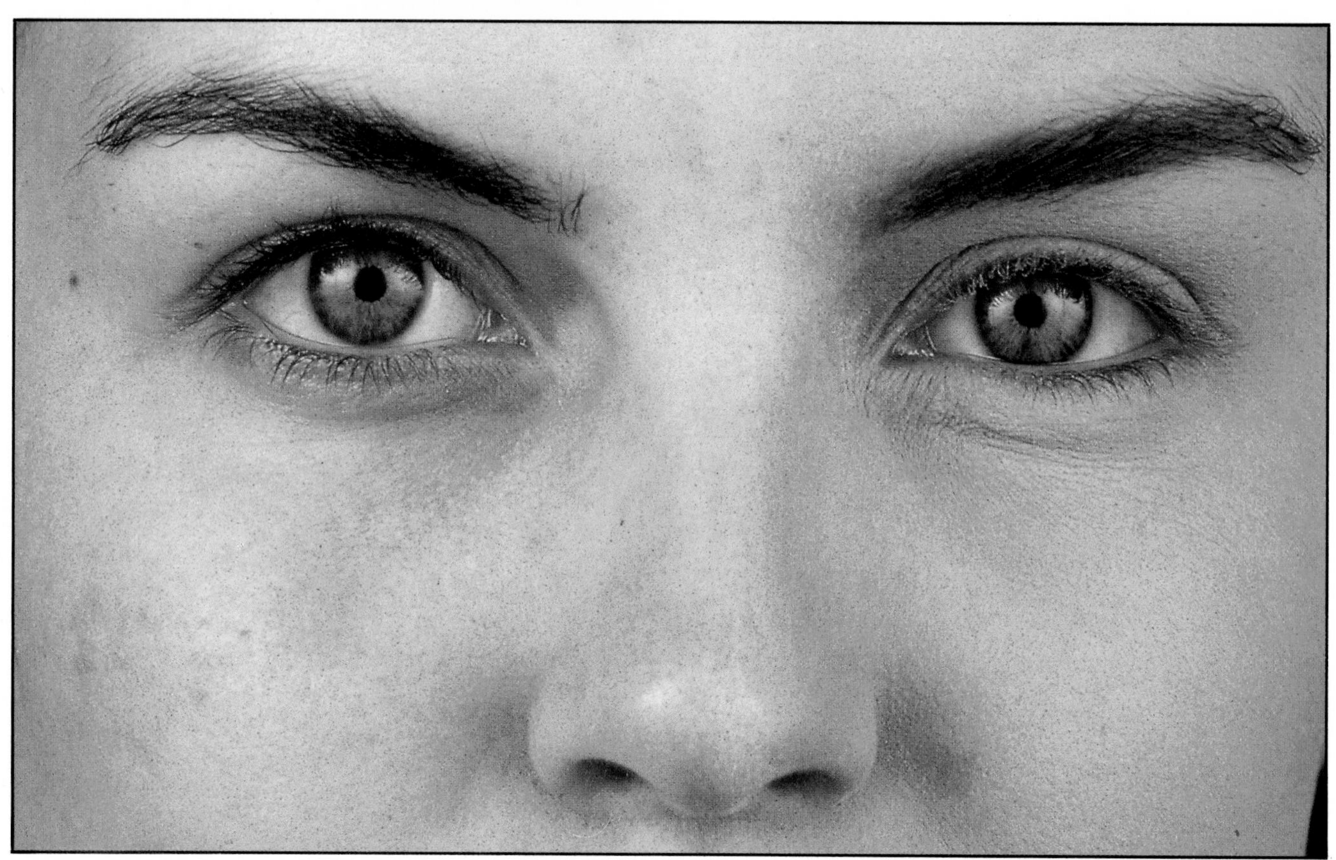

Clever use of foundation, powder (and concealer if necessary) disguises our faults and evens out skin tone for the colour cosmetics to follow.

give extra cover to skin with very obvious problems. No concealer is needed. But because the creams are heavier they are also more noticeable and so you should look to the more subtle forms of concealing before deciding that you need a cream foundation.

Solids create a mask or marble-like effect. Popular in the sixties, today they are only used for dramatic effect in photography, for theatrical purposes and fashion shows. A solid must never be used

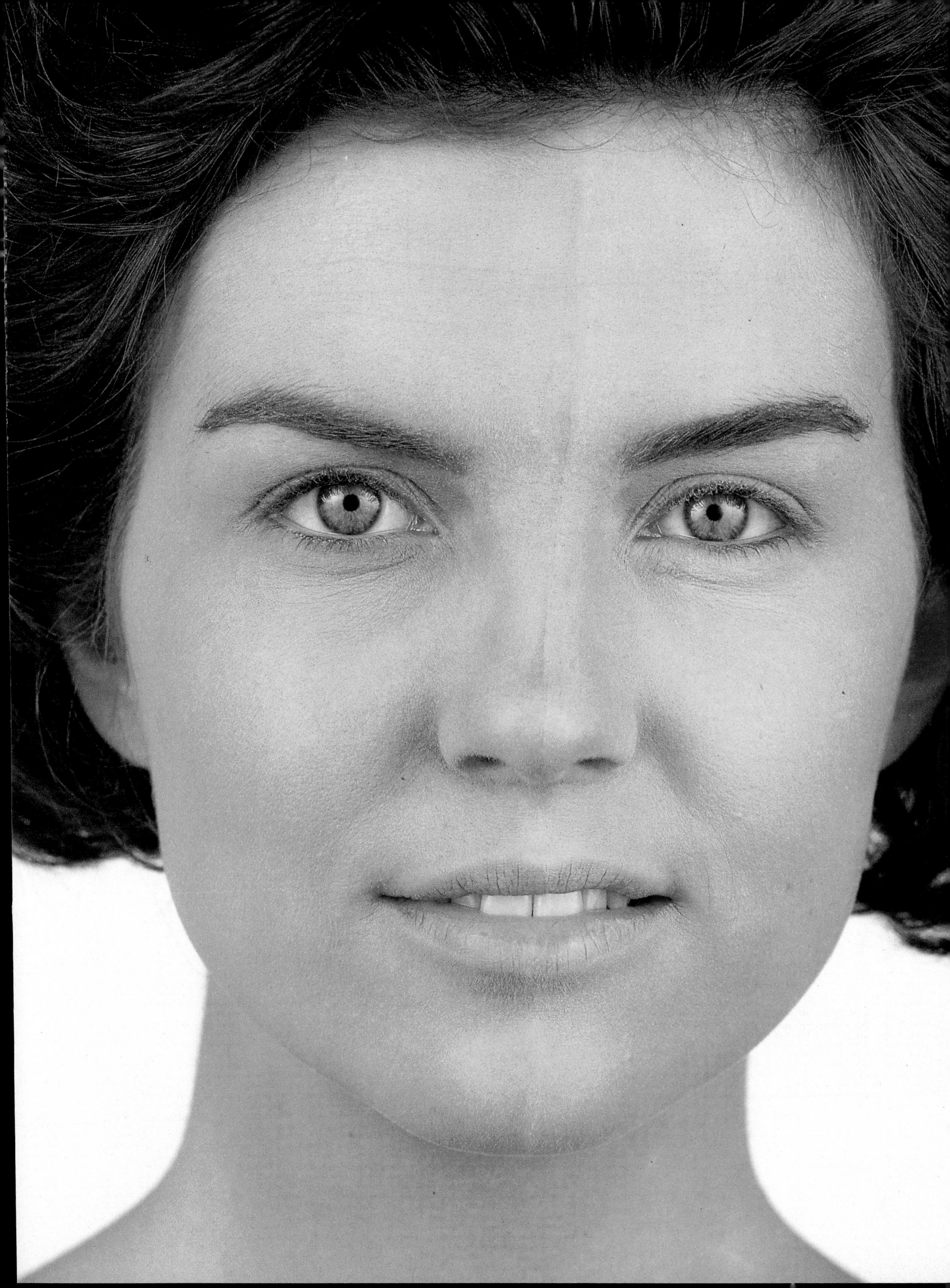

(Below) liquid foundation and block powder give a light, translucent look on older skin. (Opposite) cream foundation and loose powder cover widespread blemishes.

commonly used today. It is usually colourless, although some do carry a hint of colour. In either case 'translucent' means that it allows the natural skin tone to glow through.

Transparent powder is always completely colourless.

Textures Face powder is available in two forms: Loose, which comes in a 'tub' container, and block, which is a compressed form of loose powder and is presented as a solid block.

Block powder is the finest of the two textures and is used to 'set' liquid foundation. Cream foundation is too heavy to be set with block powder.

Many people still think that block is heavier than loose powder. A very simple experiment proves the opposite. Fill a face powder brush with block powder and flick the bristles with your fingers. You will see only a very, very fine dust. If you were to do the same with loose powder its heavier particles would be very obvious! But the ultimate test is in application. Any amount

(Right) a simple flick test proving that block powder is much finer than loose powder. (Opposite page) a perfect finished make-up using the finest cosmetic textures.

Loose powder is also important if you have very oily skin as it can be used on top of liquid foundation to help absorb excess oil. The absorption is helped both by the consistency of the powder and by the method of application, (i.e. you press the powder onto the skin with cotton wool or powder puff).

'Tools' you need. Powder puff and/or cotton wool balls.

Concealers These are necessary to 'blot' out dark shadows under eyes, broken veins, high cheek colour and simple spots and blemishes. They are generally applied before foundation (but remember that cream foundation does its own concealing).

Textures Concealers come in sticks or as thick cream with their own applicators. They are oil-based or water-based; the latter has more staying power.

'Tools' you need. Small brush to apply concealer and dry latex sponge to blend in.

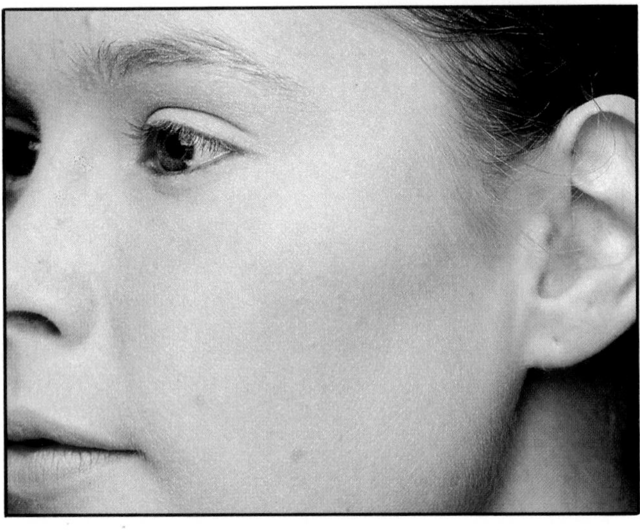

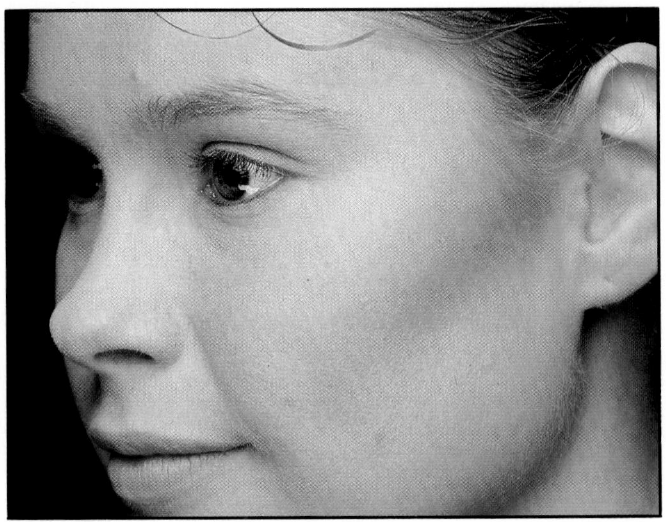

(Above) indicating correct position for blusher and (above right) finished blusher application, showing it to be one of the most flattering of the colour cosmetics. It accentuates the cheekbones and adds colour and warmth to the skin.

of block powder can be applied to a face without it being apparent. Too much loose powder will very quickly look heavy and unnatural.

So, the combination of block powder and liquid foundation creates the smoothest, most natural look and should be used whenever possible in daytime make-up.

'Tools' you need. Face powder brush for dusting powder over face. Do not use the flat powder puff which is usually supplied with blocks as this makes application too heavy.

Loose powder is heavier in texture than block and can be more obvious on the skin. But it is essential to use loose powder over cream foundation. This is because the thicker consistency of the cream texture needs the extra setting power of loose powder.

Blusher This is the first of the colour cosmetics that you apply to your face and one of the most flattering. Its main purpose is to accentuate the cheek bones and to add colour and warmth to the skin. Cleverly and selectively dotted around the face it gives the impression of a soft healthy glow, an effect which benefits all ages.

Blushers come in a great variety of colours and shades. In day make-up they cancel out the need for contours and highlighters.

Textures There is a wide choice of tetures: Solid Cream; Liquid Cream; Gels; Sticks and Pencils and Powder. The most popular and easy to apply is powder blusher. This is

mainly because of the form of application. The blusher brush is specially shaped to help you apply the colour to the correct cheekbone area; it helps you avoid too heavy an application as it gives only a fine dusting; and it is the perfect 'tool' with which to blend the blusher down the cheekbone. All other blushers are applied direct from their applicators or by fingertip. These methods give less control over shape, are likely to deliver too high a density of colour, and make blending less efficient.

'Tools' you need. Blusher brush.

No matter what your age, skin type, or skin problem, the range of cosmetics and their various textures make it possible for us all to present a more positive and 'colourful' face to the world.

Eyebrow Colour To add colour to the eyebrows.

Textures Eyebrow colours are either in the form of a pencil or a powder. Eye shadow colours can also be used on the eyebrows, (although eyeliner pencils are softer than eyebrow pencils and so do not apply colour as effectively). It is easier to achieve a soft natural effect with powder but hard pencil lines can be softened quite easily, and this technique is explained elsewhere in this book.

'Tools' you need. A short, stiff nylon brush (eyebrow brush) with which to apply powder or to soften hard pencil lines.

Eye Shadows These give colour, definition and shape to the eyes.

Textures Cream powder, as it's name suggests, is a combination of cream and powder. It is the most commonly used form of eye shadow. Presented as a powder it has a creamy texture and gives the staying power of cream with the soft look of powder.

'Tools' you need. An angled eye shadow brush.

Loose powder has become increasingly popular and, unlike loose face powder, it blends very finely onto the skin, (and is, in fact, the finest textured of all eye shadows). It is only available in frosted colours, some of which are very vibrant and therefore effective for a special evening occasion. The neutral colours are ideal as a base for day make-up if finely blended over the entire eye area.

'Tools' you need. A sponge-tipped applicator.

(Opposite page) the textures of today's cosmetics allow much easier and more comfortable application of make-up. This makes the morning routine a much less harassed affair!

(Right) a face beautifully finished with foundation and face powder. Always use the finest textures when possible, for the smoothest and most natural look. This means liquid foundation (only cream if a skin problem is severe or widespread), and 'set' with translucent block powder (but loose powder has to be used to 'set' the heavier cream foundation).

(Right) eyeshadow and eyeliner pencils have a cream powder texture and their staying power is therefore good. To keep a good point for eyelining, sharpen as an ordinary pencil and pop in the fridge for 15-20 minutes. But allow to return to normal before applying to eyes.

Block powder, unlike its face powder counterpart, tends to have a concentrated look on the skin. It can also appear dry and flaky on the eyelid and has no real staying power.

'Tools' you need. An angled eye shadow brush.

Cream shadow lasts all day but easily creases and must always be 'set' with face powder.

'Tools' you need. A sponge-tipped applicator.

Eye shadow wands come with their own sponge tipped applicator and are available in cream or powder form.

Eye liner pencils look like ordinary pencils and come in many different colours. Its texture is that of a cream powder

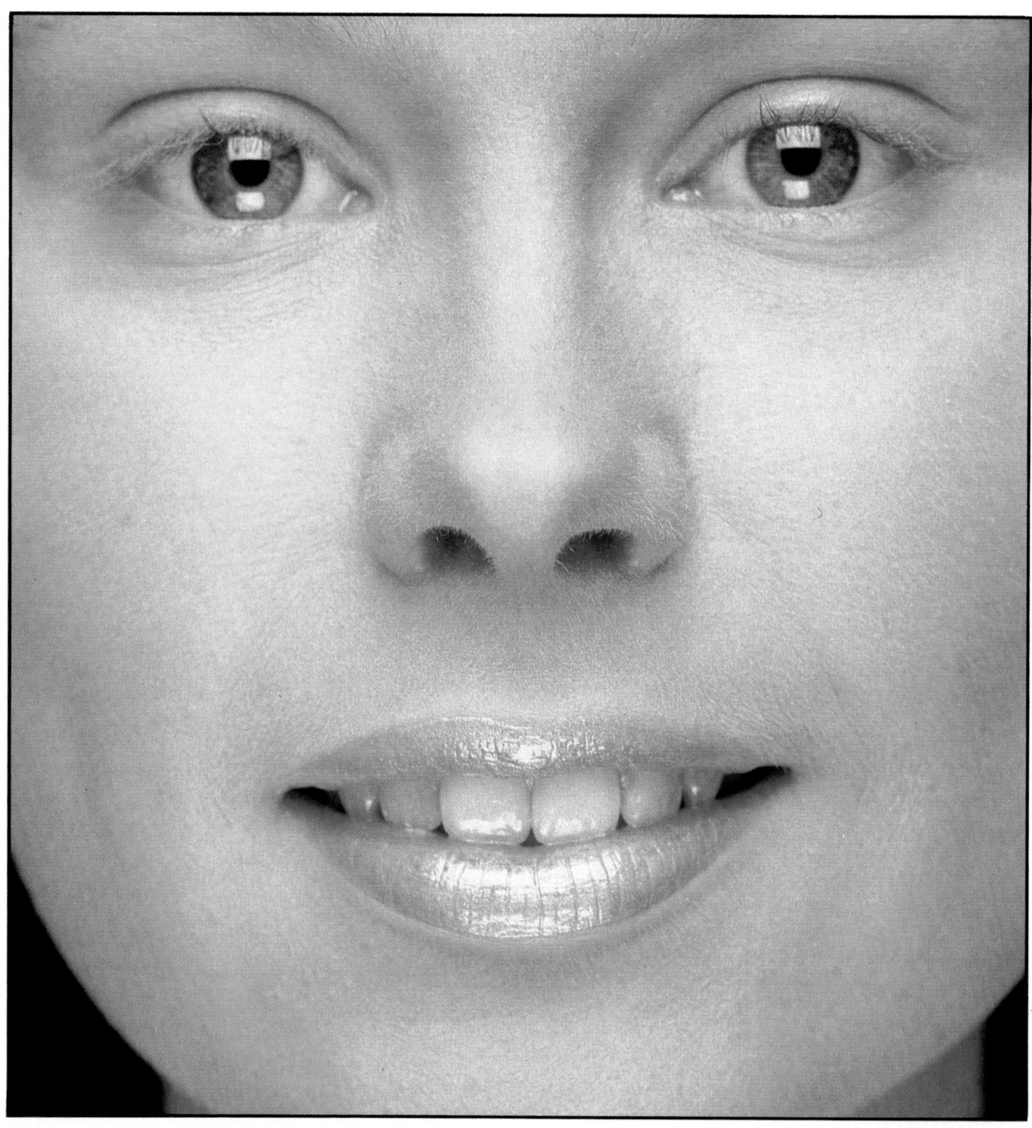

Lipstick, lipstick, everywhere... and plenty to spare! The colour range in lipsticks is marvellous and, combined with the softer textures and choice of the glossy glamour look, the lipstick is possibly the most potent of all cosmetics. Perhaps because of the variety of lipsticks now available it is an area of cosmetics that is frequently misused and abused. The guidelines are quite simple and should keep you on the right track. Your lipstick colour, texture and application should balance the rest of your make-up. Dramatic eyes need dramatic lips; subtle eyeshading needs harmonious lip treatment; be it in colour shade (lighter, darker) or technique, make sure that lips and eyes balance each other out. And don't forget to harmonise lips with clothes. A badly matched lipstick is as obvious as wearing the wrong colour bag or shoes with an outfit.

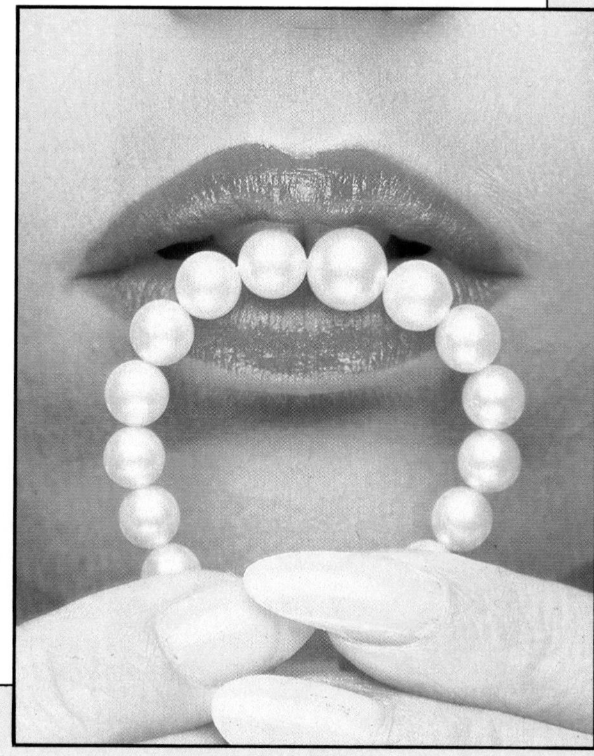

shadow and therefore it has good staying power. Keep a good point on your eyeliner pencil by using an ordinary pencil sharpener, then pop the pencil in the refrigerator for 15 to 20 minutes to harden it. But allow it to return to normal before applying to your lids.

(Above) one of the most flattering of all cosmetics. Those available today include water-proof, those which thicken and even some which lengthen lashes. (Opposite page) choose a coloured mascara to emphasise a colour theme further, or simply as extra interest in your make-up.

Lipstick This is used to balance the made-up face and to emphasise the mouth. In other words, if the eyes are exaggerated the lips should be also (with colour and outline); if the eyes are soft and natural, lipstick colour should follow suit, with subtle outline definition if necessary.

Textures The original lipstick, by Yardley, was called 'Stayfast' and quite literally stayed on for days! Today, lipsticks have a much softer texture and the majority need to be dusted with face powder to help them last a reasonable time. Soft, glossy lipsticks should not be blotted as this removes all colour from the lips. Lip pencils can be used directly on the lips but it is difficult to achieve a clean outline this way. It is much better to take the lipstick off the pencil with a lip brush. Lip gloss is a flattering cosmetic and the finishing touch over lipstick to give a soft, glamorous look. It can be tinted or clear, and can be used on its own to complement very softly made-up eyes.

'Tools' you need. A lip brush and tissues.

Highlighter This is generally used for dramatic effects, although subtle use of highlighter gives a flattering 'lift' to a face. Areas on which highlighter is used are the browbone, top of the cheekbone and the centre of the top lip. The colours are usually white or light cream.

Textures Highlighters are available as either cream or powder. Preference should be given to the one you find easiest to work with.

'Tools' you need. Contour brush.

Shaders and Contours Shaders are always brown, and are used around the face to give a slimming effect where needed, or to make areas recede.

Contours are generally brown but can be substituted with dark blusher shades. They are used under the cheekbone, more dramatically than blushers, to give a hollow look.

Shaders and contours should never be used in soft, natural day make-up. They can be used to great effect for evening make-up and in photographic and fashion make-up. The key to successful application is a *very* light touch.

Textures Available as powder or cream. A good tip for a very natural look is to use two shades of foundation, darker for the natural contours of the cheekbones.

'Tools' you need. Contour brush.

Mascara This is used to emphasise eyes further by adding colour, thickness and sometimes length to lashes. It is most commonly available in a wand with its own brush applicator.

Textures There are waterproof mascaras which are oil-based to repel water. Some mascaras have tiny filaments which add thickness and length to lashes. Others do no more than add colour.

Khol Pencil These are always in dark colours and are used inside the rim of the eye to accentuate the white of the eye for a more dramatic effect. It is an exciting technique for night make-up. However, it should only be used along with a great deal of eye shadow or it will make the eyes appear smaller. Sharpen your Khol pencil in the same way as the eyeliner pencils.

False Eyelashes These are included here as

they can be a very effective and, at times, very necessary 'cosmetic'. There are strip lashes, which are a complete line of lashes; and single lashes which usually means three lashes on a strip together. It is rare to see false lashes work successfully as the usual method of applying them directly onto the eyelid looks very obvious, and invariably precarious!

Foolproof Application Method for Strip Lashes Top lid – draw a very thin line with liquid eyeliner next to the natural lashes. This provides a base for the strip. Use either a pin or cocktail stick and apply a little eyelash glue to this eyeliner line. Hold the false eyelash strip in its centre with a pair of tweezers and apply glue to the rim of the strip. The glue already applied to the eyelid

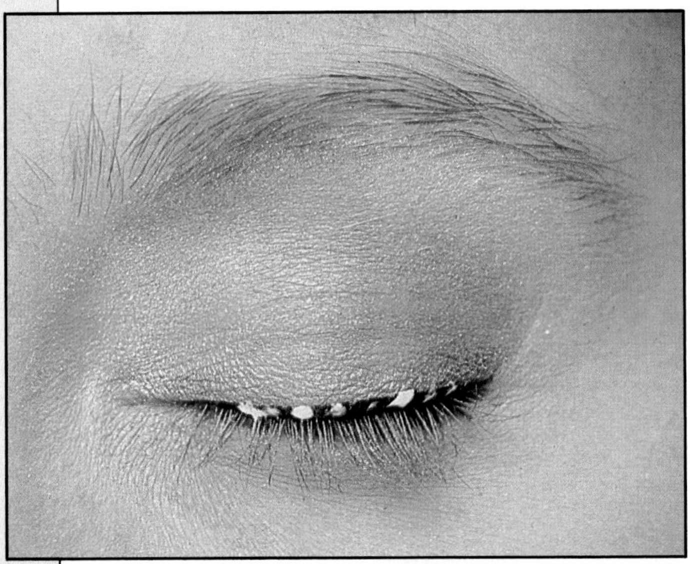

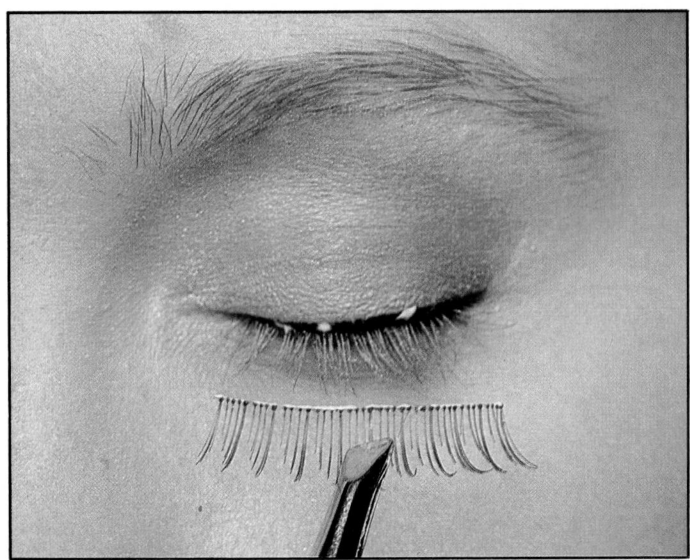

(Above) dots of eyelash glue along the base line of liquid eyeliner are now ready to accept the false eyelash strip. (Above right) eyelash strip held with tweezers and dotted with glue along its rim, ready to be applied to treated line on eyelid. (Right) a little practice will perfect this method and achieve a natural looking but glamorous set of lashes. (Opposite page) single lashes used at the outside corner of the eyes for a filmstar 'sweep'.

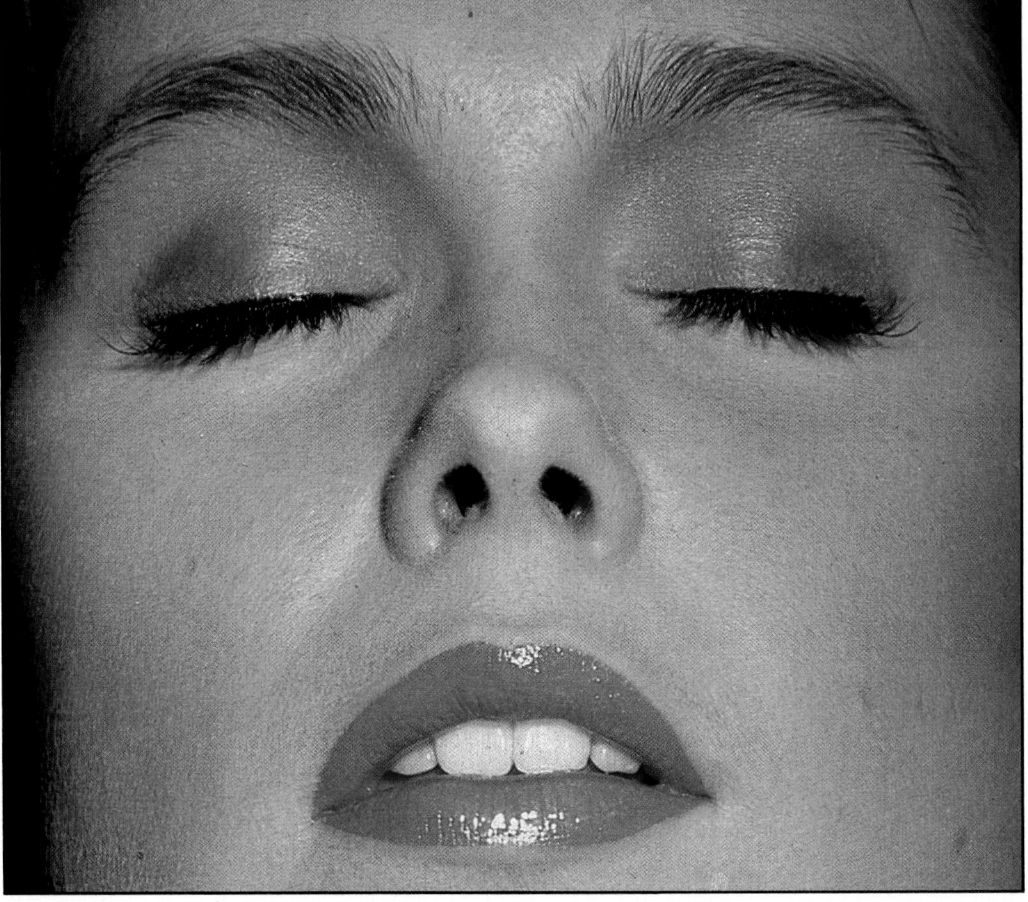

(Right) false eyelashes, properly applied (see page 24), can enhance a good eye make-up and give further versatility to your creativity. They are now available in different lengths and colours. (Far right) false eyelashes create the right 'weight' and texture, and offer contrast to this golden eye-shadow. Cosmetic colours and textures are now so varied that contrasting or toning to fashion fabrics and colours is no longer a problem. (Above) bold, dynamic colours and glossy lipstick make full impact out of the drama of black. (Above right) the serenity of white is enhanced by using softer textures and paler colours in the make-up. (Opposite) the blue hat demands a positive response in make-up. Blue shadow and a sheen on the lips make the right impact.

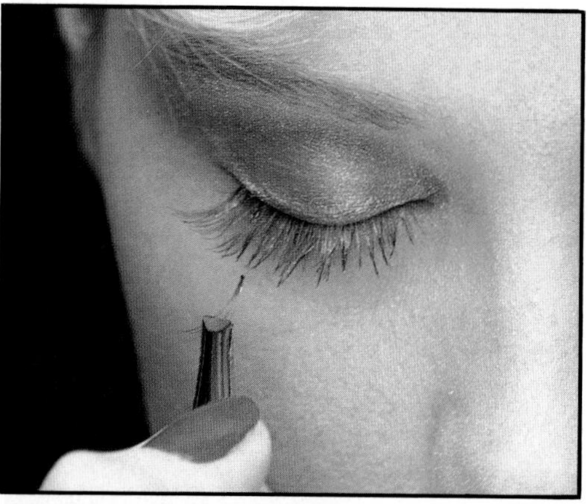

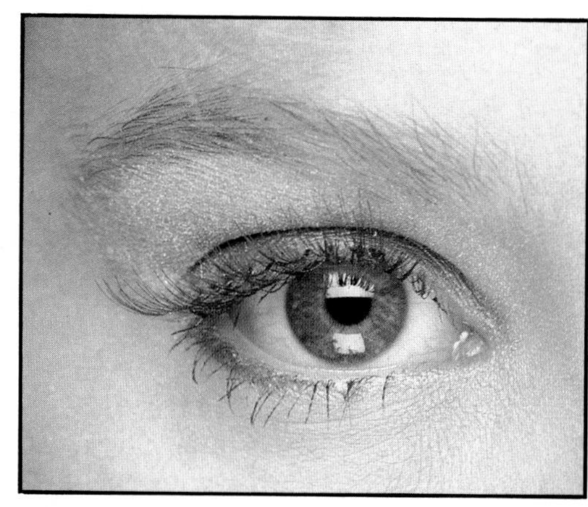

will now be 'tacky' and ready to take the eyelash strip which will stick immediately. So, gently place the strip (still held by tweezers) on to the eyeliner line. Press the centre down first and then the ends.

Bottom lid – requires the same method but the false lashes are placed underneath the natural lashes. Apply glue only to the false lashes and not to the skin. Placing the false lashes underneath the real ones gives a natural hold which keeps them in place.

Single Lashes These are used at the outside corner of the eye on top or bottom lid or both. They are attached to the natural lashes themselves and not to the skin. Hold the single lashes with a pair of tweezers and apply glue over them. Place these on top of the lashes on the top lid and press together.

Apply the false lashes underneath the real ones on the bottom lid.

False eyelashes are applied after all other make-up including mascara. A little practice will prefect this method, which gives a secure and natural-looking result.

CHAPTER 2

Tools of the Trade

(Right) correct pressure is all-important to successful application of make-up. This means a light touch, and use of the proper applicators. (Opposite page) it is worth investing in a set of real hair brushes as these are the most important 'tools' in your make-up kit.

There are many similarities between you and the artist who paints with oils. Before you can begin to work properly you have to be able to identify, understand and know how to use the 'tools of the trade': you must know about textures, what they do and how to apply them and match them for best results, and you must understand about colour, shade and light.

In fact, regard your face as the canvas for a painting. Make-up should lie on the surface of the skin as paint lies on the surface of a canvas. And because of this, the single most important factor in putting make-up on to the skin, is to apply the correct pressure. This means a touch light enough to apply the make-up successfully without encouraging the 'problems' of the skin type (e.g. dry or oily) to show on the surface of the skin. Use of the proper applicators and a full understanding of the capabilities of the different products helps considerably towards achieving the correct result.

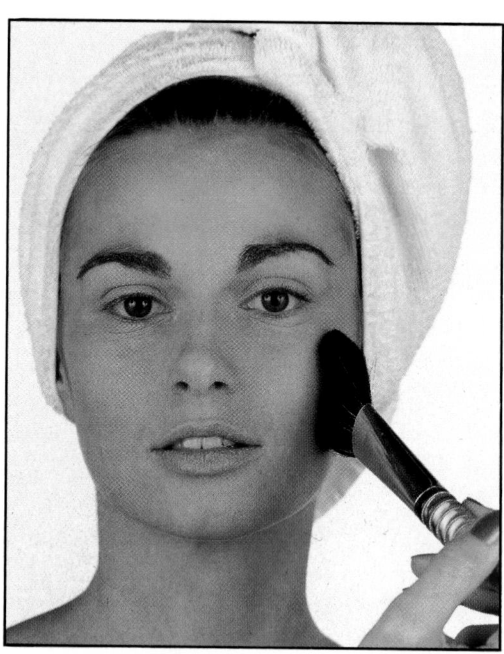

Brushes These constitute the largest and most important section of your make-up 'tool kit'. The type and size that you choose affects the crucial factors of applying correct shape and pressure to the face.

If you can, invest in a set of real hair brushes as, with careful washing, they should never need replacing. Synthetic mixtures cost less but have a relatively short life. Sable has acquired a reputation as the best type of brush, but this has more to do with status than any practicality. In fact, sable is much too soft and pliable for proper application of face powder, blusher or contour. Any other type of real hair will do an excellent job – this could be pony, boar or kid!

The length of handle of a brush affects ease of working and effect of application. Different makes vary from 3" to as much as 10" and more. A sensible and comfortable length is about 5" as this gives a good balance when held in position. Brushes over 6" in length may look impressive but do not do the job effectively. Equally, try to avoid the glamour of elaborate handles. These may look decorative on a dressing table but they become very cumbersome when held for any length of time.

Wash the brushes in mild soap. Rinse thoroughly in clean, warm water and pull bristles through your fingers to bring them tight together, (never leave hair splayed out when wet as this will ruin the shape). Leave to dry naturally. Never use artificial heat as this splits the hairs.

A. Face Powder Brush This is the largest brush as it covers the largest area (the entire face) and is not restricted to defining shape. A shorter haired brush would give a heavier, unacceptable dusting of powder to the skin.

B. Blusher Brush To apply blush powder to the cheekbones.

This looks very similar to the face powder brush but is slightly smaller as it has to work on the confined area of the

ALEXANDRE

(Above) the blusher brush is smaller and more compact than the face powder brush. It has to work within the defined cheekbone area. (Top right) to apply liquid eye-liner, a very thin brush gives precision to a thin, straight line. (Bottom right) have tissues handy for blotting lips, to pat the face after spraying with Evian water (a fresh face), and to blot mascara if necessary. (Right) a dual-purpose eyebrow brush for applying colour to eyebrows, with miniature comb for separating eyelashes after applying mascara. (Opposite) this small-angled eye-shadow brush is a must if shadow is to be applied and blended within the curve of the socket line.

cheekbones. The importance of this slight size difference is demonstrated if you try to apply blusher to the correct area using a face powder brush. You will find it impossible to keep within the defined cheekbone area. If you have difficulty distinguishing between the two brushes you can simply label them.

C. Contour Brush To apply contour powder underneath the cheekbones. Also suitable for applying shaders around the face and for highlighting.

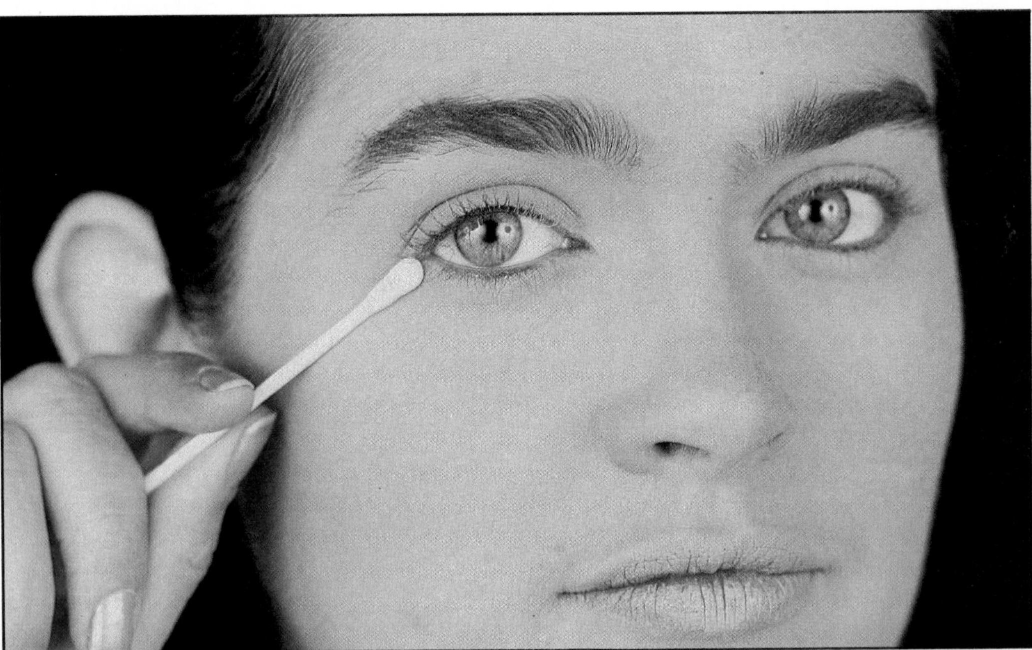

(Right) cotton buds will remove specks of stray make-up cleanly. Press, swivel and remove. (Below) a sponge-tipped applicator is the perfect 'tool' for blending loose and powder eye-shadow.

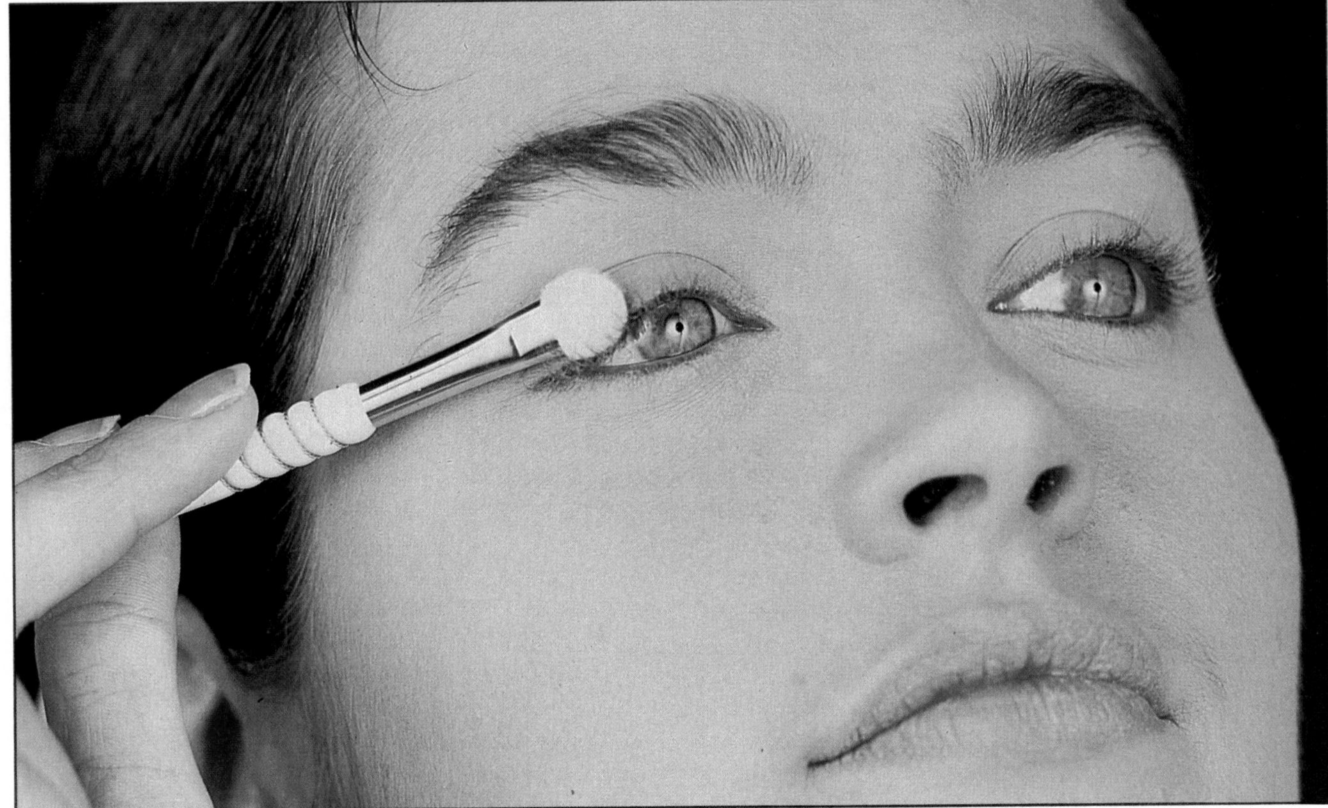

This brush is not good for blusher as it creates too much pressure on the skin. The hair should be very stiff, short and compact to give the required concentration of colour for its main task which is to contour the cheekbones.

D. Eyebrow Brush To apply shape and colour to the eyebrows.

This is like a miniature toothbrush and has short, stiff, nylon bristles. There are those which also have a miniature comb on the other side of the bristle head. This is useful dual-purpose tool as the comb can also be used to separate eyelashes, if necessary, after application of mascara.

E. Eyeliner Brush To apply liquid eyeliner or blend powder/pencil eyeliner along the rim of the eye.

A very thin-haired brush is needed to apply liquid eyeliner finely. A slightly thicker brush is necessary to blend powder or pencil eyeliner.

F. Angled Eye Shadow Brush To apply and blend powder eye shadow.

The angle of this brush is important. It allows you to follow and blend into the socket area quite easily. A straight brush makes it much more difficult to blend into the natural curve of the socket line.

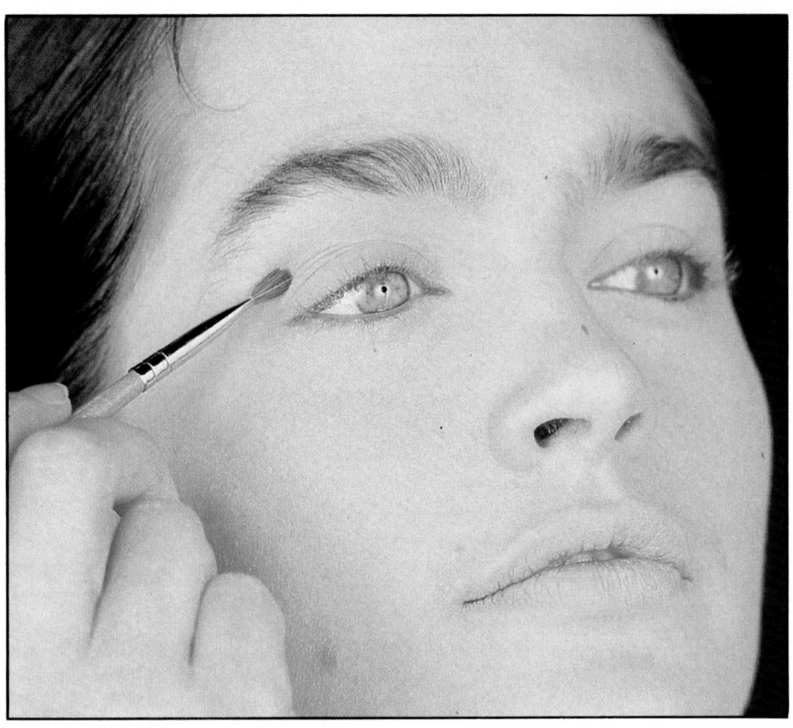

Use an angled eyeliner brush to apply shadow successfully into the hollow of your eye.

G. Fluff Brush To 'finish off' blending of eye make-up.

This is the largest of the eye brushes. It is very soft so that it can be used over the finished eye make-up without disturbing the shapes but giving an overall softer look.

H. Lip Brush To apply lipstick and ensure a 'knife-edge' line to the lips.

The brush must have short, very thin bristles to make it flat. This gives a clean outline to the lips. Cut off any straggly hairs as the brush must be even for smooth application.

Non-brush 'tools' are equally important:

Sponge-tipped Applicator To apply and blend loose and powder eye shadow.

This really is essential as it is the perfect blending 'tool' for loose and powder eye shadow. It is also used to soften the harsh lines of an eyeliner pencil.

To clean, use a mild soap liquid and press sponge gently between finger tips, being careful not to damage the hold of the plastic handle.

Make-up Sponges To blend foundation on the skin.

These come in a variety of shapes and sizes. Natural and synthetic sponges have to be moistened for use, which can cause problems of streaking. It is therefore very difficult to achieve a good result with this method unless you are very experienced.

The ideal make-up sponge is the latex rubber triangle or 'wedge'. This is used dry and therefore makes blending of foundation a relatively easy task for the beginner. Its wedge shape allows access to problem areas such as deep indentations around the nose, corner of the eye or middle of the chin. The 'wedge' has another, and very useful, function, which is a bonus of its rubbery texture. It can be used gently to erase mistakes. It takes off excess colour (e.g. too much blusher), shortens over-long lines around eyes, removes mascara or eye shadow which has fallen onto the cheekbones, and so on. In fact, your 'tool kit' would be sadly lacking without this 'Magic Wand'!

To clean use a mild soap liquid and squeeze gently.

Do not worry if stains remain on the sponge as these will in no way interfere with future application.

Powder Puff (or cotton wool) To apply loose face powder.

Either one of these is necessary to press (stipple) loose face powder onto the skin. The powder is not fine enough to be applied by brush. To clean a powder puff wash in a mild soap liquid (you can even put it in the washing machine!), and do clean it regularly or it will become increasingly difficult to deal with.

Other Useful 'Tools'

Cotton Buds: useful for removing 'stray' specks of make-up in awkward areas, e.g. mascara on top of cheekbones or browbone. Use point of cotton bud to press gently on area, swivel and remove.

Evian Water Spray: to freshen face before make-up.

Tissues: to press lips after lipstick application, and to 'pat' over face to remove excess moisture.

Section Clips: to keep hair away from face (and they cause minimum damage to a hair style).

Eyebrow Tweezers: to 'tidy-up' eyebrows.

Chapter 3

Preparation of the Skin

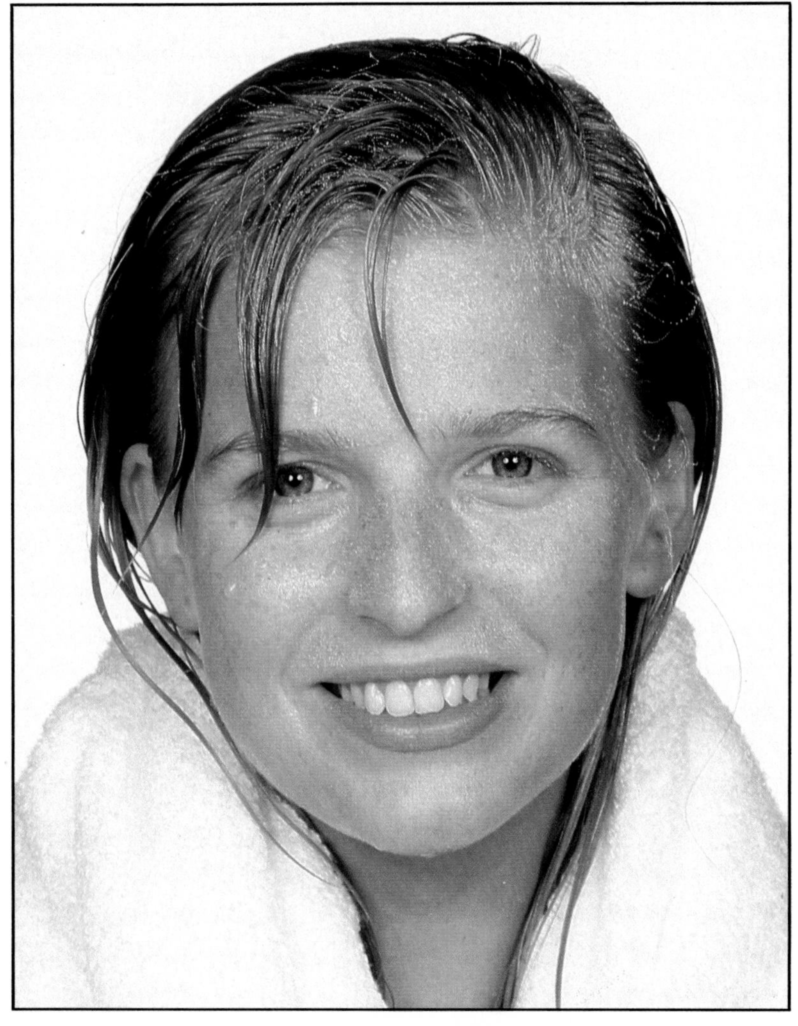

Keep your skin fresh and bright with regular cleansing to tone, and to slough off the dead skin cells which lie on the surface.

Preparation is boring! Yes, for the majority of us it surely is, but without it almost any job takes longer and the end result is usually far from satisfying. Applying cosmetics is no exception to the rule. Good preparation is absolutely essential to a perfect, finished make-up. You first have to create the correct surface to work on, and if this is done properly, even if you have an excessively dry or oily skin problem, this will not show through the finished make-up.

Cleanse, Tone, Moisturise A basic skin care routine of cleanse, tone and moisturise is the on-going preparation which contributes a great deal towards helping your skin look its best at all times. The action itself stimulates the skin and helps slough off the dead skin cells which lie on the surface and which can give your skin an unhealthy, dingy look. Ideally, you should cleanse, tone and moisturise morning and night and always before a make-up.

Regular cleaning helps to keep skin looking fresh and bright and is essential at the end of a day to clean away all the dirt that accumulates on the surface. Cream or lotion cleansers are specially formulated to dissolve make-up from the skin and are therefore very efficient. But soap and water is really just as effective and if this is the only way to make you skin feel fresh and clean, then go ahead. The only compromise that it is wise to suggest is to use a 'soapless' soap or a mild complexion bar. Ordinary soaps may be too highly perfumed or contain too harsh a detergent which will

Preparation of the Skin

(Opposite page) the majority of cleansers do an efficient job, so choose one that you're happy using. Gel cleansers are gentle to sensitive skins.

strip away too much of the skin's natural oils and so cause it to dry out. If you have a greasy or dry skin problem you could ask advice on special formulations from sales assistants; if you are allergy prone you may be wise to stay away from products containing lanolin or perfume.

Toners remove any left-over cleansing lotion and dirt and make you skin feel cool and fresh. Skin tonics or fresheners are the mildest and therefore the best. Astringents contain varying degrees of alcohol and are much harsher to the skin. They remove the skin's natural protective oil and can

Cleanse, tone and moisturise morning and night and always before a make-up.
Choose a skin tonic or freshener as the mildest form of toner. Astringents are harsh to the skin and remove its natural protective oil, so should only be used on very oily skins.

(Right) moisturising is an essential part of the skin care routine. It supports the skin's natural oils in creating a barrier against the damaging dryness of wind, sun and central heating. (Opposite page) spray over lightly moisturised face with Evian mineral water to achieve a fresh and 'neutral' base.

eventually make it dry and coarse. So, only use the latter, if you must, on very rare occasions as described in the 'Problems?' section.

Moisturising is the most important step in the cleanse, tone, moisturise routine. The skin is covered by its own natural moisturiser (a thin layer of oil called sebum) which helps to prevent excessive water loss. Use of a good 'artificial' moisturiser is extremely important as it acts as a further barrier between the skin and external drying elements such as wind, sun and central heating. This therefore doubles the effect of the skin's natural protection in keeping it supple and preventing it becoming too dry and thus more prone to wrinkling. Extra protection in sunshine is essential. Sunscreens which are water-resistant are the most effective, and of the moisturisers the water-in-oil preparations are the best (although they may be too 'oily' to wear under foundation). Ideally, you should use two types of moisturiser. A light consistency for daytime under make-up (this must be light otherwise the make-up will slide), and a heavier one to 'feed' the skin at night. The latter is especially necessary to aid dry skin. Finding the right moisturiser for your skin is a matter of trial and error but once found (and used!) it can make a very positive contribution to the look of your skin.

A Fresh Base Before each make-up cleanse and tone to remove all make-up, surface film and excess oil as these affect application and finish of the make-up. Apply a light moisturiser over your freshly cleaned skin. As this stage you now have a 'neutral' surface and it is important to apply your foundation as quickly as possible for best results. First, however, spray over your moisturised face (fill a fine spray container with Evian mineral water) and blot well with a tissue, so that you have a fresh and 'neutral' base on which to start your make-up.

Problems? If you have skin which is too oily or dry extra steps can be taken to

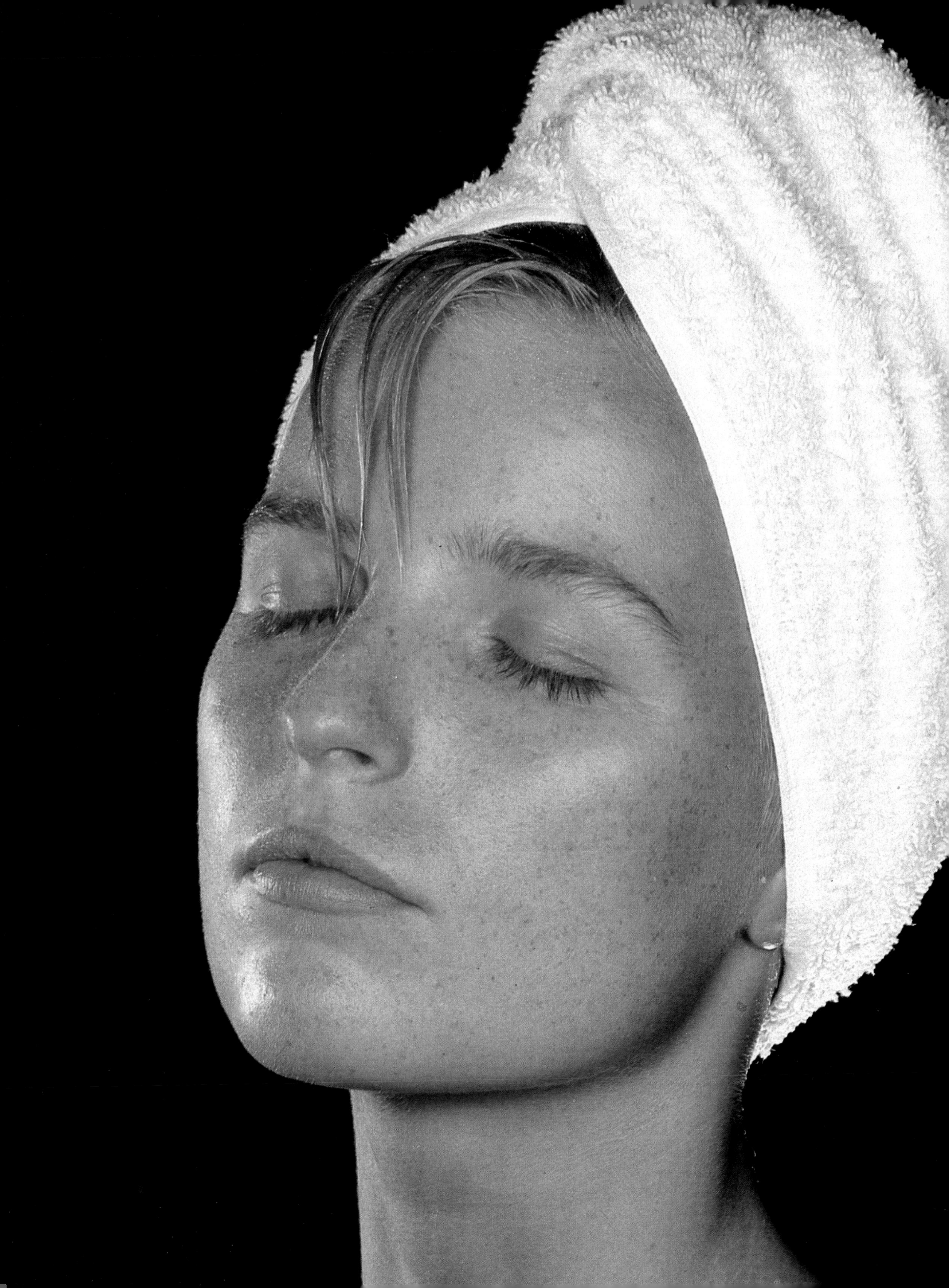

'neutralise' the surface so that these problems will not show through your foundation.

Dry skin is a particular problem as it does tend to show through make-up. Soak cotton wool in a strong (ie., high alcohol content) astringent and rub hard in circular motions all over your face. Any redness that occurs will fade quickly and meanwhile you will have created a smooth surface which will not flake through your finished make-up. However, this 'trick' should only be resorted to for very special occasions as over-use of astringents dries skin even more. Excessively oily skin makes foundation streaky and causes it to slide. The above method is equally successful in coping with this, and there is also a special film made by several cosmetic companies which is used on top of moisturiser as a sealant to stop the oil coming through. Otherwise, excess oil can be absorbed during the day by a light application of loose powder. If you only have slightly oily skin then blot your face with a tissue before using the Evian spray and then tissue off again after spraying.

(Above) to combat excessively oily or dry skin, use astringent to 'neutralise' surface before applying foundation. (Below right) pluck stray eyebrow hairs to ensure smooth blending of eye shadow, and to help towards a final, balanced look.

Whichever technique you use always finish with a spray of Evian over the moisturiser and apply your foundation as quickly as possible while the surface of your skin is still 'neutral'.

Eyebrows Eyebrows must be smooth if your eye shadow is to blend perfectly, so pluck out any stray hairs. Tidy eyebrows also help towards the final balanced look.

CHAPTER 4
Day Make-Up

(Right) a fresh 'neutral' base ready to receive foundation and powder (and concealer where necessary). Perfect the art of applying foundation and powder as they provide the back-drop for the colour cosmetics. (Opposite page) a perfect, finished make-up which can only be achieved if the base of foundation and powder is successfully applied.

In many ways this is the most important chapter of the book, because all other forms of make-up are an extension of the subtle art of achieving a day-time look. The aim is to look as natural as possible in the harsh reality of daylight, and the general rule is that it is better to under- than over-make-up. It is always much easier to add more where needed than to take it away.

Lighting Before you begin it is important to arrange the best lighting possible. Ideally, your face should be lit from every angle so that there are no shadows to distort your judgement. A theatrical mirror (the type surrounded by small light bulbs) in a windowless room is perfect, but the least practical. In fact, any room with artificial light will do, so long as the entire room is lit. Natural daylight is the most difficult to work with as shadows are thrown onto the face, but the problems can be minimised if you sit with your back to the window.

Concealer, Foundation and Powder Having created the correct surface to work on, the next step is to apply your foundation and powder. This is a part of the make-up which has to be perfected. It provides the base for the colour cosmetics (blusher, eye shadow, etc) and if the backdrop isn't right then it is impossible to create a successful make-up.

It really cannot be said often enough that the single most important factor in successful application of make-up is the correct pressure. This means a positive but light touch which does not encourage the skin's problems to show through. This is particularly important in order to get an even finish with foundation, and this is considered elsewhere, but first you have to deal with those little imperfections.

Spots, Blemishes and Other Imperfections Take a good, honest look at your skin to assess your problems. All the very common imperfections such as broken veins, high cheek colour, dark areas (particularly under the eyes) and simple spots and blemishes can all be tackled successfully with clever concealing.

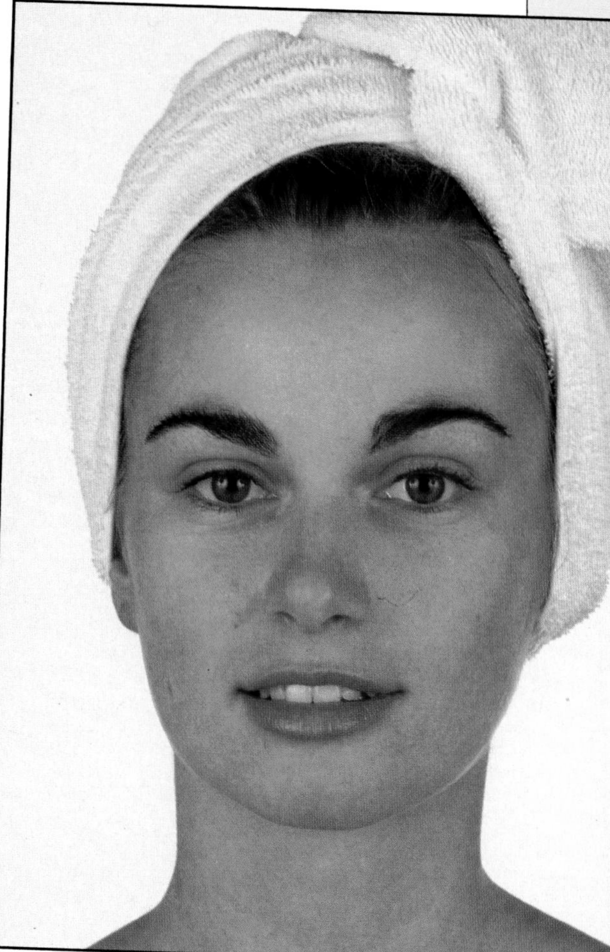

Concealers are generally applied before foundation, but can also be used on top of it. In either case it is most important to allow the concealer to become 'tacky' before blending, otherwise it will separate.

Water based concealers are best as these 'hold' to the skin and maintain coverage. An effective alternative to a general concealer is a cream foundation lighter in colour than the natural skin tone. This is not advisable for the older woman,

however, as the effect is not flattering.

Green cover sticks are popular for dealing with high cheek colour and broken veins. However, this is not a good idea if using liquid foundation, as a green tinge may show through the fine texture.

To use a concealer, take a small brush and apply it to the problem area, then press it onto the skin with a dry latex sponge. Pressing the concealer is far more efficient than blending, which will not always totally cover the flaw; the action of blending can also drag the delicate skin around the eyes.

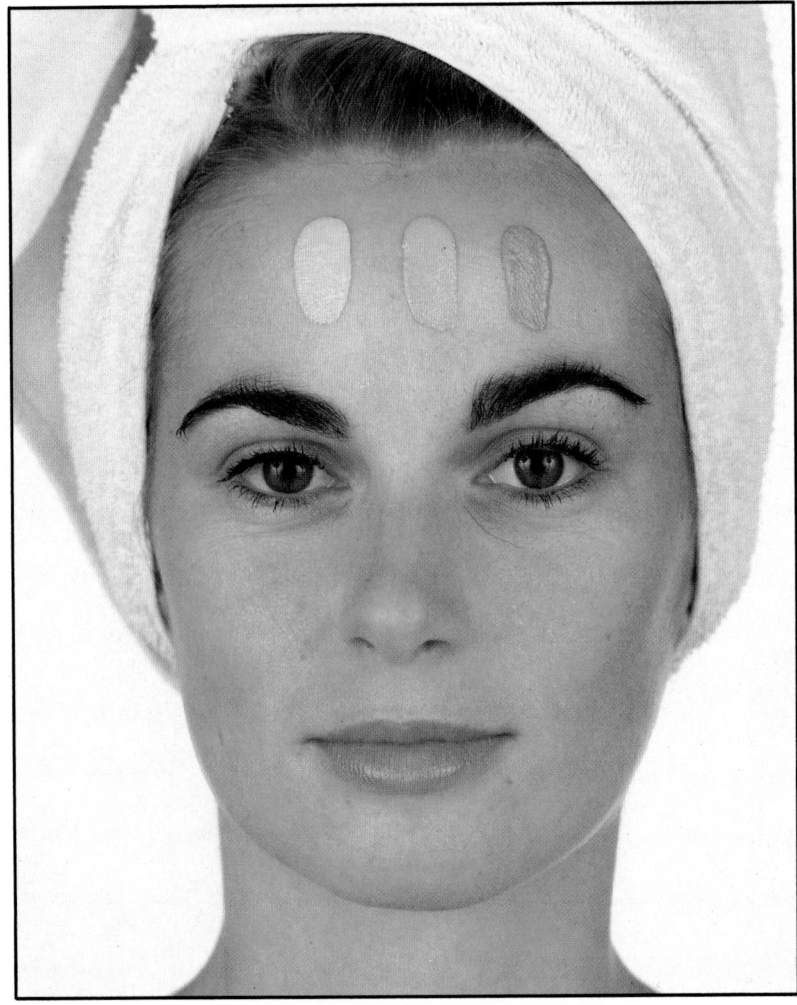

(Above) test for a foundation shade which matches your facial skin tone. (Opposite page) dot and blend foundation section by section. Blend with a dry latex sponge. Get rid of streaks with a one-inch flat brush worked left to right. Use a powder-puff to pat loose powder onto face.

Foundation If you apply too much pressure in the application of your foundation the mistake will be all too evident. It will stick to dry patches to give a heavy look; on oily patches the foundation will simply slide off, and on spots and other blemishes the make-up will appear 'caked'. The result is an unattractive and uneven finish. So avoid the heavy-handed approach at all costs!

Types to use There are two types of foundation. Oil-based, ideally only for use on dry, normal or combination skin, and water-based for oily skin. Water-based foundation dries very rapidly and therefore needs to be applied and blended fairly quickly to avoid a blotchy foundation colour.

You should always use a liquid foundation unless you have an especially difficult skin problem which requires extra coverage, in which case use a cream foundation.

Choosing shade Try to match the foundation shade (light, medium, dark) as closely as possible to your facial skin tone. There are no hard and fast rules as to where to test for this match. The back of the hand and the wrist are both used but are not ideal. Your forehead is the best testing ground (it is, after all, part of the face you are trying to tone with!) and is also the area used by cosmetic camouflage experts to achieve a near perfect result. If a good match has been made it will not be necessary to continue the foundation down the neck.

Application Foundation is applied to the face section by section, beginning with the forehead. Dot and blend each section before moving on to the next. A sensible route to follow is forehead, cheek, chin, cheek, nose and eyelids. If you dot your entire face with foundation some areas may dry before you are able to blend them, and this will create a very patchy finish.

To dot foundation use an eye shadow shading brush. This is a more effective applicator than your fingers, and makes filling-in difficult areas, such as deep indentations or the corners of the nose, much easier.

To blend foundation use a dry latex sponge for best results. Blend down the face to fade away under the chin. This downward action does not 'drag' the skin as you are simply gliding over the surface with gentle strokes. And, in blending down the face you work in the direction of the tiny facial hairs, which gives a smoother finish. If you blend upwards the facial hairs are ruffled and this makes it difficult to achieve a perfect result; also, any excess foundation will go into your hairline. Press rather than stroke the foundation onto red cheeks and other flaws as this method covers more effectively.

Eyelids should be covered with foundation to provide a good base for the eye make-up. It also blocks out veins and redness which tend to show on a fair skinned person, or the dark brown pigmentation that can be a problem with

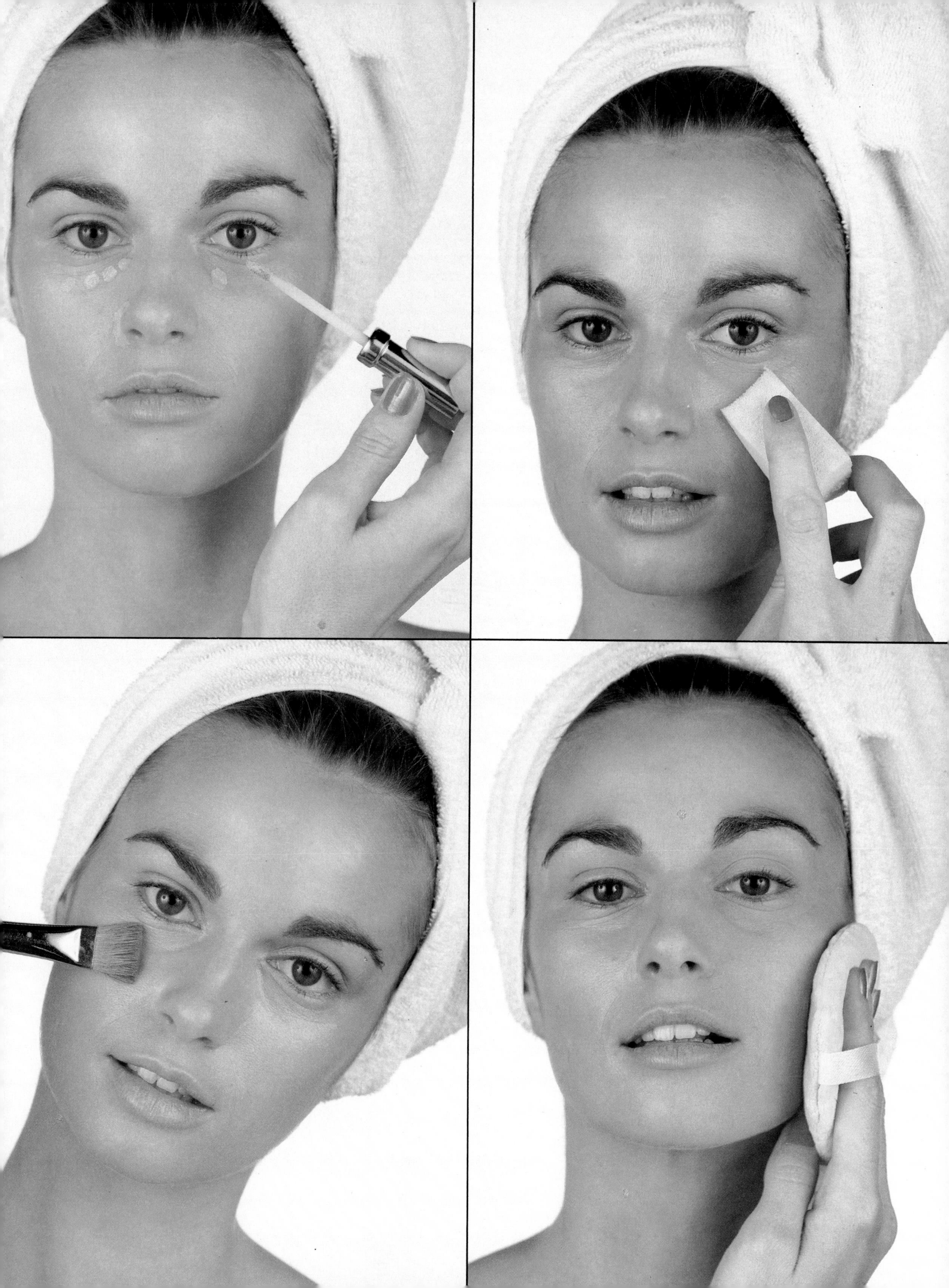

(Right) 'setting' foundation in under-eye area. A brush would irritate the eyes. (Opposite page) use of a thin-handled brush along the cheek helps to define angle and area for blusher application.

sallow skin. Do not apply too much foundation to the eyelids as this can cause eye shadow to crease. Gently lift eyebrow and blend foundation downwards towards the eyelashes.

Do not use foundation on deep lines, wrinkles or bags around the eyes as it will only accentuate these problems.

Lips are covered by foundation to give lipstick staying power and to prevent pigment in highly coloured lipstick staining the lips. Foundation should never be used to correct lip shape. This rarely works successfully and is, anyway, a very old fashioned technique.

If, when you have finished your careful application of foundation, you find that it looks streaky (usually because of oiliness) here is a foolproof tip. Take a large, flat, one inch brush and work over your face very lightly from left to right and all the streaks will disappear.

Face Powder Face Powder is used to 'set' foundation to make sure that it lasts all day or all night. Translucent is the most popular powder as it allows the natural skin tone to glow through.

Types to use If you use a liquid foundation then 'set' it with a block powder. Always use the combination of liquid foundation and block powder when you can as they give the finest finish. But remember that you can use loose powder instead of block if you have a very oily skin, as this will help absorption.

If you use a cream foundation you must 'set' it with loose powder to ensure that it lasts over a long period of time.

Application To apply block powder use a face powder brush and stroke it onto your face. Work downwards only (in the direction of facial hairs). Continue until skin is smooth and silky to touch.

To apply loose powder use cotton wool balls or a powder puff. Press the powder on to your skin patch by patch so that you do not 'drag' the foundation. This pressing action also helps absorb excess oil.

Don't be shy of applying powder (although more caution is needed with loose). To test that the foundation is well covered place the back of your hand against different areas of your face. If the skin is sticky or clammy to the touch more powder is needed.

Have faith if the initial powdering looks rather heavy, as this is put into perspective when the make-up is complete; also some of the powder is absorbed by your foundation.

Eyelids are also powdered and these are 'set' against the creases. Lift your eyebrow gently to stretch the eyelid. Blend away foundation creases and then apply powder down towards the eyelashes. If you do not first blend the foundation creases away and if you apply powder from the eyelashes up, then you simply 'set' these creases. This means that the eye shadow will crease when you apply it.

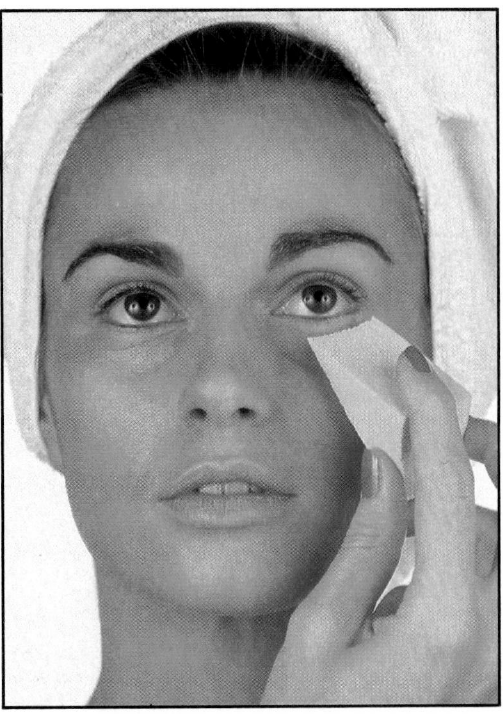

Finally, blend away foundation that has creased in the under-eye area. Dip the tip of your 'wedge' sponge into the face powder and 'set' up to your lashes. Do not use a brush for this area as it will irritate your eyes.

Quick Guide to Foundation and Powder Matches in Day or Evening Make-Up

Liquid Foundation – Translucent Block Powder

Cream Foundation – Translucent Loose Powder

Gels – Translucent Block or Loose Powder

Problem skin (too bad to be evened out by Concealer and Liquid Foundation) – Cream Foundation and Loose Powder

Very Oily Skin (with no major flaw problems) – Liquid Foundation and Loose Powder

Cream Eye Shadows and Cream Blushers – 'Setting' with face powder

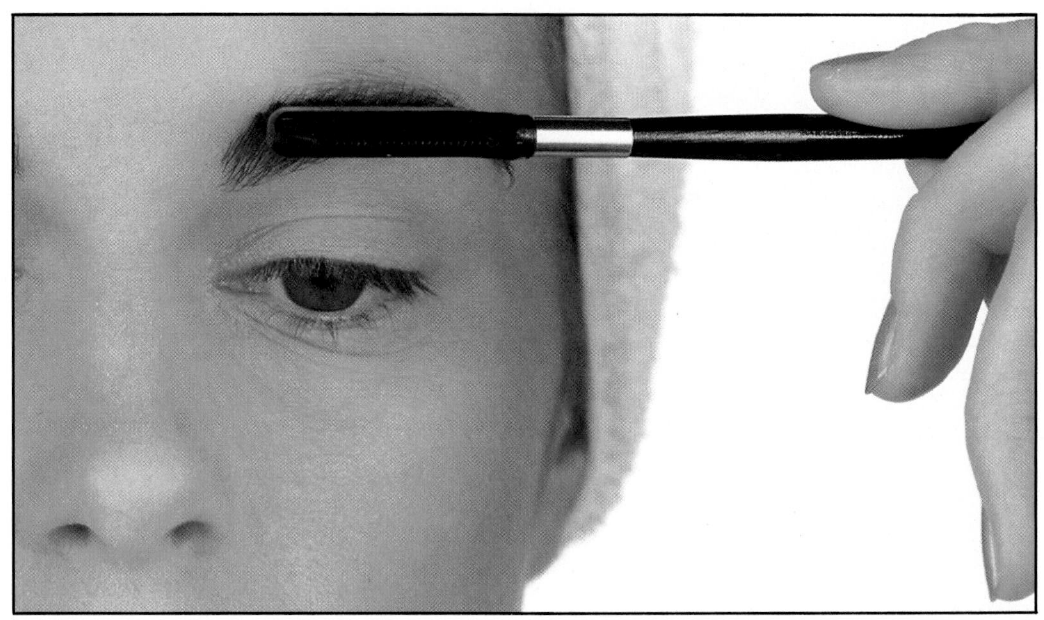

(Right) hold eyebrow brush horizontally to follow line of eyebrows. (Opposite page) alternative applicator, the eyebrow pencil being held in correct position to achieve a soft effect.

Concealer – Only needed under Liquid Foundation

Blusher If you apply your blusher at this early stage it helps give shape to the face and this makes it easier for you to decide on the correct eye make-up. The purpose of a blusher is to accentuate bone structure and to add colour to the face. It is an area of make-up that has become greatly over-complicated and you will not find in this section the normal array of diagrams showing individual techniques for triangle and pearshaped faces! The guidelines for application given here work equally successfuly on any shape of face and are also easy to relate to our three dimensional reality. But first you have to select the correct blusher for the job.

Types Powder blusher should ideally be used for day make-up. It is the finest textured of all, and as it is applied with a brush you have more control when shaping.

If you use a cream blusher it must be applied before the face powder. As with all creams, it needs to be set by the powder to stop it creasing later on.

There are light coloured blushers in pale pink or peachy shades, and dark coloured blushers. They both serve to make the cheek bones more prominent, but work in opposite ways. The light blushers act as highlighters and are applied along the cheekbones. The dark blushers make areas recede and are applied below the cheekbones.

Note: highlighters and shaders must never be used in day make-up as their effect is too dramatic and unnatural. Skilled use of the blusher cancels out the need for highlighters and shaders.

Where to apply Blusher must be kept within strict confines for a day look or the result will be ridiculous.

1. First you have to pinpoint the cheekbone. Take an imaginary line from the bulbous piece at the entrance to your ear down to the corner of your mouth. Placing a thin handled brush across the cheek helps define the angle.

Light blushers are applied 2″ up from this line

Dark blushers are applied 1″ up from this line

2. Do not apply blusher any lower down the cheekbone than the end of your nose, (imagine a diagonal line drawn from the tip of your nose across your cheek).

3. Do not apply blusher any closer to the centre of your face than the outer corner of your eye, (imagine a line, from the outer corner down your cheek to meet the imaginary nose line).

4. Do not apply blusher any higher than the temple.

How to apply Use a very light touch as too much pressure gives a blotchy, 'clown-like' appearance.

Always start at the hairline. Eighty percent of the blusher will come off at first point of contact giving a high density of colour. The centre of the face cannot take this, whereas the hair line can.

Work down the face with short strokes in the direction of the facial hair, gradually fading blusher away at the correct point. If blusher application is blotchy, finish off with face powder.

Eyebrows Eyebrows frame the eyes and affect the total look. They should therefore be worked on before you apply eye shadow. The object, as with all make-up, is to improve upon your natural features, so do not falsify your normal eyebrow shape.

Use a pencil, or a powdered shadow which you apply with a short, stiff nylon brush. In both cases colour is delicately and gradually put on to the eyebrow with short strokes. To soften a hard pencil line use the eyebrow brush.

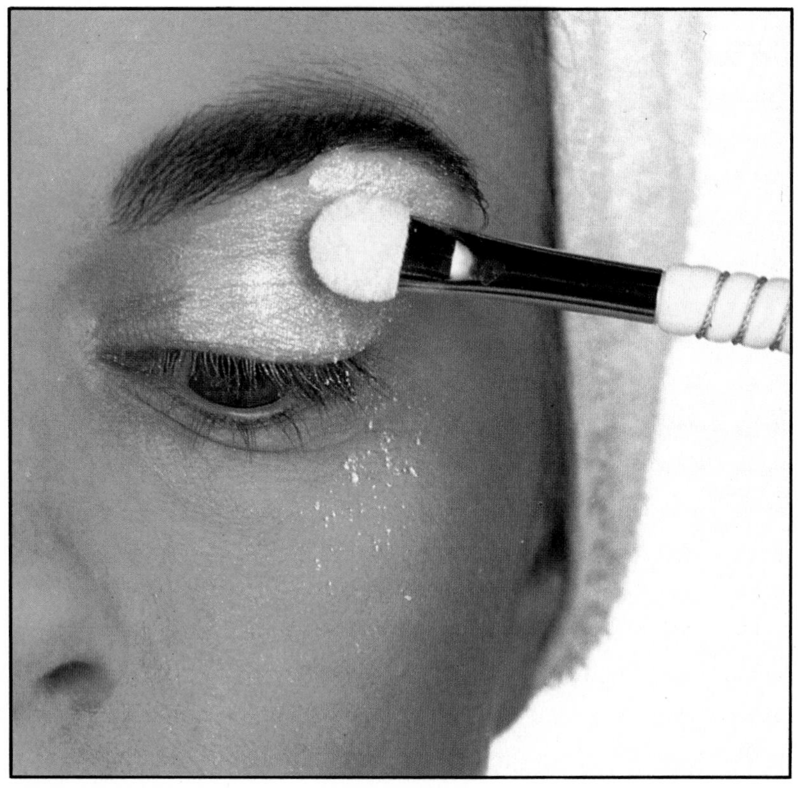

(Above) always start with lightest colour. (Opposite page, top left to right) application of darkest eye colour. Harsh pencil lines are blended with sponge-tipped applicator. Colour 3 shows contrast and application. Colour 4 defines the shape of the eye.

Pencils are slightly more difficult to use than shadows. If too much pressure is applied you will create a hard line which will look false. The 'trick' is to hold the pencil between your thumb and first finger, very close to its unsharpened end so that it is held in a straight line which could continue up to the ceiling. In this way you will find it impossible to put any pressure on the eyebrow and will easily achieve a soft effect.

If your eyebrows are a little sparse or the hair colour fair, very gently colour the hairs that are there. By this careful action you will also mark the skin itself in a very natural way. This is called 'feathering in'. Hold the pencil as in the photograph but even lower down the stem.

Eye Shadow Most eye make-up guides, like face shape guides for blusher, confuse by presenting an array of different shapes with diagrams for specific make-up. The first problem is in identifying the correct shape before you can begin work! Here is a basic shading technique which, with slight variations, will suit everybody. Four contrasting colours are required, and you can use any of the eye shadow textures, but for the ultimate smooth, soft day look loose or cream powder eye shadow gives the best results.

Colour 1. This is the lightest of the four colours you apply to the eye. Its purpose is to highlight the browbone and to give a base to the other colours.

Gently stretch your eyelid by placing a finger just above the eyebrow, next to the temple, and lift. Apply shadow just below your eyebrow and blend down towards the eyelashes. Cover the entire eyelid. Fade away all colour: pay special attention to the corner of your eye, where harsh lines can form.

Colour 2. This is the darkest of the colours you choose and is applied with a pencil under the bottom lid and over part of the top lid. Its purpose is to accentuate the eye. An eye pencil gives the control necessary to draw in the lines successfully.

Gently place a finger against the outside corner of your eye to keep the skin tight and get rid of creases. This enables you to draw a solid, straight line close to the rim of the eye. Begin at the outside corner of your eye as this is the thickest part and can therefore take the extra concentration of colour. Draw a line about three quarters of the way along the bottom lid, fading colour away towards the nose.

Draw a line along the top lid to a point just beyond the outer edge of the iris of your eye. This line is much thicker than that on the bottom lid and is extended into a triangle shape.

Blend the pencil lines with a sponge-tipped applicator for a soft, natural look.

Used correctly a pencil will not drag the delicate skin around the eyes.

Colour 3. The third colour fills the area from the beginning of the eyebrow down to the inside corner of the eye. It is darker than the base colour, lighter than the pencil, and contrasts with the fourth colour. Its purpose is two-fold. It gives a soft but greater definition to the nose, making the overall look much sharper, and it also makes the eyes appear larger.

Start at the beginning of the eyebrow and blend colour down the line of your nose and in towards the corner of your eye.

Colour 4. The fourth colour is the most important as it defines the shape of the eye.

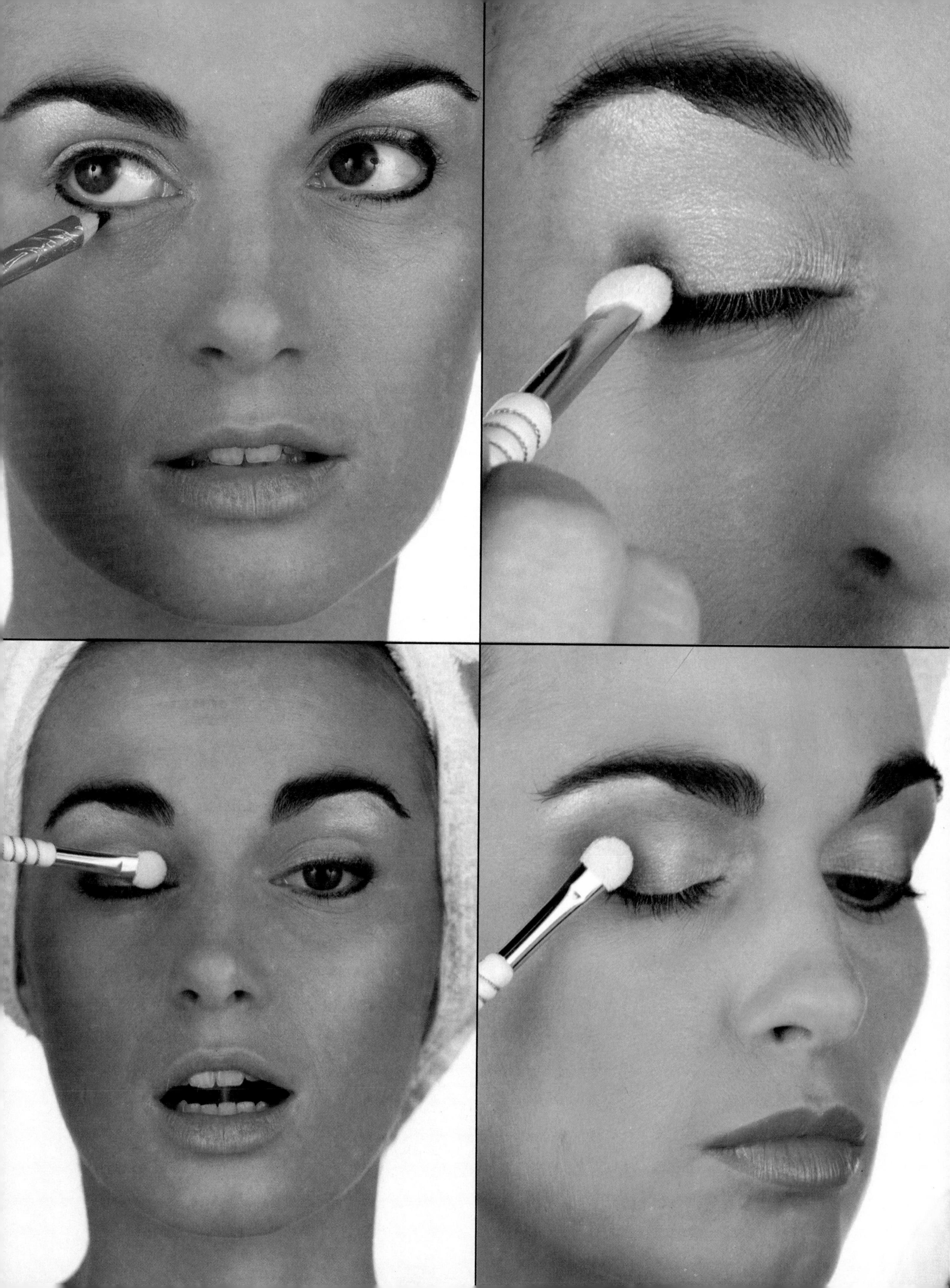

It should contrast with the third colour but still be lighter than the pencil colour.

Before applying the fourth eye shadow colour you have to decide on the shape it should take. This can only be properly decided by looking at a visually balanced face. So it is wise at this stage to put on your lipstick (technique explained in Lipstick section).

Apply the eye shadow to the top lid over the area covered by the eye pencil, next to your eyelashes. Most of the eye shadow colour will be unloaded at this point.

(Above) a lip brush gives a clean line. Lay it flat against the lips and follow the natural outline. (Opposite) when mouth has been contoured, fill in where necessary.

Blend the shadow with downward strokes, but work up over the pencil area towards the eyebrow. The decision as to how high to take this colour is determined by the degree of your socket line when your eyes are open. If you have no visible socket line blend the colour higher towards the eyebrow. If you have a large socket area blend the colour slightly lower. In both cases the shape of the eye shadow should be soft and rounded; it should not be extended beyond the natural eye socket area in a dramatic, winged effect.

You take this colour across the browbone to blend with the nose line colour for the finished effect. But keep checking the shape you are creating throughout your application of this fourth colour. The finished shape should be soft and rounded, and should not extend towards the temple in a winged effect.

Why this technique is special The usual method of applying eye shadow is to take it right across the eyelid following the socket line. This makes the face appear broader and the eyes seem smaller. The illusion is similar to that created when a plump person wears a dress with horizontal stripes; it makes her look much bigger than she actually is. The special technique described above keeps the face in proportion and makes the eyes appear larger. What is more, the effect can be used successfully, with slight variations of eye shadow shape, on every type of eye.

Lipstick Choose a lipstick colour which tones with your blusher. This gives a well co-ordinated effect.

Apply lipstick with a lip brush for a knife-edge line. You can use a lip pencil but it is more difficult to achieve a sharp outline; however, colour can be taken off the pencil with a lip brush.

Lips must be closed to give a firm surface. Take plenty of lipstick on to the brush (this makes it easier to achieve a good line). Lay the brush flat against your lips and move evenly along following the natural outline. When the mouth has been contoured in this way, fill in where necessary. You will have to open your lips to colour the corners of your mouth properly.

Now blot the lipstick by placing an open tissue full against your mouth and, using the flat of your thumb, press the tissue over your lips. Be careful here not to apply too much pressure or you will take off too much of your lipstick.

If you see a need to accentuate your lips, outline the bow of the top lip with a fine lip pencil and blend with a lip brush.

To give lipstick extra staying power blot with a tissue and dust with loose powder before applying a second coat. And, for a soft, dewy look, finish off with a little lip gloss, (but do not take this to the edges of your mouth as it may cause the lipstick to run).

Mascara This is the final stage to your make-up and one of the most flattering of all cosmetics. Even the loveliest of lashes can be further enhanced and glamorised by a coating of mascara.

Look down into your mirror and begin

(Above) the tip of the mascara wand successfully coats lower lashes. (Opposite) delicate use of blusher on chin, nose and forehead to finish off with a warm glow.

application on the top side of the top lashes to deposit most of the mascara here. This also takes off any powder that has dropped from the eye shadow. Now look up and finish off the top lashes with a coating from underneath. Use the point of the mascara wand (brush) to coat your bottom lashes.

Use a tissue to remove excess mascara from the wand (brush) to avoid clogging your lashes. If, despite precautions, the lashes do become clogged, place a tissue underneath your open eye, close your eye, and comb lashes with an eyebrow brush. To remove specks of mascara from your cheek take a cotton bud and lightly swivel on the mascara speck and remove.

There are lots of lovely mascara colours to choose from these days so it is worth indulging to make your eye make-up even more attractive.

The Finishing Touch To complete your daytime make-up add finishing touches with blusher on chin, nose and forehead. This helps towards a warm, delicate glow.

Day Make-Up

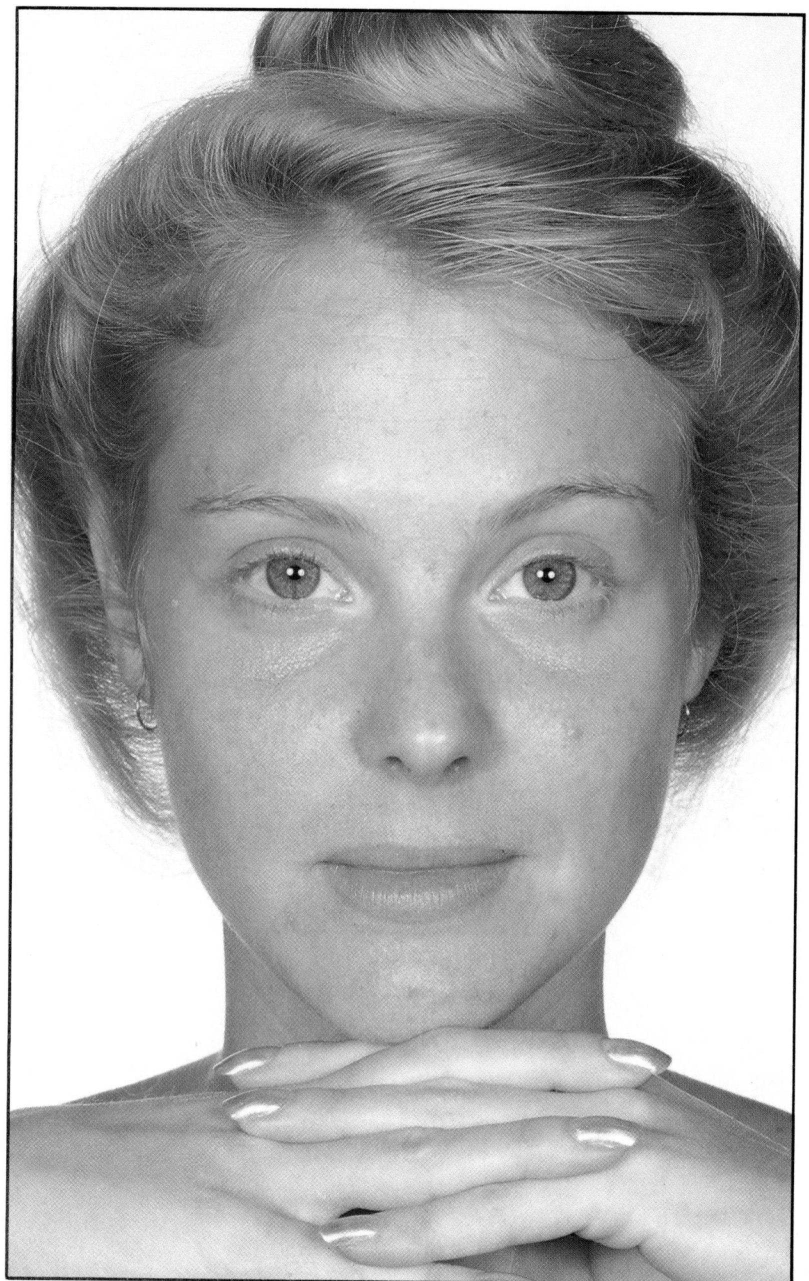

(Left) the bare canvas, in need of clever concealing work, foundation and powder. (Below) blusher applied in the early stages gives shape to your face and helps to create a balanced eye make-up. (Bottom left to right) the four basic steps to eye make-up shape and colour, when successfully mastered, can be adapted by you to suit any mood and occasion. Lips can be painted to perfection with the precision of a lip brush. Add lashings of mascara for the final, glamorous touch. (Opposite) the total transformation to a soft, glowing and natural day look.

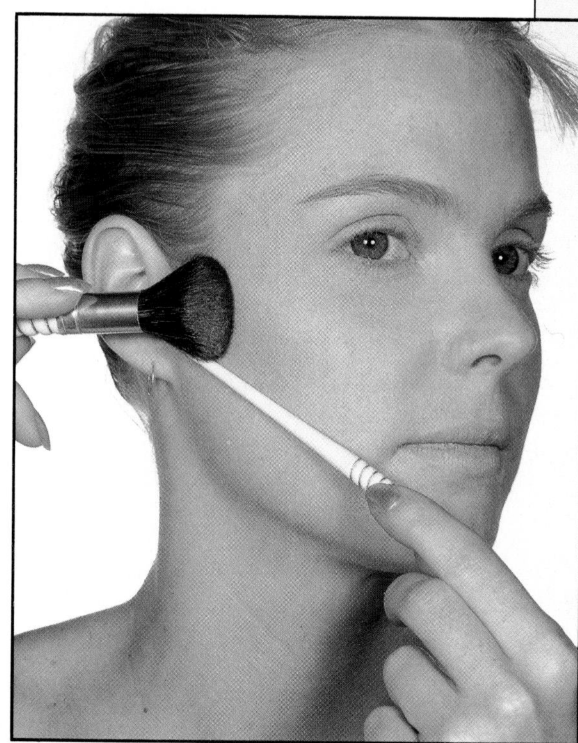

CHAPTER 5

Evening Make-Up

(Right) bold lips and subtle but effective use of frosted eyeshadow and false lashes for a truly glamorous evening look. (Opposite) a softer approach, but equally stunning especially in candlelight!

Evening make-up need not be any different from day make-up. But the more flattering quality of night lighting and the mood set by glamorous evening fashions gives you licence to be more adventurous.

The general rule about evening make-up is that it requires a heavier application to ensure that facial features and make-up colours stand out in some of the more dimly lit night-time settings. It is, in fact, an exaggerated form of day make-up, but with a wider choice of colours (mixing natural and synthetic) and the use of more dramatic shapes and textures.

Evening Make-Up

Evening Make-Up

Foundation and Powder Evening make-up is generally put more to the test than day make-up. For instance, to withstand a night of dancing and some perspiration it is crucial that the base is dependable.

So, for the more demanding occasions, use a cream foundation and 'set' with a light application of loose powder. This heavier finish means the base is less likely to 'move' during the evening.

For extra glamour substitute translucent face powder for one with a gold, bronze or frosted tint.

Blusher There are two ways to create an attractive and dramatic effect with your blushers.

1. Take the light coloured blusher (the one that is applied *on* the cheekbone) up onto the temple and/or forehead. You can even take it over the entire eye area using it as your base eye shadow colour. Or, bring the blusher round into the eye area and blend with your base colour.

2. Apply dark blusher to the underside of the cheekbone for a 'model girl' look.

Contouring For a really dramatic look, shade under the cheekbone. But only a young person can get away with this rather theatrical effect. You can use either a contour (underneath the cheekbone) with a dark blusher as second colour, or choose two shades of blusher in pink and plum.

(Above) for frivolous party mood the 'synthetic' look (e.g. pinks, lilacs etc.) and (opposite) matched to an outfit, creates the ultimate in total co-ordination.

The technique is the same as that described for blushers.

Dark shade, only about $^1/_4$ inch in width.

Lighter shade, about $^3/_4$ inch in width.

Eye Shadow Colours can be darker than those for day eye shadows, but the colour graduation remains the same (i.e. base is lightest, eyeliner darkest, nose line and fourth colour to contrast with each other. Here are some suggestions for a good evening look.

Colour 1. Instead of a base white use a colour. This cancels the need for colour three (the nose line) as the base colour now introduces the definition and slimming effect in this area. If you do use white as a base then the other three colours must be darker than for a day time look or they will not stand out enough.

Colour 2. Blend the pencil with the eyebrow (stiff, nylon) brush instead of a sponge tipped applicator to keep the line more dramatic.

Almost anything goes in evening make-up. Use gold eye-shadow everywhere. On lips, eyes, cheeks and even to highlight other lipsticks.

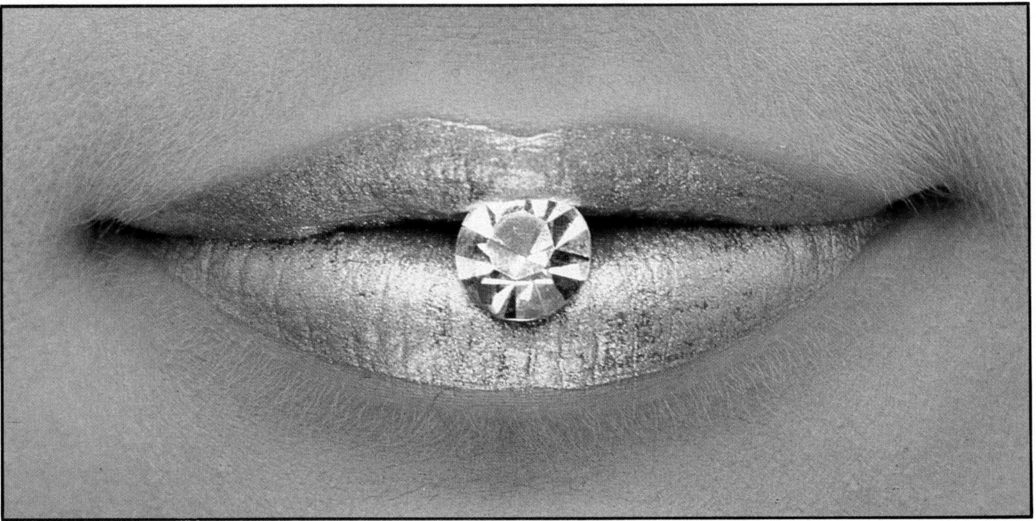

Evening Make-Up

Colour 3. The same area as for day make-up is covered. However, if you use a colour for the base this step will not be necessary.

Colour 4. The same technique as for day make-up but create a different shape. Take the colour higher towards the eyebrow and sweep it outwards to make a pointed (winged) rather than a rounded effect.

Khol A wonderful way to exaggerate and enlarge the eyes. But only use khol pencil along with lots of eye shadow, otherwise it will have the opposite effect and make your eyes appear smaller.

Apply khol all around the inside rim of the eye. Use the same technique of application as for ordinary eyeliner.

Lipstick The colour of the lipstick must balance out eye and blusher colours. So, if

The before and after of an evening make-up. Bold use of colour linked to outfit, and bold use of blusher and highlighter for a sparkling effect.

Evening Make-Up

Heavy use of a colour eyeshadow all round the eyes, and basic day look techniques adapted for a touch of drama.

darker colours have been used, the lipstick should also be a dark shade. Add plenty of gloss for a glamorous evening look.

Lip Liner A more dramatic evening look can take the boldness of a lip liner. This is applied before the lipstick. You can draw directly onto the lips or take the colour off the pencil with a lip brush. Alternatively, you can use a darker colour lipstick than the one you use to fill in the lips. In either case, simply trace the outside line of your mouth.

Mascara Choose a coloured mascara rather than black or brown to further complement night eyes. Apply more than for a day look to give extra emphasis and also because you have to contrast against darker eye shadows.

False Lashes These can really come into their own in an evening make-up. Apply three or four single lashes to the outer edge of the top lid for a sweeping effect. Or, apply full strips to top and bottom lids.

Highlighting As a finishing touch use a highlighter to give a general 'lift' to your face. The browbone, top of the cheekbone underneath the eye, centre panel of nose, and lower cheek following the jaw bone,

Evening Make-Up

are the usual areas. This can only be successful with a very light touch and"careful blending.

Highlighting must never be obvious, and plenty of practice is necessary to perfect this most subtle of techniques.

Shading As subtle a technique as highlighting, and equally difficult to achieve successfully, shading should only be used in evening make-up (daylight makes it almost impossible to 'hide' the shaded areas), and only if you are quite young.

The main reasons a shader may be necessary are to slim down a nose or jawbone.

As this technique is the most difficult part of any make-up, the easiest way to attempt it is to use a shade darker in foundation in the areas above applied with your main foundation colour.

Remember any obvious shadow line will be concealed by the application of powder.

Use of theatrical make-up enables you to be daring and creative. Black skins complement frosted and synthetic colours beautifully. They can also take dramatic use of contours and highlighting in the evening.

CHAPTER 6

Colour in Make-Up

Matching, toning, co-ordinating, contrasting. These are words so commonly used in connection with colour and which terrify so many people. The fashion houses long ago began to break all the colour rules which many of us held sacrosanct – 'blue and green should never be seen' – leaving the less confident of us really in a sea of colour! But understanding colour and how to use it in the art of make-up is really quite straightforward, and it is important to grasp it if you are to achieve the ultimate of total colour co-ordination between your make-up and clothes.

(Left) the synthetic colours of pinks, blues, lilacs, purples. (Above) a completely natural look using only earth and autumnal colours.

Colour in Make-Up

The only colours which are included in both the 'natural' and 'synthetic' colour categories are white, black and red.

Colours fall into two categories. The naturals, which comprise all the earth and autumnal colours, and the synthetics, which comprise every other colour known to make-up e.g. pink, lilac, purple, etc. The only colours which are included in both categories are white, black and red. Simply, the guidelines are, for a day make-up keep to one or the other colour category and you will always achieve a good, co-

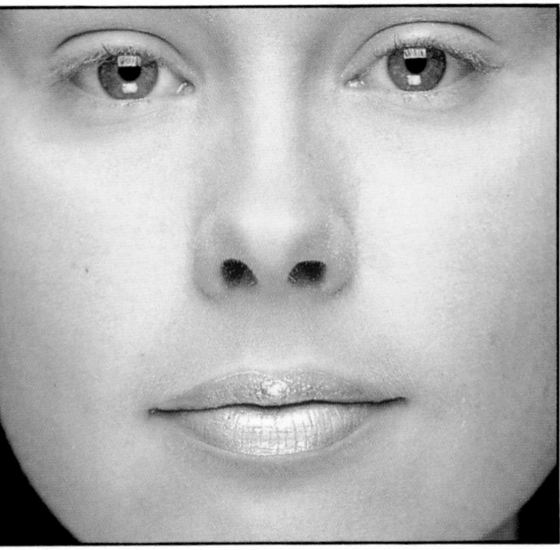

A beautiful, muted effect using 'synthetic' colours on lips and cheeks. Ideal for daytime, goes with any outfit, and is quick to apply.

ordinated look; for an evening occasion you can afford to mix the two categories for a more exciting, vibrant effect.

The Muted Look With this technique the colour you choose for your cheeks and lips dictates whether the overall colour effect is natural or synthetic. The art is to use just two muted, neutral shades on your eyes, which are able to adapt to or 'reflect' the stronger tones of the blusher and lipstick. So, for example, a white eye shadow covers the entire eyebrow and lid while the second colour, say grey, outlines the outside corner of the eye and smudges up slightly onto the lid. You can now choose either synthetic colours (e.g. pink lipstick

and plum blusher) or natural colours (eg., coral peach lips and a rusty, coppery blusher) and either combination will work equally successfully with the soft, neutral eye shadows.

The technique has many advantages. It lessens the confusing choice of up to four different eye shadow colours. It solves the problems of co-ordinating with an outfit as you cannot really go wrong with this method. And, possibly most important, it is very time-saving on a busy morning!

Complexion, Hair and Eyes There is much nonsense spoken about matching make-up colours and general complexion. Here are some simple and effective guidelines.

Eyes. Any colour of eye make-up should work with any shade of eye. If it does not, it usually means that it has been

applied too strongly. In which case, it can be softened down in stages if you dust translucent block powder on top until the right depth is achieved.

Hair. The only hair colour that can cause real problems is red, although this caution applies more as a person becomes older.

Skin. Pale skin, no matter what the colour of hair, is best complemented by synthetic colours. Sallow skin, or a skin that has a tan, is more suited to the natural colours.

Above all, your use of colour should be fun, imaginative and versatile within the given guidelines. Suntans disappear, seasons change and so do fashions, and in order to keep up with this constantly changing scene you have to adapt your choice of make-up colours to suit the mood.

(Below) 'natural' make-up, again using earth and autumnal colours. (Opposite) use of 'synthetic' colours.

Disco and Elaborate Evening

Use frosted make-up, mix colours that spark your imagination, paint on marks (opposite and overleaf). Match lips to eyeshadows outrageously; be pale and interesting but make the lips bold (subsequent pages). Use your cosmetics as a paint box, for now is the time to be really creative.

Now you have mastered the basics of the art of make-up you can really enter into the world of art if you so desire. Fancy dress, disco, almost any special occasion gives you licence to be free and easy with your imagination. Be exotic, mysterious, fantastical, frightening – but above all, have fun.

Disco and Elaborate Evening

CHAPTER 8

Fashion Make-Up

(This page and opposite) Spring and Summer for softer and bolder use of seasonal colours. (Overleaf) for an autumn woolly, autumn make-up colours; and a strong, frosted eye make-up makes a pale winter face more interesting.

A 'fashion look', whether it be in clothes, make-up or hair, is a style of the moment. The 'moment' can last from months to years. And these 'styles', 'fashions', 'looks', are mainly inspired by the famous names on designer clothes labels and by the great fashion houses. A popular style of clothing, for instance, can encourage famous hair salons to create a complementary hairstyle; and the colours adopted as fashionable for the various designer clothes collections dictate the make-up colours through each season.

In America, the ultimate fashion look is total co-ordination of a person's make-up and clothes' colours. Certainly, make-up

suld always reflect or match the mood of an outfit. A dress which is bold in style or colour should be matched in impact by the make-up and, if the dress is softer in style and colour, the make-up follows suit. The most dramatic changes of colour are seen from season to season. Autumn and winter fashion colours tend to be darker and heavier; stronger make-up colours reflect this and better compliment a pale, winter face. In spring and summer the brighter colours appear, along with pastels, whites and neutrals. Make-up therefore should be softer and lighter, both in colour and application. Also, the more colourful warm weather complexions and tans are more in harmony with the 'natural' outdoors look.

Make-up should reflect the mood of an outfit for a complete fashion look. (Opposite) this soft, glowing, natural look is ideal for the softer fabrics and styles of spring and summer fashions.

Maxi

More dramatic use of colour and technique to complement bolder fashion colours and styles.

CHAPTER 9

Model Make-Up

A combination of photogenic features and clever use of cosmetics and techniques can transform a model girl into a multitude of different people. Look at these photographs and those on the next four pages for an idea of the clever use of make-up combined with photographic and fashion skills in creating a total 'look'.

Make-up can give you confidence, but first you must have confidence in it. Confidence in its power to project and enhance for you; even to change your image completely if that's what you want. The most potent example of the use of make-up is in the world of commercial photography. Make-up is expertly applied to a model specifically to help create the right 'image' for a product or company. It may have to be

Some very different make-ups created by experts to adapt a model's features to the mood of the message or product that she is to 'promote' on the magazine pages. See also overleaf.

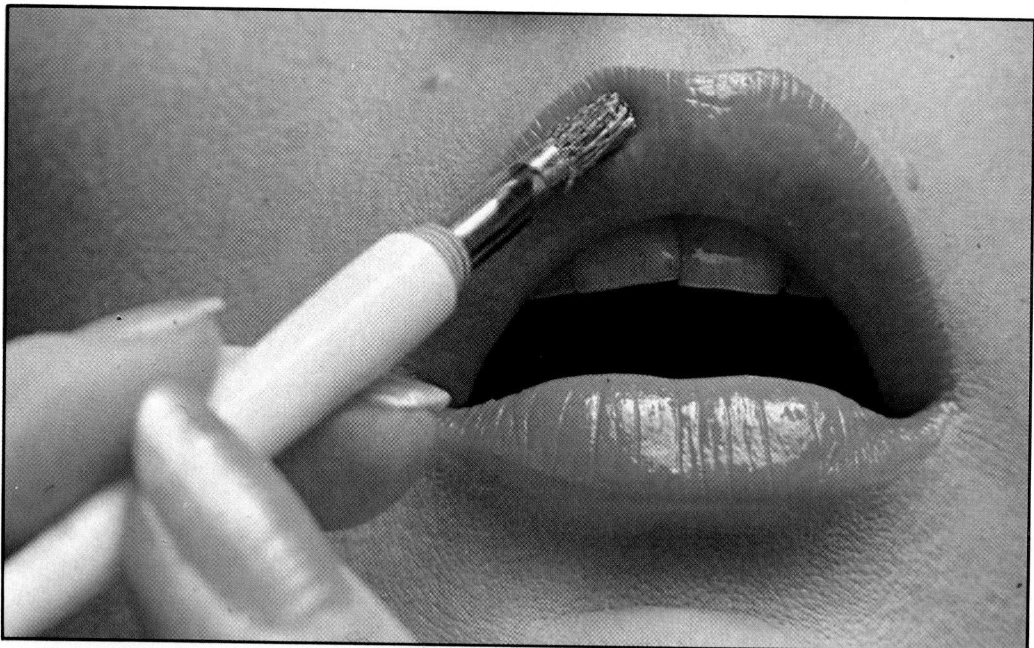

sophisticated, futuristic, old-fashioned or girl-next-door. And the majority of photographic models can be adapted with the use of make-up to all four looks. Thumb through a model's portfolio of photographs and it is very difficult to believe that it is the same girl in every shot.

It may also be hard for you to believe that many models are quite ordinary to look at in the 'flesh' but, with their photogenic features and the magic of make-up, they can turn into beautiful, sophisticated women on the fashion pages.

CHAPTER 10

Make-Up for Coloured Skin

Black skin complements both 'synthetic' and 'natural' colour. The most stunning effects can be created with frosted products (this page and opposite).

Black skins tend to be oily, although if exposed to cold weather they can also suffer from dryness, and so require the protection of moisturisers. It is therefore most important to find the right base and, if this oily-dry combination is a problem, time spent on researching a suitable foundation formulation will pay dividends.

The shade of a black skin can range from beautiful mahogany to ebony black. Today there are an increasing number of products specially formulated for black skins. This is important as cosmetics designed for white skins tend to change colour when applied to a black skin. Foundations and powders, for instance, can turn greyish, or too red or yellow. If you are lucky, a bronzing gel or tinted moisturiser might be enough to protect and to even out skin tone. However, black or white, a complexion will almost always benefit from the classic base of concealer, foundation and powder.

Concealer, Foundation, Face Powder The techniques are the same as for day make-up for a white skin, but, if you prefer, you can substitute the concealer with a foundation lighter in shade than your all over base shade. Always apply concealer/foundation before your base foundation.

Foundations for black skins are oil-based, but less so than for white skins. This off-sets problems of dryness without adding unnecessarily to oiliness. Choose your shade of foundation, i.e. light, medium or dark, to match skin tones. Follow the basic rules for powder but do not over-do the initial application. White skins can take a heavy, one-off setting over foundation, but on a black skin too much powder looks obvious and greyish. It is, therefore, far better to 'set' a couple of times throughout the day and also to apply with a brush as this helps avoid a heavy look.

Shading and Shaping These techniques can be very successful on a black skin for day make-up as the contrast to skin tone is very subtle. For best results use a sheer, liquid foundation which is darker than your base. This could mean a very dark brown or nearly black foundation colour for an extremely dark skin. Shade down sides of nose, along jawline, under the cheekbone and inside the eye-socket area. Of course, if you do use a foundation as shader you

Highlighter dotted along top of cheekbone and blended in, works beautifully on this lovely Indian skin tone. (Below) full use of vibrant 'synthetic' colours gives this skin tone a stunning effect and contrasts with jet-black hair and the boldness of black leather. (Opposite page) an Indian wedding make-up. Vivid colours with a creative design around the cheekbones and eyes match the shimmering, exciting colours of the outfit to the full. Kohl pencil is used to emphasise and dramatise the beautiful eyes, while bold, red lips balance the make-up and match the boldness of the rich fashion colours.

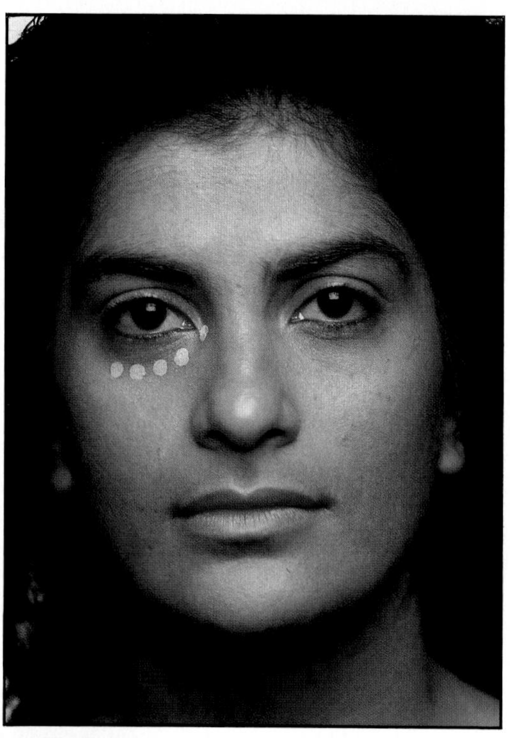

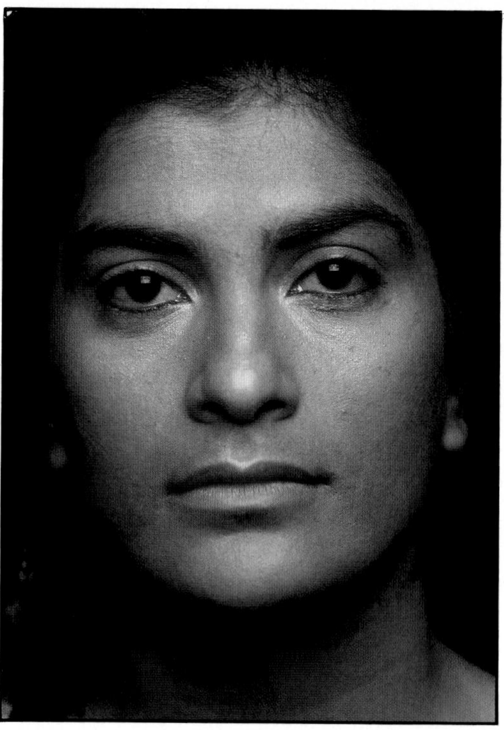

must 'set' with powder after its application on top of the base so that both are secure.

Blushers and Highlighters The same methods are used as for white skin. But choose non-greasy, creamy blushers or gels. Avoid powder blushers especially if you have undue oiliness.

Highlighters can be very effective. Try a light dusting down the bridge of the nose, around the eye area, above cheekbones and just above the upper lip.

Eye Shadow Bright, vivid colours look best on black skins, although day make-up will always look softer than on a white skin as there is less contrast for colour. Do not be tempted to apply more colour to obtain contrast as this will look unattractive in daylight. Obviously, for evening eyes you can use extra colour, and golds, coppers and frosted shadows look very good. These can even be dusted around the face for a more exotic effect.

Follow the same format for making-up eyes as described in the appropriate chapter, along with the following thoughts:

1. A white base is too dramatic against a black skin. Choose a colour or leave natural skin tone as base.

2. Although black or brown can be used to effect as an eyeliner, you could also try navy blue.

3. Take care to choose a colour prominent enough to outline the nose.

You may be lucky enough to have a natural khol effect around your eyes.

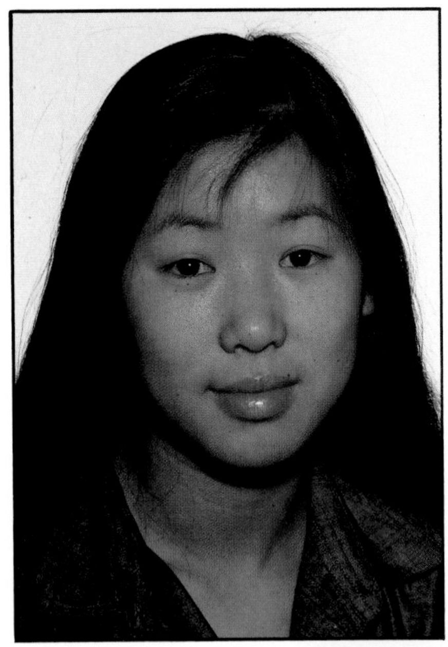

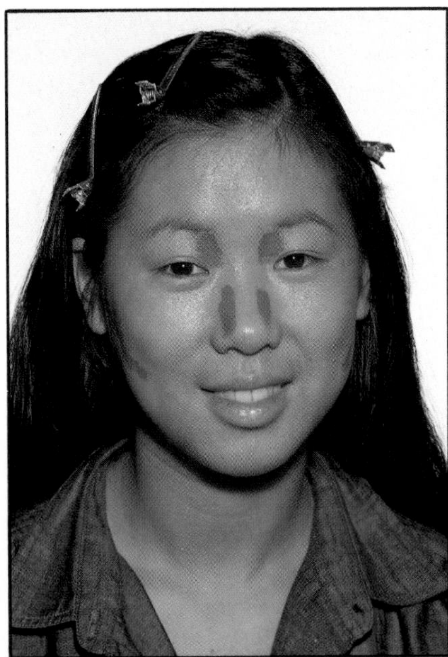

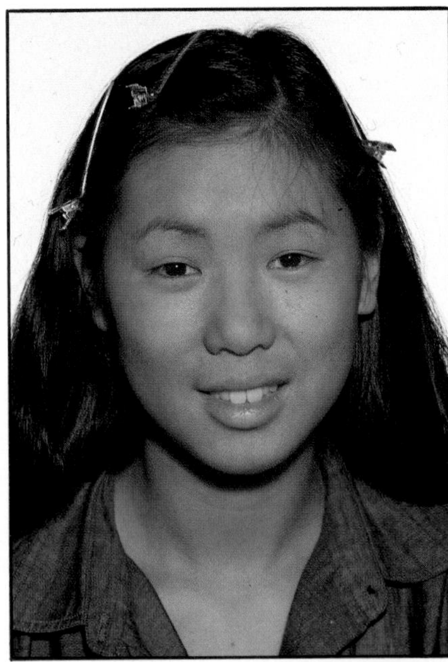

As a shading technique on a darker skin, use a foundation colour darker than the base. Apply down sides of nose, along jawline and under cheekbones. Highlighters can be very effective also (above centre, above right). (Right) to create a socket line use light shadow next to lashes, and darker shadow on the outer corner of eye. (Opposite) bright, vivid colours and frosts can be used to great effect.

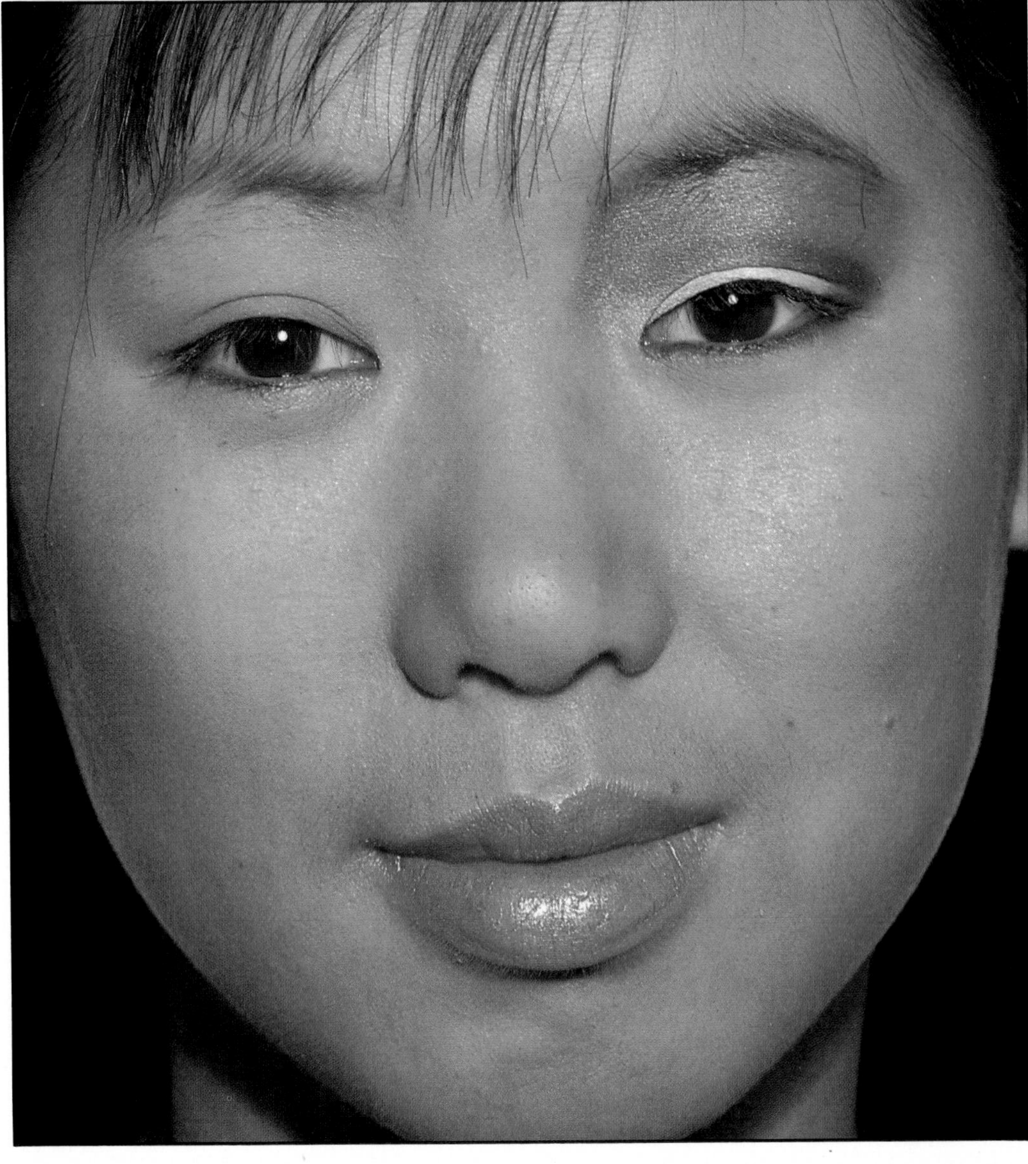

Make-Up for Coloured Skin

(Right) dramatic use of foundation and powder emphasise the pretty mouth and eyes of this Oriental girl. (Opposite) full make-up with use of blusher, highlighter and frosted eye-shadow for a glossy evening look.

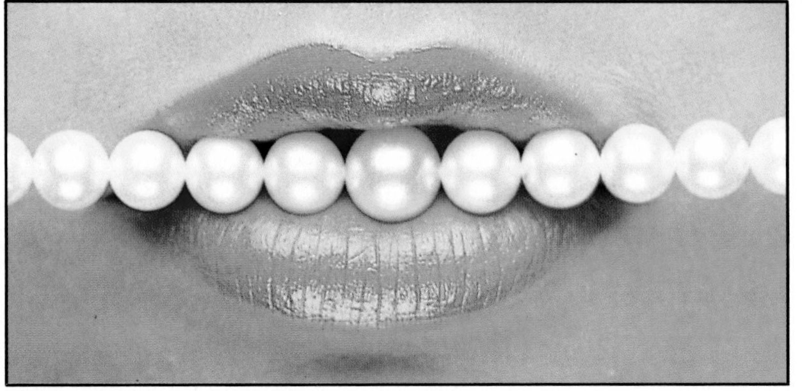

Experiment with using a colour over this if you think it will better complement you make-up. And if you do not have this natural effect then introduce it using lots of black or other suitable colour.

Lipstick Many black women have ample and beautifully formed lips which do not need exaggerating. But if you wish to slim your lips then trace the outline with a dark brown or black lip pencil and fill in with lipstick. To soften the outline apply foundation over the top, and powder to set.

CHAPTER 11

Questions and Answers

(Opposite) skin will never be affected by make-up if it is diligently cleansed at the end of each day.

1. Does make-up cause spots and blemishes by clogging the pores of the skin?

No. Spots form because of certain hormonal activity which occurs at different times of life. In fact, make-up acts as a barrier against some damaging environmental conditions such as wind and dust.

2. Why do lipsticks sometimes change colour after application.

Invariably because of an acidic skin. This is usually indicated by naturally dark coloured lips. Use brown-tone lipsticks such as beiges, corals, apricots and peaches.

3. Why do foundations sometimes change colour?

Acidity again! Acidic skins tend to bring out the orange in foundations. Stick to beiges and light tans and use a mild astringent first as this neutralises the acid effect of the skin.

4. Why does colour disappear so quickly from some faces?

Because people with very oily skin absorb make-up to a greater degree than those with dry skin. Setting with loose powder will delay the process but some touching-up may be necessary.

5. What can be done about disguising very dry skin?

This is the most difficult of skin types to deal with when applying make-up. But you can take certain precautions to 'neutralise' the skin before foundation and powder are applied. Also, good moisturising beforehand and an oil-based foundation will help minimise the problem. Never use loose powder on dry skin.

6. How can glossy lipstick be made to last longer?

They really cannot, as they do come off all too easily. Use harder textured lipsticks, powder for extra staying powder, then apply a lip gloss.

7. Are there any general guidelines on make-up for the older woman?

Keep make-up light, and this means colour, texture and application, whether for a daytime or evening look.

Avoid cream foundations as they do age an older skin. Never use foundation around eyes as this accentuates wrinkles etc.

8. How do you prevent lipstick 'bleeding' outside the lip line.

Blot lipstick with a tissue and dust with loose powder before applying a second coat.

A beautifully made-up face is a subtle work of art — but don't stop there. Healthy, well-cut hair doubles the impact of your make-up efforts, and for ultra-sophistication, make full use of the lovely colours available in nail varnish for a truly co-ordinated effect.

Questions and Answers

This book has explained the basic techniques and professional ground rules from which all good make-up is created. Experience and the confidence that follows gives you the licence to experiment with this highly creative skill and to perhaps, one day, develop your own individual style.

SKIN CARE

Skin Care Contents

Introduction
page 134

Understanding Your Skin
pages 136-145

Skin Types
pages 146-153

A Healthy Routine
pages 154-169

Special Treats for Your Skin
pages 170-183

Diet and Exercise
pages 184-195

Body Watching
pages 196-207

The Care of Hands, Feet and Legs
pages 208-223

Hair Care and Styles
pages 224-237

A Healthy Skin for Life
pages 238-249

The Finishing Touch
pages 250-256

Introduction

Skin Care – not just a pretty face – a beautiful body as well – total care for the whole of you – a serious subject which is exciting and fun – a positive approach to caring for yourself from top to toe.

Identify the problems and needs of your skin, be it face, body or feet, and with these practical answers and good ideas to help you, have fun in your own home, achieving smooth, supple skin; the greatest asset a woman can have.

CHAPTER 12

Understanding Your Skin

Smooth, soft skin will enhance anybody, but it won't happen by itself. Constant care and nourishment is required throughout the year to combat the cold of winter and the heat of summer, and to replace the natural moisture and oil which the elements take away. Hands and feet need particular attention during summer.

Skin Care – a simple enough statement, but what does it mean? Obviously, care of the skin – but life is never that easy!

The skin we worry about most is the skin that shows – the face – but we must not be fooled, there is much more to it than that.

Skin is one of nature's wonders – we all have it and we all owe a lot to it. It is also one of the most important parts of our body.

Firstly, it is the packaging, and we know from our experience of other things – for example, the products we buy – that packaging is very important. It is what first attracts us to something, and it must be appealing and desirable.

Secondly, it is vitally important to our well-being. It protects us from the elements and it keeps us warm or cool, regulating our temperature extremely efficiently and reacting to everything that happens around us.

It is only when something goes wrong that we begin to notice if there is a problem – a rash, or a spot – but it is only our skin, or our body through the skin, trying to tell us something.

Just think how much we can tell about our environment by how our skin reacts. We shiver when it's cold, we perspire when it is hot; fear and excitement, tension, nervousness and pleasure all show on our skins, not to mention how we react to the different ways we are touched. So do not underestimate its importance; look and listen, and learn to work with skin, not abuse it.

Remember we cover 95% of our skin

Don't forget the areas which tend to get dry and look dingy. A gentle scrub with a rough-textured sponge will awaken your skin and improve your circulation. If you bend and stretch while you are doing this, you can combine care for your skin with a useful daily exercise routine.

most of the time, but there is always a situation when the usually unseen may be revealed. So let's be ready for it – smooth and pleasing to touch and see.

Mirror Check – take a long look in your mirror. What do you see? That same familiar face looking back? Disenchantment, lack of inspiration, we have all felt like this, but it gets us nowhere, we must be positive and strong. Let's face it, if we feel this way we are not really looking at ourselves critically – the image is too well known to us so we stop really checking. Take a deep breath, move into a clear light, daylight is best, and start to open your eyes.

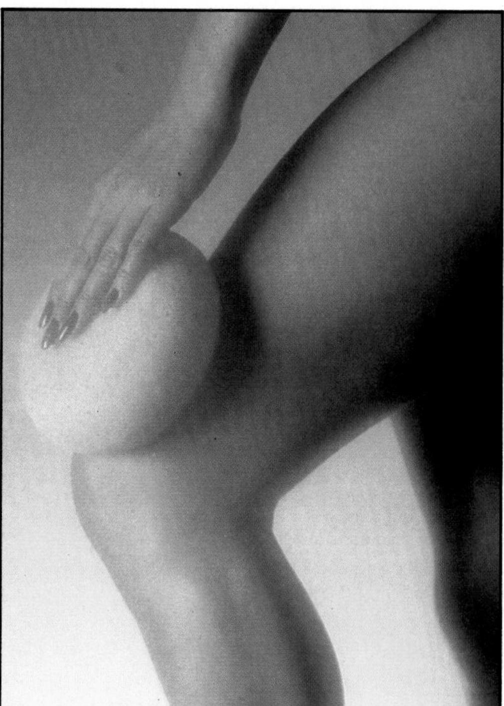

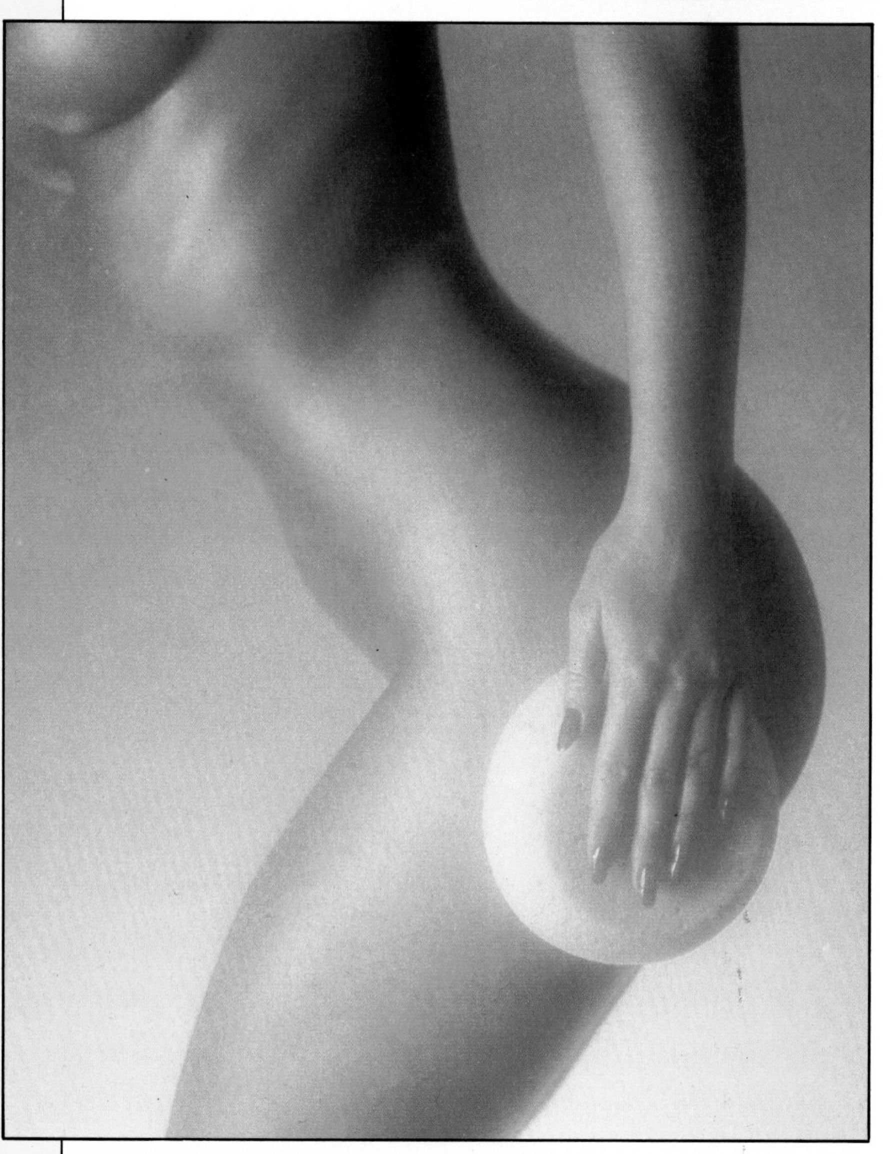

Just how does your skin look: fresh or dingy, clear or spotty, dry or greasy? Is the texture of your skin good and smooth? How are the laughter lines? Are your lips moist or dry, smooth or lined? Eyebrows: do they need attention? Do you look the way you would like to look or do you know there is room for improvement? If we are all truthful we know in our hearts there is always something we can change for the better, it's just admitting it and taking the first step. Don't be overwhelmed, don't try and do too much to begin with – let's make a list, a plan of action, and forget all the old excuses; who are you fooling?

Jot down all the good points and all the bad, and begin to work out how you can improve. It is also important to be aware of other things such as your diet, your environment: smoky, centrally heated

Understanding Your Skin

Don't take your skin for granted. Watch how it changes in response to your skin care routine. Close attention will tell you what your skin lacks, and therefore needs, so learn to understand what it is letting you know. That means a regular check in the mirror in natural daylight: be extremely critical and act accordingly. Take special note of hair and eyebrows: nothing should escape your eye.

offices can be disaster for skin, as well as just unpleasant to be in. Are you sleeping well, do you get enough exercise, are you mentally calm or do you have unusual worries or problems? Are you healthy – what are you eating and drinking – how long since you had a break? All these things have a marked effect on the skin, as it reflects the way you feel. The more that is going on, the fitter and stronger you need to be. There is no room for depression.

Skin Care can seem unexciting but it should be a challenge and great fun, so think of it as a treat – your special moments. Pamper yourself, set a little time aside every day, your own time; you've worked hard, you deserve a little relaxation. Think how much others will appreciate a new, sparkling, relaxed you; think how much more confident you will feel because you are in control. Feeling good is the basis of your personality and the image you portray – so start today.

Skin Variety would seem to be the spice of life. There are almost as many variations of colour, texture and type as there are people. Just as no one looks the same, not one of us has exactly the same skin, or identical problems; some skins are much tougher than others, and some are far more sensitive. Your life style and where you live will also make a difference: skin which is subjected to extremes of temperature will inevitably suffer, cold and wind will dry out even an oily skin eventually, and long spells in a very hot, sunny climate can make skin age very rapidly.

The skin is not like a plastic coating; it lives and breathes. It consists of seven layers which are continually changing; new layers are produced in the dermis (the lower layers of skin) and gradually move upwards to become the epidermis (the top layers of skin) eventually being shed when they reach the surface. Keeping the skin clean and well moisturised helps to give a smooth surface; a dry skin crying out for care can be seen in the little lines around eyes and lips, and if nothing is done these will become deeper and eventually impossible to repair.

The skin also has a natural elasticity which, as one gets older, will diminish, so care in the handling of skin right from the beginning will pay off later. It is possible over several years to stretch and harm the skin by rough, uncaring treatment.

Understanding Your Skin

Two stunning results of attentive skin care on young faces. The end product depends upon the original type and condition of the skin itself, but even ageing skin can be dramatically improved.

There is nothing one can do to stop the skin ageing, but the more care you take, the slower it will happen. We all want to grow old gracefully, and knowing what to do and how to care for it, hopefully will mean we always look at least ten years younger than we really are.

The next few pages are to help you work out your skin type and put together a good routine that will work for you. Never stop watching your skin; note every change and act quickly. Understanding your skin's needs is more than half the battle.

Chapter 13

Skin Types

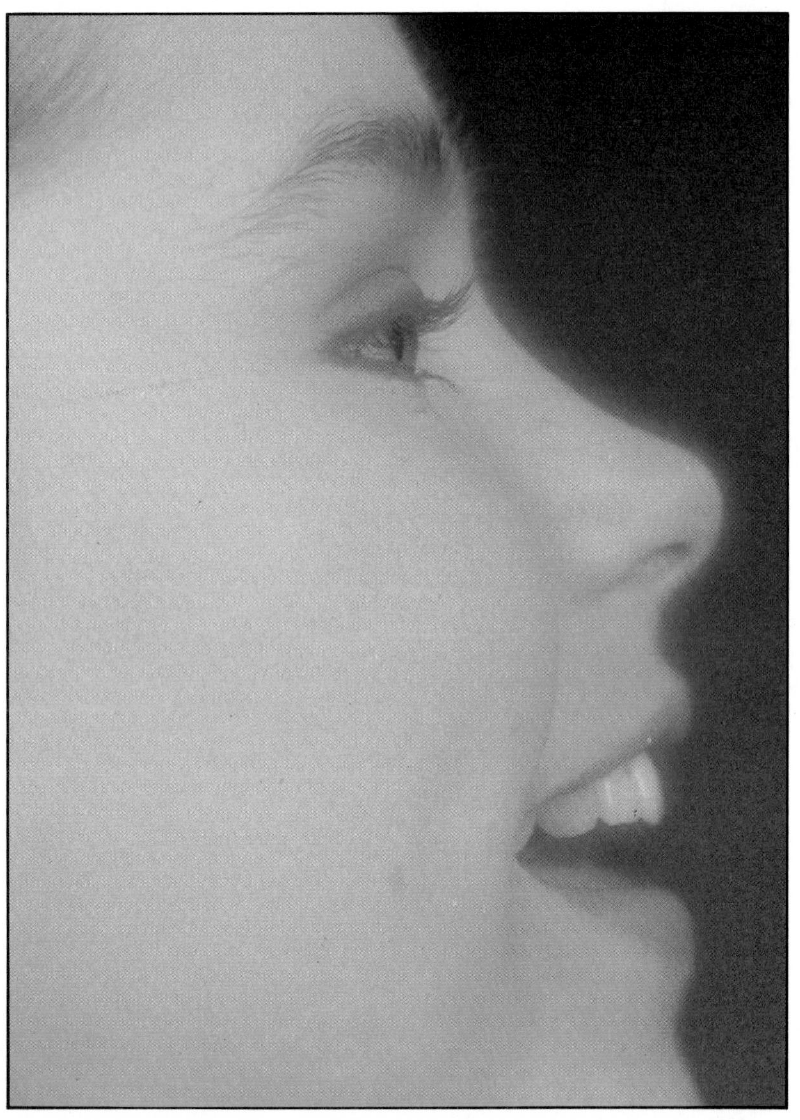

Dry skin must be tended very carefully, so watch for the first signs, such as lines around mouth and eyes. Left unnourished, these will become permanent wrinkles. Delay this by starting to replace lost moisture at an early age, thus keeping this type of skin looking its best.

Dry Skin An all-over true dry skin is almost always found on a blue-eyed blonde with a very fair complexion. Sometimes it can be a light red-head with freckles and pale skin – these skins are extremely fine and very sensitive and they take a great deal of looking after, but a fine, pale skin can be the most beautiful when it is cared for and in good condition.

A good cleanse, tone and moisturize routine is essential. This type of skin responds well to gentle, regular care; mild products are usually best as dry skin can be very sensitive to harsh or strong products. Unperfumed ranges are ideal. Dry skin is also extremely sensitive to the weather, hot or cold, to central heating, diet, food and drink.

Always treat dry skin with care; don't pull or stretch the skin, especially when removing make-up. Watch carefully to see the effect of any new products, and if the reaction is not good – i.e. the skin becomes drier, red, itchy or sore – stop using the cream or lotion immediately; you could be allergic to it.

Dry skin needs monitoring constantly, so note every little change and act on it quickly.

The worst enemy of dry skin is lack of moisture. This causes the surface of the skin to appear tight and lined. Real problem areas are around the eyes, forehead and mouth, the lines at the side of the mouth and also around the lips. Never forget to moisturize these areas well; and never forget the neck – another very vulnerable area. Fine lines, if ignored, can soon become permanent and unattractive; so whenever you cleanse or moisturize your face, smooth the products on to your neck: think of it as an extension of your face.

Dry skin can be hard work at times but truly the most rewarding. When it looks good a fragile, pale, peaches-and-cream complexion – the kind written about in romantic novels – must be worth a little time and effort.

To keep this skin in good condition never go out without some kind of protection, summer or winter, as this skin needs a slick of moisturizer or a light foundation at all times to act as a barrier against pollution and the elements. Remember, nearly all priceless things are fragile and delicate!

Blemishes and spots can be a problem with oily skin (below right). Diet will contribute towards avoiding this, but a good skin care routine incorporating a tinted foundation will help to conceal imperfections. If you like to wear a fringe, make sure your forehead is well cleansed so that oil is not trapped beneath the hair. If that problems persists, limit yourself to a few whisps instead of a full fringe.

Oily Skin The oily skin type is usually found on a darker, more sallow skinned person with dark brown to black hair. The excess oil will be found all over, but is often more concentrated on forehead, nose and chin. This is simply due to over-active sebaceous glands. What is causing them to work overtime can vary – it may be a harsh, astringent cleansing routine, it can be a stuffy, airless environment and sometimes it can be an over rich diet: all these are worth checking on.

This skin needs firm but not harsh handling. You need to be very careful in choice of products, which should be efficient enough to deep cleanse, thoroughly removing dirt and oil from the pores, but not too strong – if products are astringent and contain a high percentage of alcohol, they strip the skin of oil. For a short while this is effective, then, because the glands think the skin is drying out, they produce even more oil and the problem then becomes even worse.

Young skins can be oily due to the changes taking place in the teenage years – most people find their skin settles down after this – but there are, of course, the exceptions who find the problem continuous. Great care is needed to keep an oily skin healthy; the only consolation is that as you grow older a dry skin gets dryer

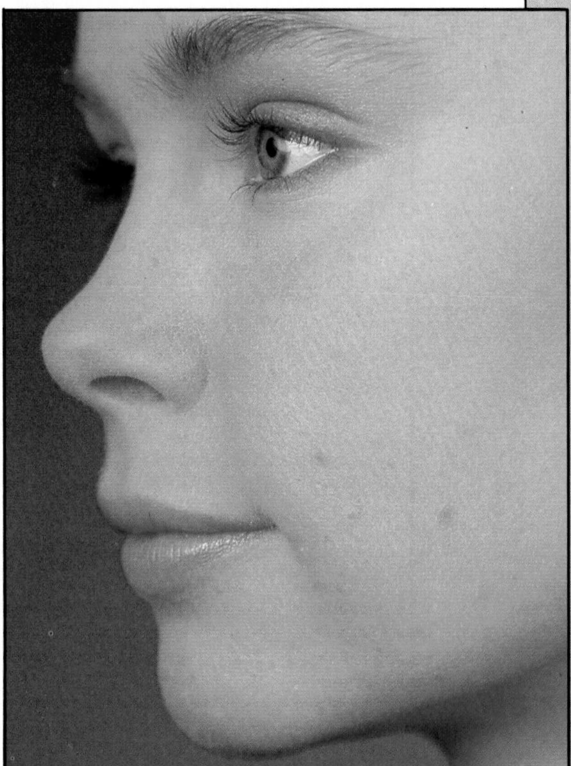

but an oily skin becomes normal!

The oily skin areas to watch are open pores down the centre panel. Also look out for blackheads and blemishes. All these can be greatly helped by keeping the skin clean and freshened. Blackheads are always the sign of a badly cleansed skin; they are a build up of oil and dirt in the pores, and these then lead to spots; so keeping the skin clean is the secret. Oily skin is a pretty tolerant skin, not usually highly sensitive to products and their ingredients; it nearly always loves sun, and ages less than other types. It is a good skin type but it needs the help of a firm hand; don't let it get away with anything – you are in charge.

Check that normal skin stays normal. Watch the nose and chin areas, and don't forget the neck – soft, smooth skin must not come to a sudden stop. Make use of any extra time you have, to ensure that hands and feet are up to scratch.

Normal Skin Normal Skin is probably the most coveted skin type. Any skin colouring and hair colour may have normal skin, and we all assume that, if we had perfect, normal skin, all would be wonderful.

If you are lucky enough to have a truly normal skin look out! Things can change, so don't be lulled into a false sense of security. You have the best so look after it; you need to keep the balance of your skin by using products for normal skin, watching for any changes and acting quickly if they occur.

Normal skin is very tolerant of all situations, but make sure it gets its fair share of fresh air and good diet – and don't abuse it. Like an old friend, you can be tempted to

Combination skin refers to facial skin where outer parts are dry and the centre oily. Special treatments are essential in these cases to keep the skin in tip-top condition. Treat the two skin types separately to give a balanced, finished effect.

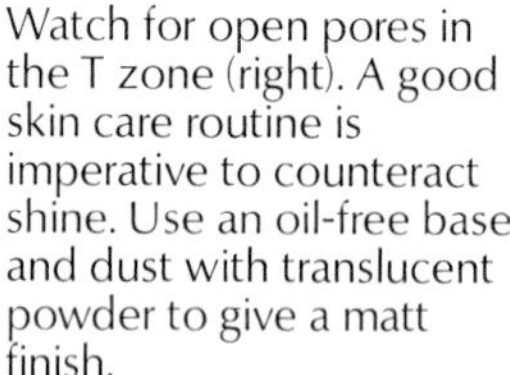

Watch for open pores in the T zone (right). A good skin care routine is imperative to counteract shine. Use an oil-free base and dust with translucent powder to give a matt finish.

take it for granted, so give it a special treatment every week; don't let it feel left out, you have the best so take time to keep it that way.

Pay special attention to the neck, and make sure this area is not drier than your face; it may be necessary to invest in a light throat cream to use once or twice a week. As you have a little more time than others with tricky skin routines, don't waste it. Spend extra minutes on hands or elbows which may need a bit more help.

Combination Skin This type of skin is usually found on a medium blonde or dark brunette with a variety of skin tones. It is probably the most common skin type and often the result of a poor skin care routine, or general neglect. Combination skin is very seldom an impossible problem, more usually a case of confusion and lazyness.

The word combination is the clue, meaning two skin types combined together on one face. Usually, the two types are dry/normal or dry/greasy, with the dry areas on the outer parts of the face (cheeks) and eye area, and the centre panel or T zone being normal to oily or greasy. The best way of tackling this skin is to treat it as normal, using products for a normal skin gently to cleanse the skin. Use a toner for dry skin on outer parts and one for oily skin down the centre to balance out the differences, followed by an application of moisturizer for normal skin just where it is needed, around the eyes and on the outer, drier parts, leaving the centre panel free; this way you can correct and balance the two skin types.

This skin really responds to special treatments. The T zone – called this due to its shape across the forehead and down the central panel – is the oilier part and a mask or scrub can be used on this area to make sure it is kept really clean. It works well if you use two face packs, one down the centre for oily skin, and one on the outer part for dry skin; this way you can treat the skin perfectly for both areas.

By taking care and understanding this type of skin you should see a real improvement, and, with time, achieve a normal skin. It is extremely important to watch for any change and tailor your skin care routine to the daily needs. Don't just repeat routines out of habit – there must be a reason for anything you do to the skin. Combination skin needs waking up and stimulating into action; you must be the inspiration to get the system working and then keep it going.

CHAPTER 14

A Healthy Routine

Different types of make-up need different cleansing routines. For soft, natural make-up (opposite page) use a quick, gentle cleanser. Heavier, more dramatic day or evening make-up (above) requires more careful removal. Eye make-up can be smoothed away gently with special remover, and a second cleanse should take away every remaining trace. Although make-up never harms the skin – in fact it protects it – every scrap must be removed at the end of the day to give the skin a chance to breathe.

Cleansing Clean, fresh skin free from blemishes is what we all strive for, and the basis for this is a good cleansing routine. Regular cleansing is more important than the products you choose to use, as skin needs constant and watchful attention.

Choose a product specially formulated for your skin type and use it! It is incredible how many people complain about products and on questioning have only used a product once; two to three weeks is needed to give a new cleanser a fair trial.

Cleansing is the general term for cleaning the skin: removing all make-up, dirt and grime from the atmosphere, and natural oils that build up during the day; also removing the dead layers of skin which are always on the surface, waiting to be gently removed, as a build up can give a dingy look to the skin and cause an uneven surface.

Eye make-up may need to be removed with a special eye make-up remover. Be very gentle around the eye; never pull or drag the skin – patience here is a virtue. There are oily or non-oily products and it is up to you to choose the one that suits you best, but the non-oily products seem to irritate the eyes least of all. Waterproof mascara can be a problem. Use the manufacturer's recommended remover to avoid making the eyes sore by rubbing.

Remove your cleanser either with tissues or damp cotton wool using upward movements – firm but gentle – and don't forget the neck.

A Healthy Routine

A gentle scrub with a skin soap and brush will help to clean oily areas – forehead, nose and chin. Make this a once-a-week routine. Massage the cleanser into the skin (bottom right) and remove with gentle upward movements with either tissues (opposite) or damp cotton wool. When removing eye makeup with the special remover, do so gently, taking great care not to pull or stretch the skin (below), since over the years rough treatment can cause lines.

If you need to wash your skin to feel clean use a wash off cleanser; a cream which is water soluble so you get the best of both worlds, and remove make-up by opening the pores with gentle massage so as to float out the deep down make-up and dirt (that no soap can do), rinsed off to give a fresh feeling and closed pores.

Don't forget the oily T panel. Cleanse this with special skin soap and brush to make sure there is no build up of oil or dirt, at least once a week.

Remember it's not what you use, but how often you use it. Skin needs constant attention.

Tone – cool and refreshing, even the most sensitive and fine skin needs to be toned after cleansing. The final trace of cleanser needs to be removed, the skin needs to be cooled and pores need to be closed after cleansing.

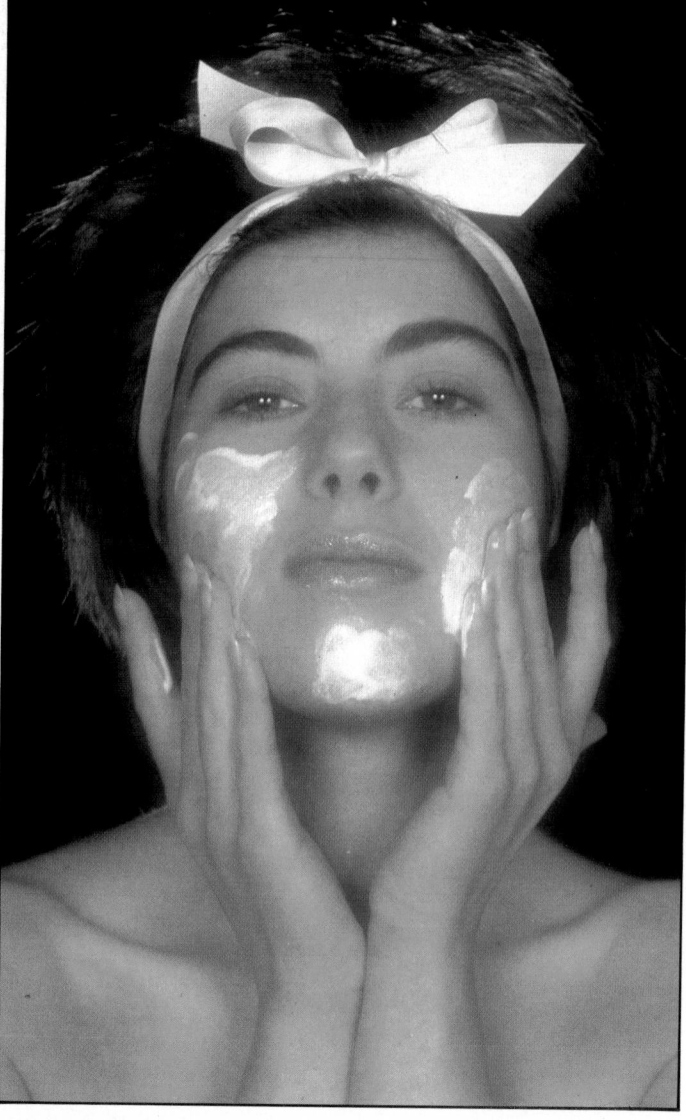

A facial splash with warm water can serve as a pleasant, sensual treat as well as a necessary antecedent to the application of toner.

Choose a product for your skin type; a toner should never sting or burn, it should just be cool. Apply to damp cotton wool to dilute strength if necessary.

Splash your face with warm water if you wish before applying toner. Be careful of very cold water; on a sensitive skin this can cause broken veins. Extremes of heat on the skin should be avoided.

These days toners can also balance the skin. This means the liquid is able to balance the 'P.H.' value of the skin. The 'P.H.' indicates the ideal natural balance of the skin between acid and alkaline: too acid means dry, too alkaline can mean spots, so we need skin that has a little of each. These P.H. balancing products help to prepare the skin for moisture and make-up, and

A refreshing spray with mineral water makes skin feel great (right). Follow this up with toning (above left), and moisturizing (above right), taking special care under the eyes. In any areas where lines are more obvious, apply a little extra moisturizer; the forehead and centre of brows can usually do with a little extra help. Remember to take moisturizer down over the neck. None need be wasted – even hands can benefit from any surplus.

Eyebrows frame the eyes and should balance with the eye shape. Follow the basic routine, trimming a few hairs from under the brow every day to keep them in check. You may alternatively need to extend the brow line by pencilling a fraction at the end. Brows become extremely important if hair is taken away from the face or tucked under a turban (opposite). If your hair usually covers the brows, remember to make adjustments when wearing a new style.

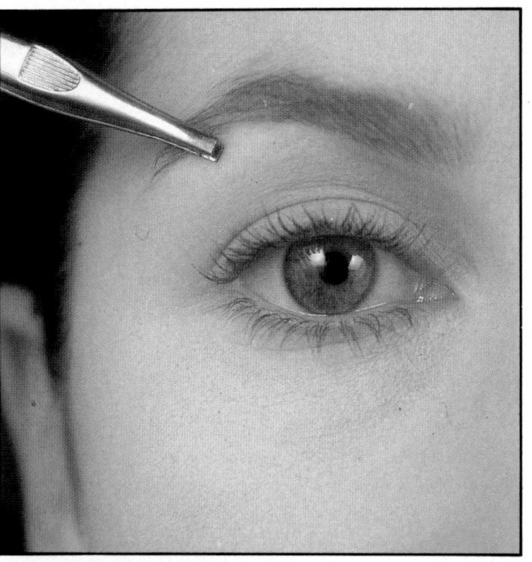

and smoke all have an adverse effect on our skin, drying and ageing it.

Fresh air is a rare thing these days, so we must compensate by replacing the moisture lost in all these different ways. Spray the skin with mineral water, cool and refreshing, either from an aerosol or spray, which is cheaper; drink several glasses of water a day and spray the rest on your skin, blot and then apply your moisturizer or under make-up base to prepare the skin for foundation. Skin in good condition will show now more than ever and needs the minimum of foundation. A good skin, well cared for, is a fantastic investment; it's the basis of your total look, and well cared for skin always looks younger. Some people read palms: maybe they should read faces!

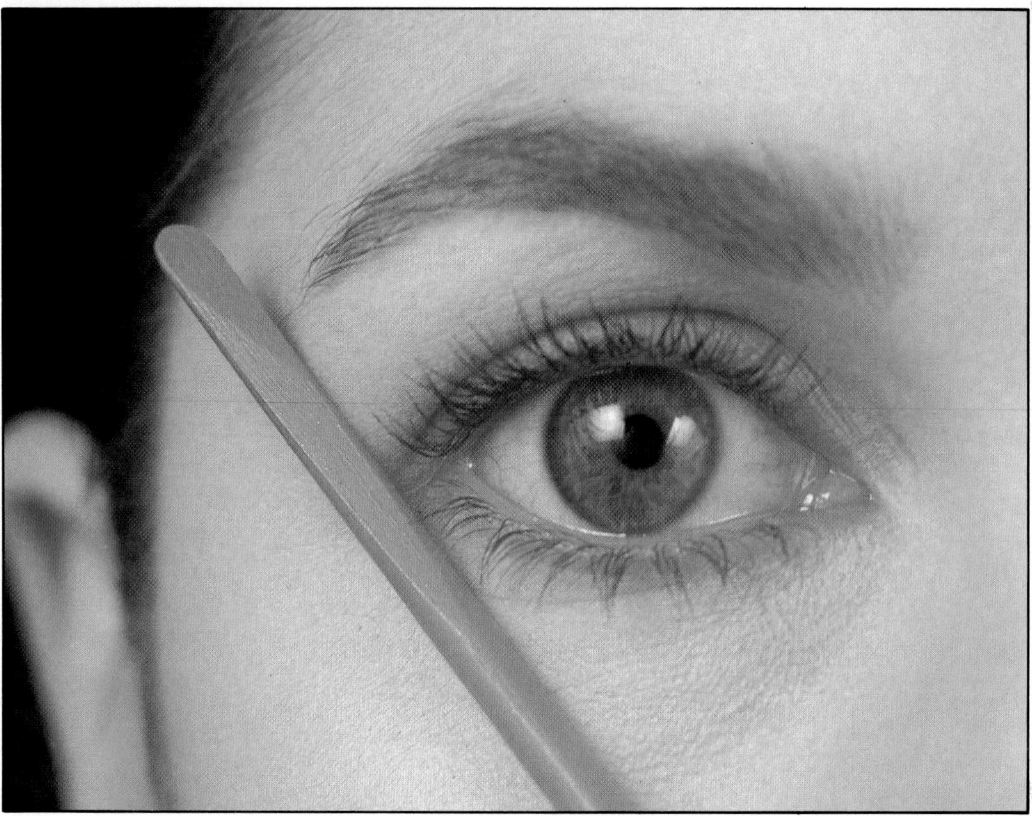

products will apply more easily on the skin and won't tend to change colour so readily. These products also seem to be free of perfume and more natural, which can only be a good thing for your skin.

Moisturise – replace the water loss – skin needs moisture as sure as your plants and flowers need it, and for the very same reasons. The elements – wind, cold and hot sun – dry out the skin, and central heating and air-conditioning don't help either. Polluted atmospheres, and chemicals we use every day: air fresheners, hair-sprays

Eyebrow Trim – eyebrows are the frame to the picture – so beware: do not remove without care! Eyebrows add character, and frame and balance the eyes.

Ideally, eyebrows should begin in a line above the corner of the eye – clearing the hairs which grow into the centre, over the bridge of the nose. They should finish on a line drawn from the corner of the nose to the corner of the eye and extended upwards. The browline is usually short of this point and needs to be pencilled in. Under the brow you need to clear any hairs which are 'stragglers' below the main body

Fresh, natural skin is great for a day look, but at other times a soft, subtle make-up can enhance features which are naturally good. Apply soft, warm, brown shadow on lids, and top with gold highlighter (below). Then consider, for instance, a cool, blue pencil under lower lashes and on the rim of the eye to add interest (below right). Coral blusher gently fluffed onto cheeks and temple will add a natural, all-over flow (opposite).

If your brows are very 'solid' and dark in colour you may need to thin or 'weed out' the hairs. This means taking out from the body of the eyebrows a few hairs every now and then to lighten the overall appearance of the brow rather than to pluck them very thin and still leave them dark. This way you can have them bushier but not so dark, and this is usually much more attractive: a better frame for the eyes and not so severe. Don't underestimate eyebrows, they are important; they give a professional look to your make-up so preparation is crucial. Once you have achieved the ideal shape don't leave it; trim the odd hair every day before you start your make-up. This way they never get out of hand, and you can keep the shape with no real bother. If you have real problem eyebrows it is a good investment to have them trimmed professionally so that you can follow the line and learn from the ideas

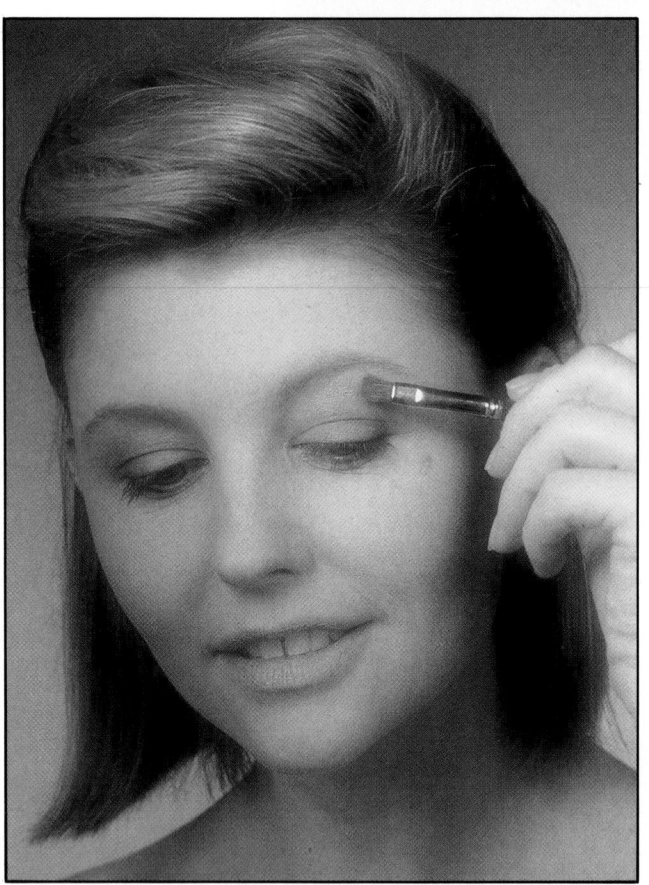

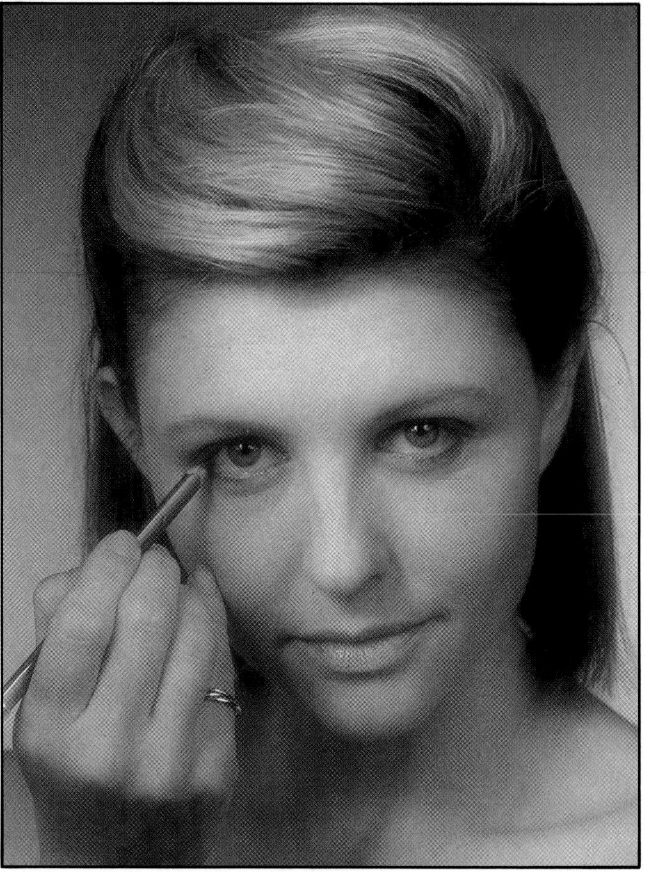

of the brow, but don't take too many – just tidy – never take from above the brow as a general rule – this will only lower the brow line, which is the opposite of what you need to do! In very rare cases one could do this if one brow was very much higher than the other, but expert help may be needed to set the pattern.

and tips. It could be money well invested; you can learn so much from watching a trained hand at work!

Make-Up Good skin, well cared for, can look fantastic. A fresh look can be ideal for daytime but don't forget, always apply moisturizer before you go out to maintain

A Healthy Routine

With a final touch of colour on the lips, a warm, peachy gold reflects the colours used on the eyes without becoming overpowering (below). Hair gently curled to frame the face completes the more groomed, softer daytime appearance (opposite), compared with the original look (below right).

the moisture levels; with a little mascara and a slick of gloss on the lips you have a very natural look.

Even very good skin can need a little help from make-up – you can enhance and add to a good skin to make it look even better – and a touch of light foundation will add a glow of colour and blend in any differences of tone – apply a touch of translucent powder all over, then on the eyes.

Add cool, blue pencil under lower lashes and on under rim of eye to add sparkle to the eyes. If they are blue, use light green, if they are green or brown, a clear colour adds impact without being too heavy.

Gently add a little soft coral blusher to the cheeks. A natural glow gives a very healthy look, and it helps to keep the make-up looking fresh; a touch on the temples also warms and softens some face shapes. Use a big brush as it helps to apply the colour evenly. If you have a long face, put a touch of colour on the chin. Warm corals and peaches are more natural than bright colours and pinks.

Use a warm, rusty brown shadow on the eyelids and blend upwards and outward to the eyebrows. Add a touch of gold highlighter onto the brow bone and a touch of rusty brown under the bottom lashes to balance.

Outline the lips in a natural brown colour and fill in with a natural tone. Peaches and golds are good, they add soft colour and also a little life – beiges and browns can be a bit too lifeless and make your natural make-up look dull.

Bathtime – a real treat – your piece of daily luxury, so don't waste it!

Plan and use every minute of it to the full: do everything you have to do and then relax for as long as you possibly can. Use this time really to unwind: do a few exercises while the bath is running. If you don't like the idea of a soapy, bubbly bath which may be drying on the skin, scatter in some dried flowers or herbs or a couple of drops of flower oil or flower water; they will give out a wonderful aroma, and these perfumes can actually help you to relax during the day and to sleep at night. Choose from any number available: lavender, rosemary, jasmine or camomile are just a few. It is important that you really enjoy the perfume you choose or it will not have the best relaxing effect.

If you have time for a long soak a herbal pillow can be fun. In the bath, rest your head on a soft pillow filled with herbs; the steam will warm them so they give off a wonderful aroma. You can then drift and dream, this is what your special time is all about – total relaxation. If possible, play your favourite music; all these things calm and relax you, helping you to cope better with day-to-day problems. They will never completely melt away, of course, but you will be so much more refreshed and strengthened – and able to manage.

A bath, listening to music, exotic aromas, and a cup of tea, may seem silly, out of the question, decadent! You are wrong: this is your time, spend it as you want. Solitude is a very old-fashioned word these days but it is a good one. We should learn to cultivate peace and quiet; being alone for a little while is essential and stimulating; it gives us time to be ourselves, think over our own thoughts, sort out problems away from anyone else, and this is difficult to do during a normal, busy day. At the end of a busy day you are expected to bathe! So take this time and use it to the full – exploit and use the freedom – and emerge calm, clean and refreshed in body and mind: a new woman!

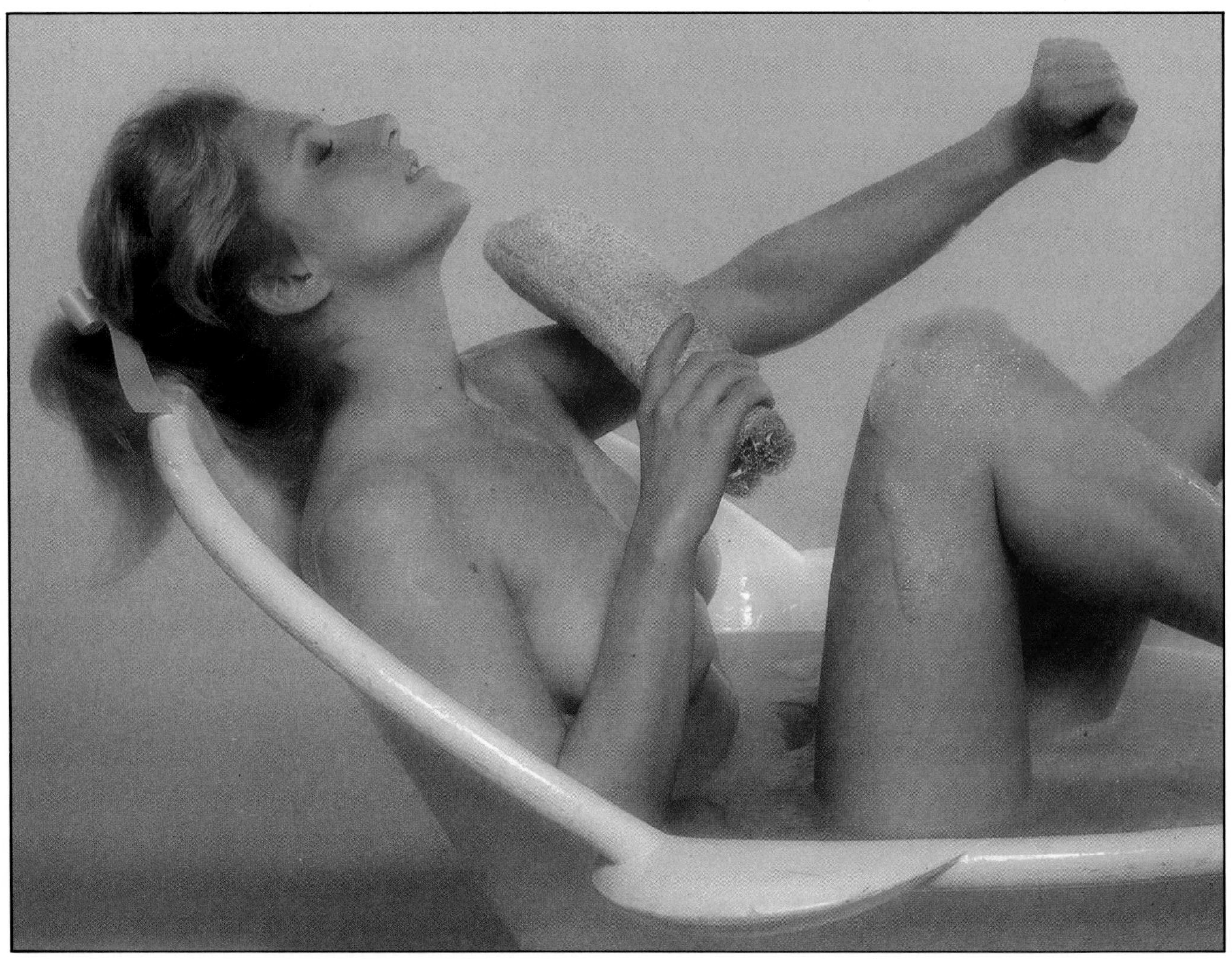

Make pleasurable as well as efficient use of bath time: relax, refresh yourself mentally and physically, and enjoy the opportunity for solitude and reflection.

CHAPTER 15

Special Treats for Your Skin

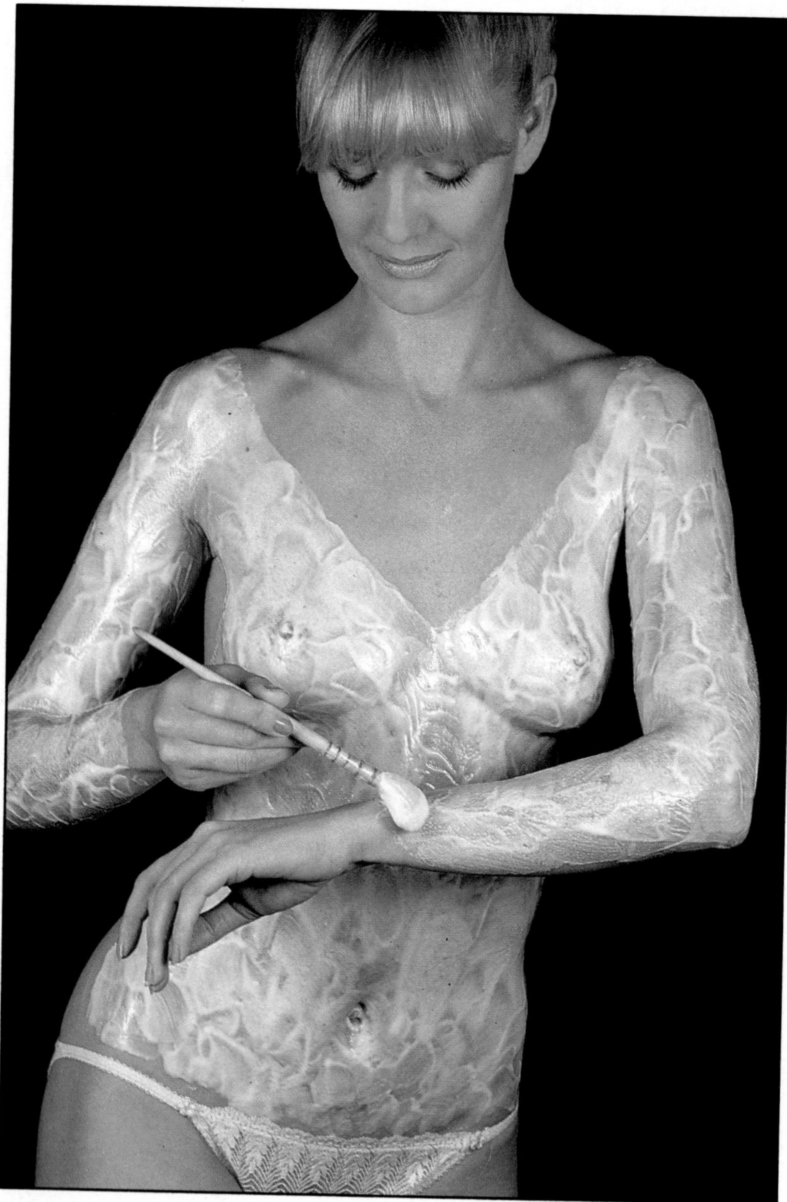

Combine a new diet with a skin care routine: taking time for steam treatment (opposite) or body masks (above) may help take your mind off food. Sip a cup of herbal tea to help you relax.

Beauty is said by some to be only skin deep, but we have a great deal of skin so let's look after it. We tend to cleanse and treat the skin on our face and neck but forget the rest of our body. Watch out for dry areas: elbows, knees – all skins suffer from the effects of the elements, especially in the winter, and most of it doesn't see the light of day till summer, and then we can have a shock.

It is important to cleanse the skin well – don't miss your back and shoulders – they need a firm touch as they can become oily under warm sweaters and woolies. A medicated soap can be very useful; used daily with a back brush it will help to keep skin free from blemishes which can be a problem here.

If you have a little extra time, a great treat for the skin is to do a body pack. Using natural yogurt as a base, you can add oil or lemon juice to it: for dry skin add a little almond oil, for oily skin, on shoulders for example, add a little lemon juice. Yogurt is wonderfully soothing to skin, a fantastic help on any skin problems or eczema, and the best help on sunburn as it will promote healing as well as cool down the skin – for this you could add a little honey – and don't forget, it is as good to eat as it is for your skin.

Steam and Heat A warm, herbal infusion gently to steam the face can be not only very pleasant but can also help with your skin care routine. The idea is to steep a selection of herbs and dried flowers in a large bowl – the water should never be boiling, just hot – this brings out the perfume of the herbs and also won't break your favourite bowl! You will need to let them 'rest' for 3 or 4 minutes and then you should place a towel over your head to trap the steam. This will contain the aroma of the herbs to stimulate the skin and, along with the warmth, will open up the pores and relax the skin. This is also great for easing sinus problems and, if you have a cold, it will help you to breathe more easily. After a few minutes, rest and then repeat. The skin should feel stimulated and glowing, never uncomfortable, and will be in the right condition to ease away any blocked pores or blackheads now that it is relaxed.

Special Treats for Your Skin

A creamy face mask applied with fingertips can really do things for a fine, sensitive skin, nourishing and moisturizing without being harsh or astringent (above). A gentle steaming with a warm towel (opposite) helps to tone up circulation and make skin glow.

If your skin is rather fine and sensitive be very careful not to overdo it. If the water is just warm it will still have a good effect; just like in the sauna, some people can take more than others.

Another way of stimulating the skin with warmth and steam is to use a hot towel. Soak a face cloth or small towel in hot water, wring it out, and place it over the face. Repeat this several times till your skin starts to glow; this will have the same sort of effect as a steam, but it is not quite so pleasant unless you add some flower oil, or rosemary oil, to the towel. This is a good treatment to get the circulation going and to stop skin looking dingy.

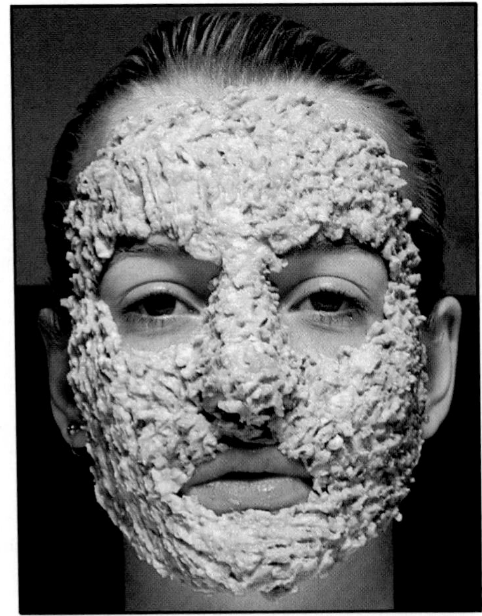

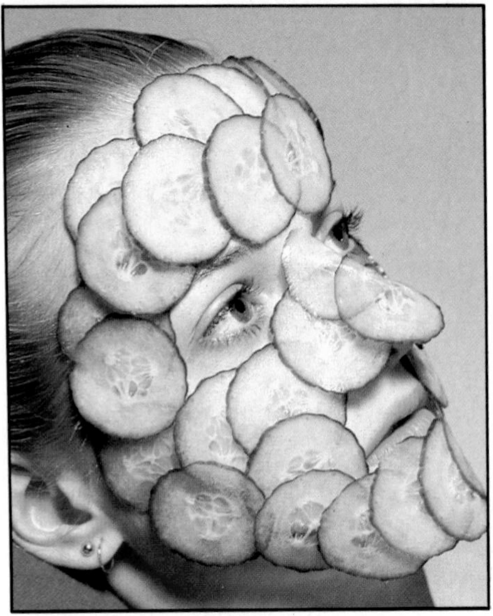

Today's face masks allow you to move your face muscles safely after application (above), while home-made ones come in a riot of colour. Don't be afraid to experiment with a whole variety of ingredients, such as mashed avocado (top right), cucumber (above right), or sliced strawberry (opposite). Some proprietory brands even have a refreshing, minty aroma (right)!

Face Masks Don't let us forget the face mask. Modern formulae have put paid to the old face masks which used to crack if you smiled; they still exist but most of the best, nowadays, are in a cream form so they are easy to apply and quick to remove, and they are also much more gentle on the skin. Choose one for your skin type and follow instructions. You can make your own, using a base like yogurt to make application simple, and add to it – for dry skin: almond oil, advocado (mashed), honey or egg yolk; for oily skin: strawberries (mashed), egg white, tomato or cucumber, one or two drops of lemon juice can also be added. If you have a combination skin, you can use a mask for oily skin down the centre and a dry skin mask on outer panels.

You may find it easier to apply a mask with a brush. Either follow time instructions

Body massage – the part of skin care you can share. It may not – indeed, need not – be totally professional, but it's free, enjoyable and doesn't require an appointment, so there are obvious advantages.

on the product or, if it is 'home-made' leave on for a good 15 minutes.

Massage is another way of stimulating the skin and toning up the circulation. You can give your face a quick massage every time you cleanse off your make-up. Gently massaging the skin when you cleanse it warms the skin and opens the pores so that the cleanser can get into the skin and float out the dirt, grime, and old make-up. A quick wipe over or wash cannot do this efficiently; a deep cleanse is necessary at least once a week to back up your day to day cleansing routine. For massage, you need a slightly creamier cleansing cream that will stay on the skin a little longer than the usual light cleansing cream.

Apply cream over the entire surface of the face and neck and, using long upward movements, gently but firmly massage the neck to the jaw line, including the sides as well, then move fingers over the chin area and upwards over the cheeks, using both hands. Still work on the centre of the forehead, easing out to the sides, then slip around eyes from the outer corners inward and over closed lids. Finish by working down the top of the nose and then the sides, finishing with the top lip and mouth area. Repeat all these movements 3 or 4 times each and if there are areas which need extra help, like the forehead if it is rather lined, spend a little extra time on these areas.

If you follow these easy steps, you will find that the skin feels good and relaxed afterwards, and, for a complete treatment, you can follow this with a face mask if you wish.

Do take note though: if you have not recently, or have never treated your skin to a work-out you may experience a few blemishes about a week later. This just means that your treatment is working! The stimulation will help to clear the skin and throw out impurities and, if the treatments are done regularly, the skin will settle down to your routine. It is best if you have a very special date to plan any treatment, either at home or in a salon, well ahead to give the skin plenty of time to settle down.

Vary these treatments from summer to winter, watching your skin for any change and balance and understanding what it needs.

Body Massage This kind of massage is extremely relaxing but a bit tricky to do alone, so the obvious answer is to find some help! This won't be the same kind of massage that would be done professionally as this takes years of training, but smoothing over the skin with firm and confident hands can have a very soothing effect. Start by giving a friend a massage and then another day they can do the same for you. Don't plan to swop massages at the same time – it would spoil the effect to have to snap right back into action. Afterwards, you need to enjoy the good, relaxed feeling and even to sleep.

It is a good idea to cover the bed or sofa with a large towel and also to have another one to cover the rest of the parts of the body that you are not working on, for warmth.

Massage can be done with cream or oil. Oil is easier as it will stay on the surface of the body longer, but if the skin tends to be naturally oily you can use talc. It is important to use one of these to help your hands to move smoothly over the skin.

Massage Routine Start your massage sequence with the toes and feet. You need to use firm and confident movements here as many people are very sensitive, and if it tickles it will not be relaxing for them. Massage each toe on one foot, then the

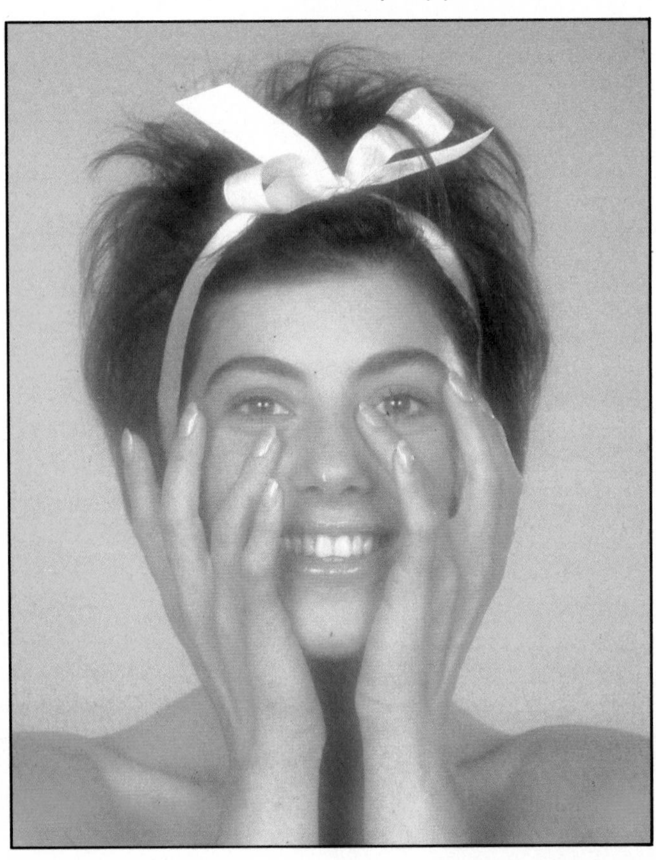

Give yourself a gentle but firm finger-tip massage, working inwards under the eye, and down the centre of the nose (above, left and right), then some upward strokes on the neck towards the chin (right). More upward strokes on the centre of the brow should be followed by drawing the finger outwards to the temples (far right). Cheeks and chin need upward, lifting movements (overleaf). Follow these steps every time you cleanse. They will help to prevent the skin being stretched, however quickly you need to operate. Once a week, however, spend more time deep cleansing and attending to problem areas.

Special Treats for Your Skin

foot itself, working up to the knee, then repeat this on the other side.

Then from the knee to thigh, spending extra time on areas where there is excess flesh – as well as smoothing here, a gentle kneading movement can be used.

fingers, hands and arms. Return to the back and repeat this again; the back, shoulders and neck are the areas most affected by tension so spend extra time here, especially across the shoulders and back of the neck – a gentle kneading movement is good, followed by a smoothing movement to finish. This should take about 15 minutes.

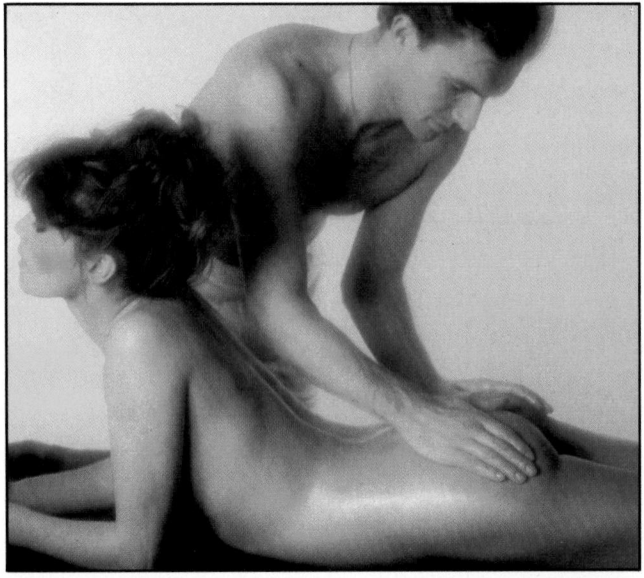

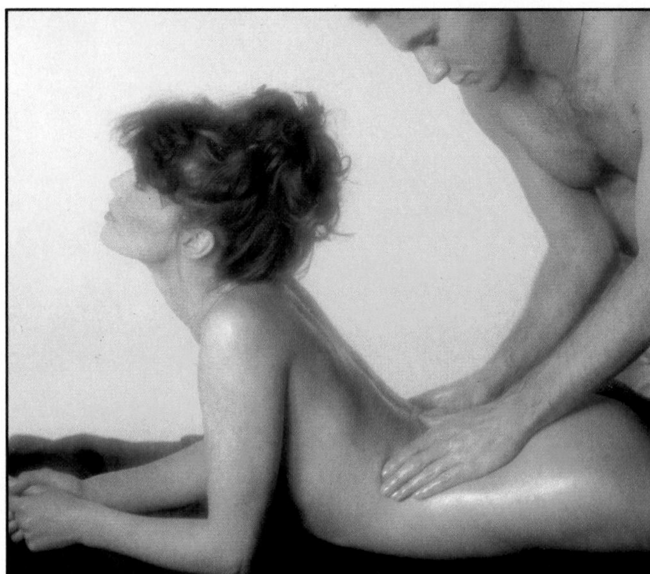

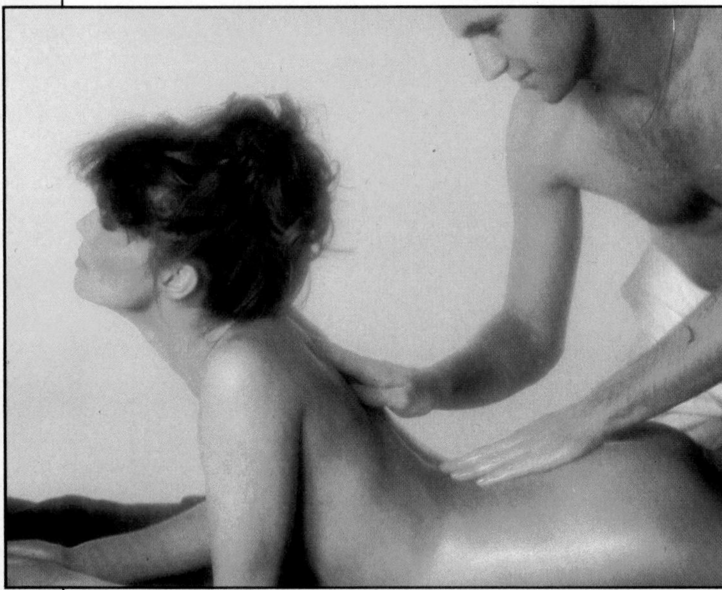

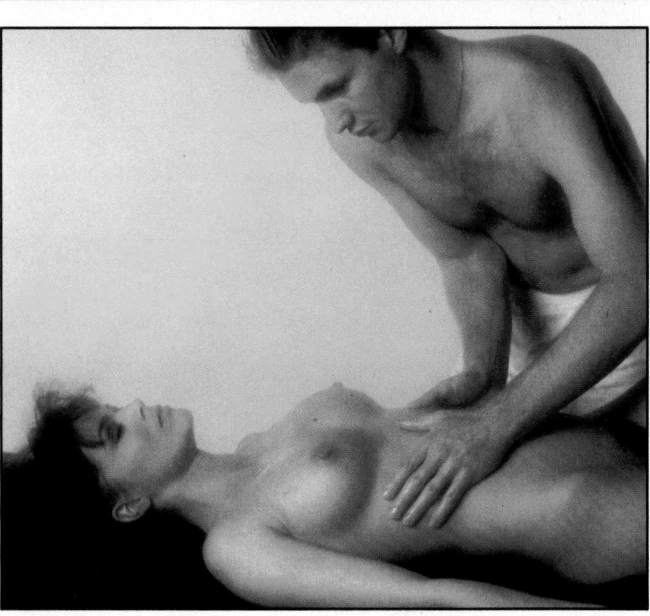

Educate your man in the art of body massage. Make him aware of areas where gentler treatment is essential, but learn to enjoy the various degrees of firmness which will help to tone up different parts of your body.

It is best at this stage if the person you are working on is lying on their back to begin with – this is more relaxing.

Never massage too firmly on the stomach area – you need to be extremely gentle here – the same goes for the chest area on a woman, but for a man it is OK.

Then turn over and repeat the sequence, from the feet up the backs of the legs.

When you get to the base of the spine, work gently up the centre of the back, and then on each side in turn. Then work on the

When you have completed this they should be totally relaxed so cover them over and let them doze for a little while.

The best person to swap massages with is obviously your man – so start helping him to relax and understand how enjoyable it can be – and how easily he will be able to do the same for you. Today, stress and tension are our worst enemies, so let's try and overcome them, and also have a smooth, supple body as a bonus.

Diet and Exercise

For a good, balanced diet you cannot go wrong with plenty of fresh fruit and vegetables. Vary these as the seasons change and you will not become bored. And, provided prices are reasonable, you will feel able to buy and experiment with the ever widening variety now available. Soups, salads and vegetable stews can be great fun – in summer or in winter.

Skin and Diet It has been said many times that your body is what you eat and I think, nowadays, we all tend to agree even if we don't follow this policy 100%.

The skin on your face, more than anywhere else, actually shows whether you have a good diet. Many people advise us only to eat good, fresh, high fibre, low fat foods, not to drink alcohol, tea or coffee, and all will be well. I am quite sure they are absolutely right – but they have forgotten to take one thing into consideration – we are all human!

Try and plan what you eat. Don't buy convenience foods in a rush, they can be expensive and are not all that good for you. Don't overcook food; in particular, eat vegetables raw whenever possible and make sure that you include eggs, cheese and fish in your menu; they contain the different minerals and vitamins that we all need. Fruit is also important; we all know now that oranges are rich in vitamin C but other fruits have useful things, bananas for example contain potassium and, like all fruit, natural sugars.

Crisp, fresh foods are great for teeth and body, contain natural sugars and vitamins in a handy pack, and offer the best convenience food you can buy – *and* you don't have to throw away the packet. They provide very filling snacks, yet are low in calories, so don't give you that 'over-full' feeling. Much better for hungry kids than biscuits and chocolate, and certainly quicker work for you.

Dried fruit and nuts can be a good substitute for chocolate; they are not necessarily lower in calories but are much better for you, providing natural sweetness as well as extra roughage.

Your skin will only look good if the body is working well.

The foods to avoid
White bread
Convenience foods
Too much fat
Tea and Coffee
Sugar
Too many dairy products

The foods to choose
Wholemeal bread and flour
Low fat milk and yoghurt
Fresh fruit and vegetables
Fish
Brown sugar or honey
Liver
Fruit juices
White meat
Nuts and dried fruits

The foods to avoid are those that tend to make the body sluggish and inefficient. You need the roughage and fibre in crispy fruit and vegetables and wholemeal flour to get your digestive system going, but be careful how many dairy products you have as they tend to contain some of the things to avoid; good in moderation but don't overdo it. Milk, cream, meat and eggs, for example, have a high fat content, just the same as butter and chocolate. Be aware of

Exercise should be fun. You need space to do it in, and clothes in which you feel comfortable. You should also be warm and relaxed before you start since tense, cold muscles can easily be pulled. So limber up as a dancer would – slowly to begin with, starting with a few deep breaths to calm yourself. (Overleaf) holidays can be ideal for exercise. Use the beach early in the morning for a long run, then do your routine undisturbed. Plenty of fresh air and space will give you a healthy appetite and allow you to enjoy every minute of a full day.

what things contain, this is very important to your choice of foods. Some of the things we were always told to steer clear of can actually be better for you – brown bread and jacket potatoes, baked beans and wholemeal spaghetti served with vegetables and without rich, creamy sauces or butter can be not only low in calories but also extremely healthy. It's things like chips that are bad news because the potato's skin or fibre is removed and they are coated in fat in the cooking; you have thrown away the best part!

If the digestive system is working well, the impurities are not retained in the system and your skin will show this by appearing fresh and clear. Your eyes will appear brighter and you will sleep better, and this can only help the way you feel and

And, because you are relaxed, you'll sleep so much better.

look. If you feel more active you will then naturally do more, which will keep you fit and get you out into the fresh air: ride a bike, go for walks, all these things are so much more fun than sitting in front of the T.V. with a bag of crisps!

It is, of course, a question of balance – start by looking at your diet over a week, or even a month, and note the good days and bad days – we all have them and they compensate one for the other. If you have a day when you eat all the wrong things – sweets, white bread, too much coffee – then make the next day a day of salads and fruit juice. This way, over a period of time, it will balance out. Try to avoid bad eating habits, i.e. eating the same wrong things every day. Cut down on tea and coffee, sugar, fat and salt, but don't try to do without them completely. Watch the amount you eat: I believe we all eat not only the wrong things but far too much.

Exercise Toning and strengthening your body is important – you may be asking at this point what this has to do with skin? To my mind, there is not a lot of point in having smooth, soft skin from top to toe if it doesn't look good. Apart from that, exercise is good for the well-being of your whole body, and that includes the skin.

If you have never done exercises before, take note – don't go mad, take it easy, as all too often we get carried away by a rush of enthusiasm. Making a body do things that are totally alien to it can be dangerous, so we must start slowly. If you have any doubts or reservations check with your doctor first, to make sure that it is a good idea. You can exercise at any age but a certain degree of care must always be taken.

Exercise is very good for you because it makes you use muscles and parts of the body that in our modern lifestyle never get called on. It helps your breathing, it gets the system working and the effect of this is a general sense of well-being. It helps to relax you and strengthens both your mind and body so that you become fitter and better able to cope with your day-to-day affairs. It also makes you aware of your strengths and capabilities as a person. The discipline is good training for the other parts of your life; it helps you realise that when it comes down to it, you are in control of your own body.

There are many ways of taking exercise: joining a health club to work-out; joining a dance class; all kinds of sports and swimming, or just on your own at home – you must choose. Some people like to exercise in company, while others prefer to do it on their own. The important part of the whole idea is that you do some kind of exercise, and as a bonus it can even enhance your social life as well, by bringing

Exercise to your favourite music to help you keep the 'flow' going. It's best to keep to a sequence that you can vary just a little as you go – it's easier that way, and less confusing. This is particularly important if you are not so young – you must embark upon exercise gradually.

you in contact with people who share the same ideas.

Some General Exercises To give you all the information on exercise is in itself a subject for a book, so here are just a few very general exercises to help you begin. There are endless exercise programmes available on tapes, in books and magazines. You must choose the one that seems to fit your needs best. The only thing I would say is, whichever one you choose it must be fun and enjoyable and you must take it step by step, a day at a time, and never force yourself into a position you cannot easily achieve.

Here are a few basic steps for you to follow to start you off.

Exercise 1 Stand with feet apart and raise right arm up and over head, this stretches the side and top of the body. Let your left hand slide down the left leg – gently pushing over till you feel the pull on your waist – change to the other side. Repeat this several times.

Exercise 2 Rise up onto toes and gently, arms out at sides, bend knees till in a sitting position, hold for a count of ten and raise arms above head. Repeat this 6-10 times.

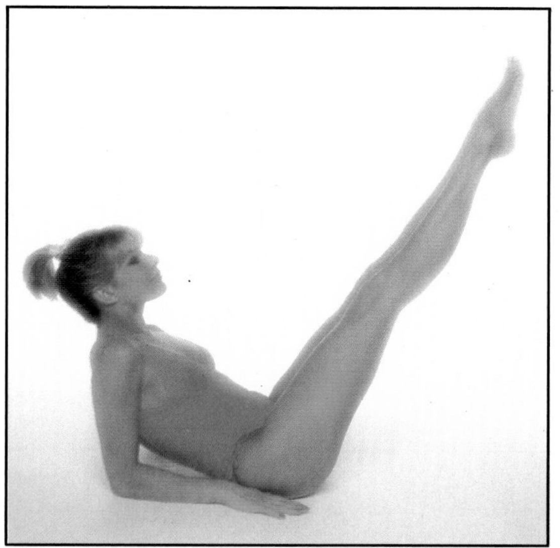

Exercising may make you feel uncomfortably hot – this means the routine is working. But you can take precautions, like tying your hair back: it can be very annoying if it falls around your face, and you may not want to wash it every time you exercise.

Exercise 3 Lie on floor with hand supporting head and raise one leg as high as is comfortable. Repeat this 10 times and then change to the other leg.

Exercise 4 Lie on floor and support back on elbows. Lift legs together as high as possible and hold for a count of ten. Repeat this 6-10 times.

Exercise 5 Stand with feet apart and bend from waist to touch the floor, at first trying ten bends. Rest and repeat five times. Eventually, you may be able to put your hands flat on the floor; this will come with regular exercise.

Exercise 6 Sit on the floor and reach to touch toes, again try to touch ten times and then repeat five times.

Go gently to begin with, each day you will stretch a little further.

Body Watching

Sleep and Relax A good night's sleep is a wonderful thing – if you always sleep well be extremely thankful, it will show in your face. Sleep helps us gather our strength and rejuvenate ourselves ready for the next day. You need to be relaxed and calm in mind and body to get the maximum benefit from a night's rest.

Don't go to bed if you are tense and uptight, plan for sleep: don't eat and drink too late in the evening – the body doesn't like to rest while still working. If you sleep badly, try eating early and just have a light meal. If you have problems, try and solve them logically before retiring, work out what can be done and plan to do it first thing in the morning. Try and clear your mind, make a list of the problems and what action you must take, you will achieve nothing if you are tired and bad tempered the next day.

Take a warm, but not too hot, bath with some nice smelling oils. Soak for a while and let the warmth and lovely scents relax

Sleep and exercise may seem total opposites. Not so – exercise at the end of the day, followed by a warm bath, can help the body to relax and allow you to enjoy restful, refreshing sleep. Tension and worry are the main causes of sleepless nights, but a good routine prepares the mind and body for sleep. If sleepless nights present a real problem, check all the ideas suggested here, and do consult your doctor if you are still worried. This should put your mind at rest and so get to the root of your problem.

Sleep is important for fresh, lively skin, but don't panic – we all need differing amounts of sleep. Remember that eight hours is only an average – some people will need ten hours, others as little as three or four.

you. Sip a cup of herbal tea afterwards, camomile is a great one for those who can't sleep. Sometimes it helps to talk things over with a friend, ask others for their opinion; it may throw some new light on the problem and help you to work things out.

If you can't sleep it may be very simple; you may not need to sleep. Some people need very little rest so don't force yourself – take up a hobby, read, study, make use of the extra time you have. When your body is tired it knows and it will demand sleep. Comfort is essential – make sure your bedroom is warm but not overheated, and that the bed is comfortable – you cannot relax unless it is. Forget your problems – you can either do something about them or not – and either way sleep will help your plan of action, so relax, sleep and dream.

If you could go on holiday tomorrow, would your body be ready? If not, why not? Don't leave things to the last minute. Check and maintain your body continuously: hiding the things you dislike is simply self-deception – all must be revealed in the end! Always aim high, and don't be satisfied with second best. Pride in yourself should be the most important thing to you.

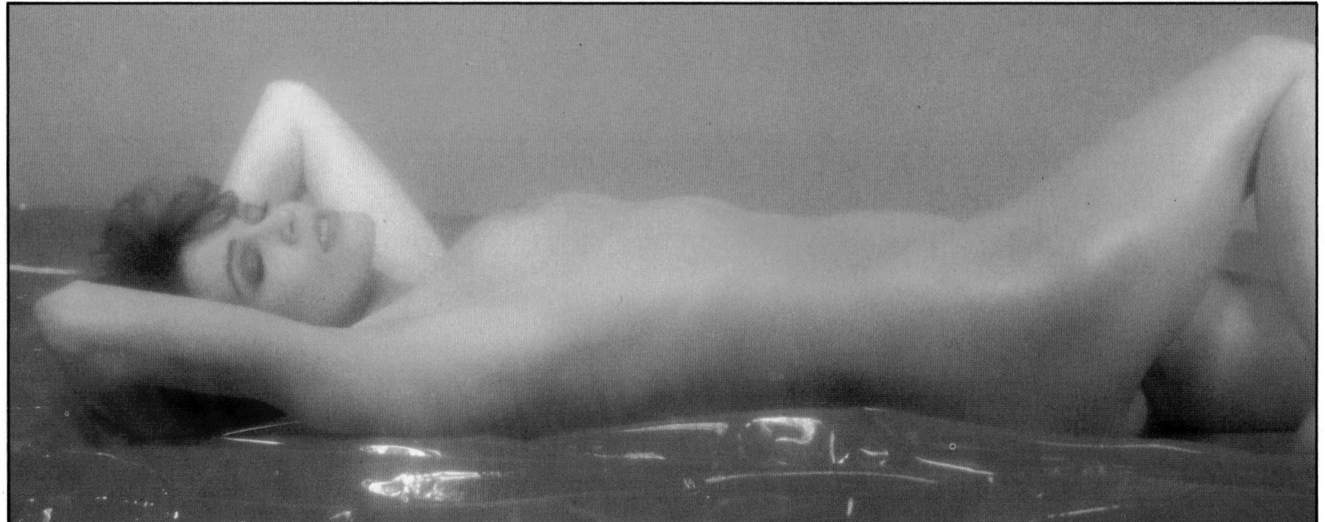

In the morning you and your skin will be fresh – if you look good everything will be seem much better. Your skin replaces its new cells and renews itself while you are sleeping, so give it a chance to work for you.

Body Watch This is something we should all be doing. Don't be lulled into a sense of false security; a beautiful body never stays exactly the same, it needs maintaining just like your car, but as with that, you don't wait till it stops before you do something. Every month you need to have a service! Check on hair, nails, skin and legs, underarms and hair colour. See if you need a check at the dentist. Do you need anything from the doctor? Plan ahead if it's summer. You may need to check jabs for holiday trips. This way nothing gets left too long. Make sure you have all the things you need: vitamins, shampoo, cleanser. Spread buying these over the weeks so you can take advantage of special offers. Buying make-up and skin care products in a hurry is never a good idea, you need to think and plan to get the best value for money and the products you really want. You sometimes get great suntan lotion offers in winter, so buy then and keep it till later in the year, it will be fine for months.

The quality of your skin is obviously important for those special, even formal occasions (above), but be aware that you cannot afford to let things slip at other times. A healthy glow in your skin will help keep you looking sophisticated and positive even when you are at your most casual (opposite).

Work out when you might take a holiday and, if necessary, go on a sensible diet two months before rather than wait and then starve yourself for a week in a panic. It's much better for you and your skin. At Christmas, lose a few pounds in advance so that when, like everyone else, you add on a few it won't matter. This way you can enjoy everything and still be in control. Have a spot cover handy for Christmas as the rich food may upset your skin.

Check, also, on what you are eating, and if there have been some bad days in the past month try and watch things now. A very good idea is to take one day a week when nothing else is planned and just drink fruit juices. Try mixing mineral water (Perrier) with your fruit juice, this not only gives it a sparkle but cuts downs on calories.

Some people find one day's fasting a week keeps their weight stable; it also rests your system and helps it to deal with impurities, this is why you always fast at the

After checking legs and underarms and removing any unwanted hair, give your body an overall tone with the sponge (this page) to make sure any creams used are completely removed. A back scrub (opposite page) offers an effective method of keeping the skin in this area in good condition. Remember that backs, shut in warm winter woolies, tend to suffer, and circulation needs waking up.

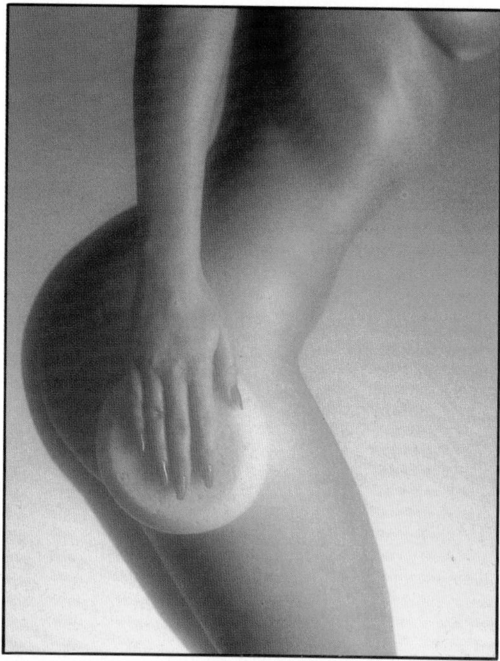

beginning of a visit to a health farm.

Think of calories as money. Some foods are very good value, high in fibre and nutrition, low in calories, so don't waste them any more than you would waste your money. Balance is alway the word to keep in mind.

Body Bits Take an afternoon or evening when you are on your own to give yourself a top to toe treat.

Massage the problem areas like hips and thighs and go over any parts of the body where the skin is not so smooth with a loofah or rough towelling back-scrub. Use a medicated soap on any oily patches like back, shoulders and tops of arms as these often get left out in a day to day routine. The days you choose to fast are good days for this – it will also take your mind off eating!

Have a good look at your feet. Any dry skin can be worked on here with a rough stone, as mentioned in the pedicure routine.

Do any hair removal. You sometimes need time on your own to do this, so plan a good, quiet time for it, so that you are not disturbed – it's not the best of beauty routines to do with an audience.

Give your eyebrows a trim and make sure they are still a good shape – keep an eye on fashion trends, you may need to grow them a little, or fine them down; styles change here as with clothes and hair. Face masks and body treatments are good on these days, but plan ahead – you may need to buy some special products, but don't use this as an excuse for not doing the treatments as you will only be cheating yourself; you will feel so good afterwards it really is worth a bit of organisation.

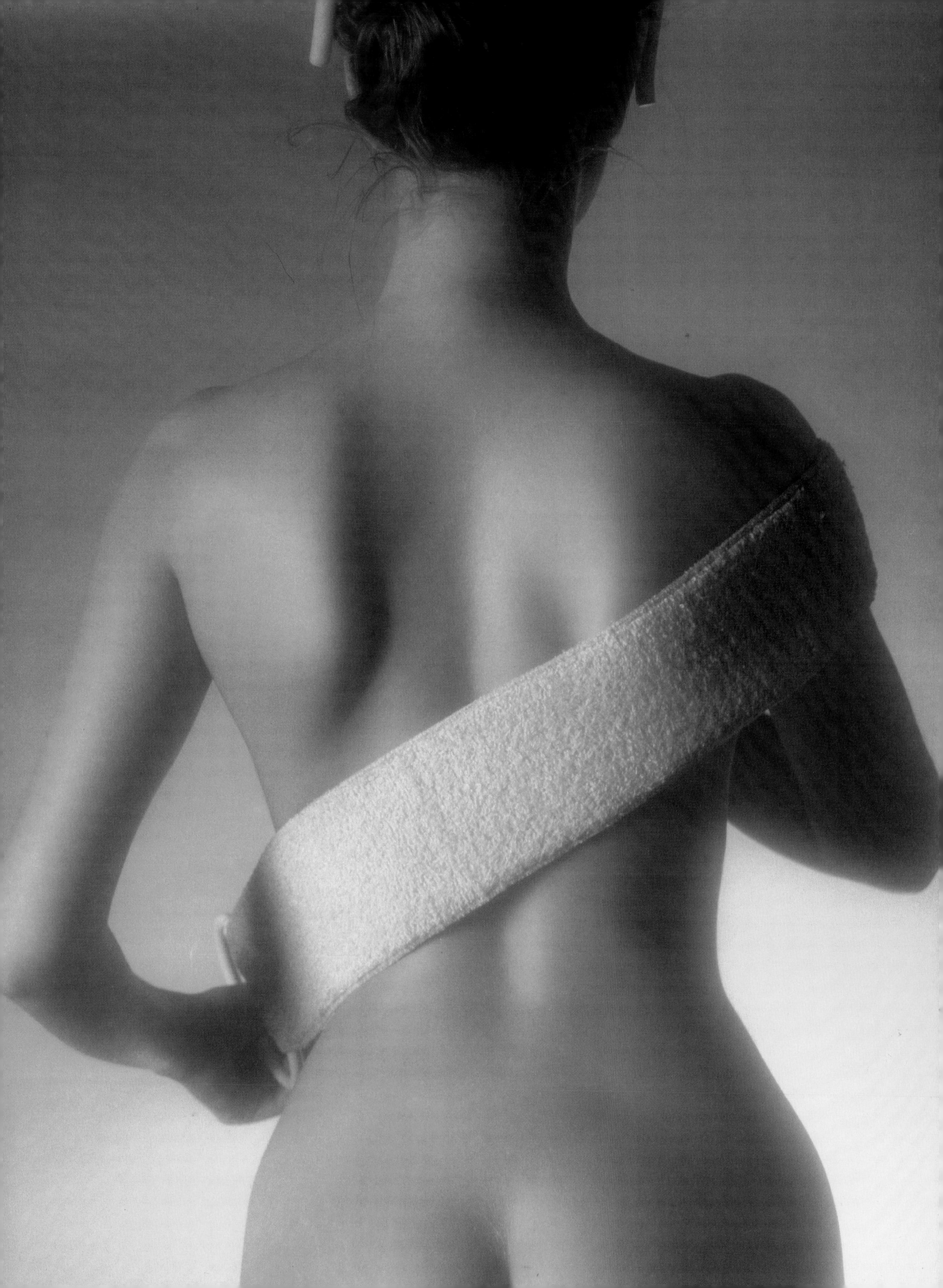

To freshen skin that feels and looks tired, and to keep a check on young skins, a face scrub (top pictures), used once a week, can work wonders and give skin a healthy glow. These creams contain tiny, gritty bits which gently stimulate and cleanse skin as you massage. This leaves the skin fresh for a natural day look (opposite), as well as smooth enough to be ready for a more elegant evening effect (right).

The Care of Hands, Feet and Legs

Hands are the most rewarding part of the body to care for. Improvements can always be effected providing the care you lavish on them is regular. Follow these easy steps and you will see an instant improvement. You really couldn't ask for a more immediate, beautiful and beneficial effect.

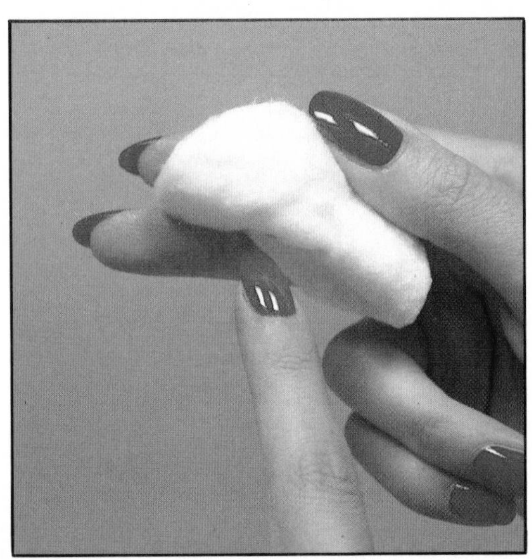

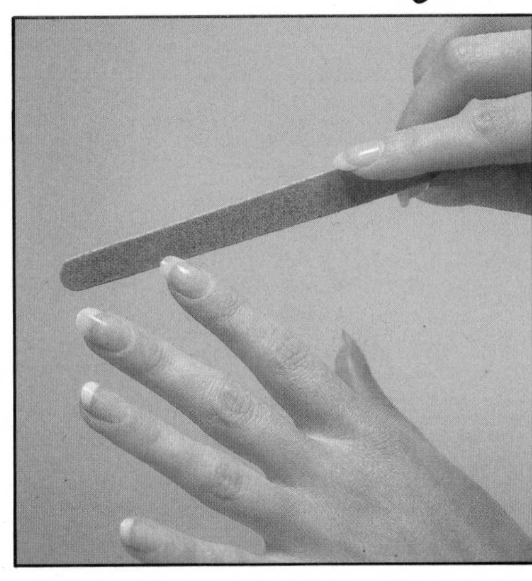

Hands Some people say you can tell everything from someone's hands. If this is true, it is time to take note and take action. Beautiful hands can be the most attractive part of a woman's body, so look after them. You need to be able to show them off with confidence, you cannot wear gloves for ever!

Hands don't need to be exotic to be attractive, just well groomed and pleasing to look at – and remember, jewellery does not look good on hands with bitten nails. If you have good hands and nails you are very lucky, but if this is not the case, you can always improve them with a little care.

First of all the skin must be smooth and supple: skin that is cared for will eventually produce good nails. It is also important to maintain a good diet and not expose the nails to the hazards of housework. At least once a week you should attend to hands and nails by following this simple routine:

1 Remove any old nail polish.

2 File nail to desired shape. Don't file away the sides of the nails as this will weaken them and encourage them to break.

3 Soak hands in warm water for 5-10 minutes. If the nails are very dirty a little mild

Think carefully about the nail colour you choose: it should tone and blend with your outfit and lip colour and be part of your total outfit (opposite page). If you have time to change your nail colour for every outfit – great If not, don't compromise: choose a neutral shade that will blend with everything.

soap or shampoo may be added to the warm water. Brush the nails gently with a nail brush.

4 Dry hands gently, pushing back the cuticles with the towel. This can be done every time you wash your hands, and in that way cuticles never become a real problem.

5 Ease back the cuticles with a rubber-tipped cuticle stick, or cover an orange stick at the rounded end with cotton wool. Never treat this area too roughly. Cuticle cream can be used if you wish.

6 Clean under the nails carefully with a cotton wool-covered orange stick, it will help if you make it slightly damp.

7 If there are any loose bits of skin around the cuticle which might pull, clip them away, but don't actually cut around the cuticle as this will only make the skin grow thicker.

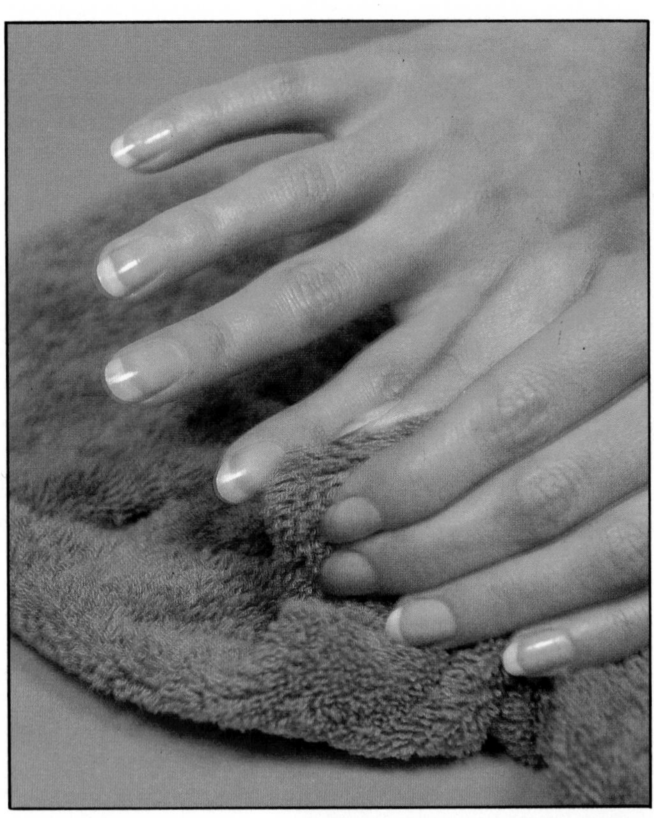

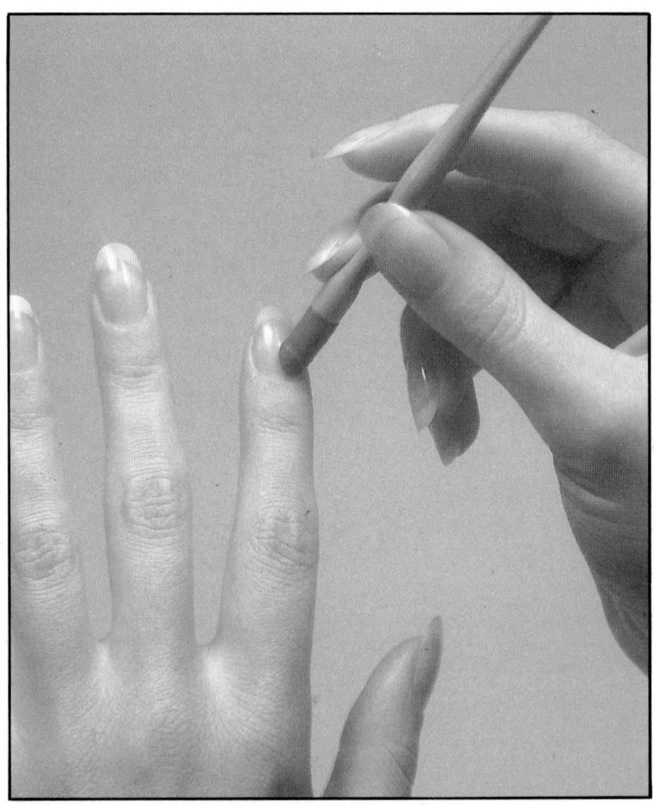

The manicure routine should always be gentle: at no time should fingers or nails hurt. Always cover the orange stick (right) with cotton wool as a protection. Clip any rough areas of skin and make sure you never cut the cuticle.

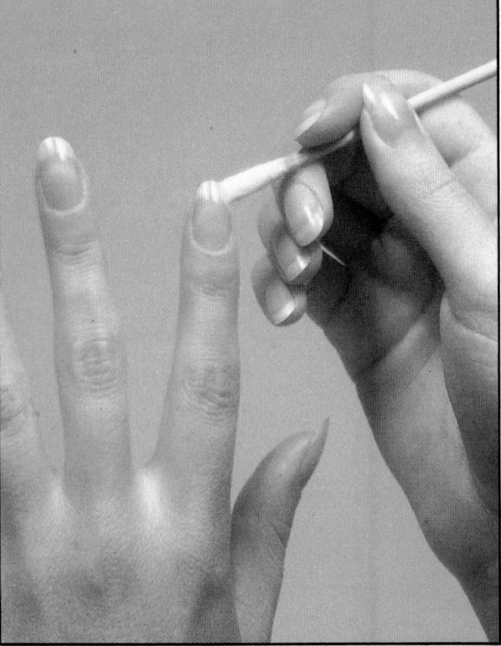

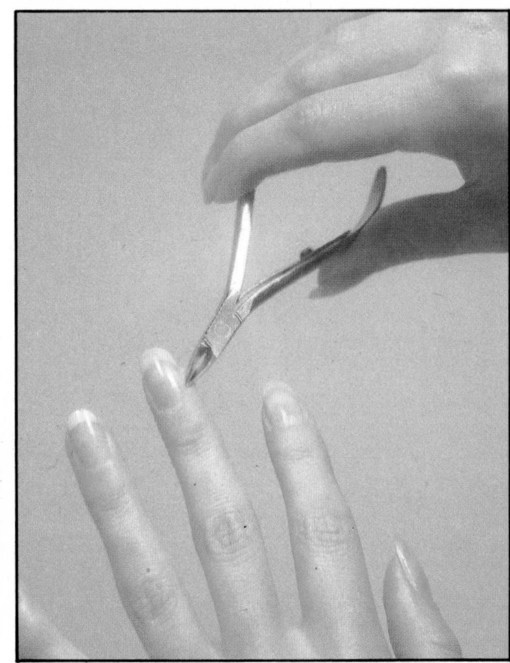

MOET
Cuvee
CHANDON

Applying polish to last is an art – it needs patience, and time between coats for it to dry well. Applying a base coat *and* a finishing top coat (this page) is the only way to achieve a professional effect.

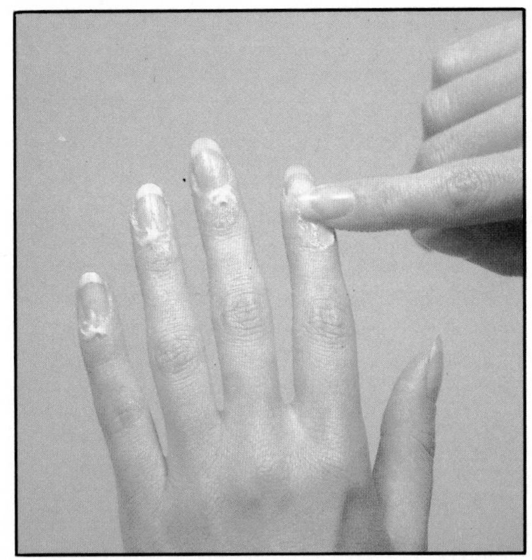

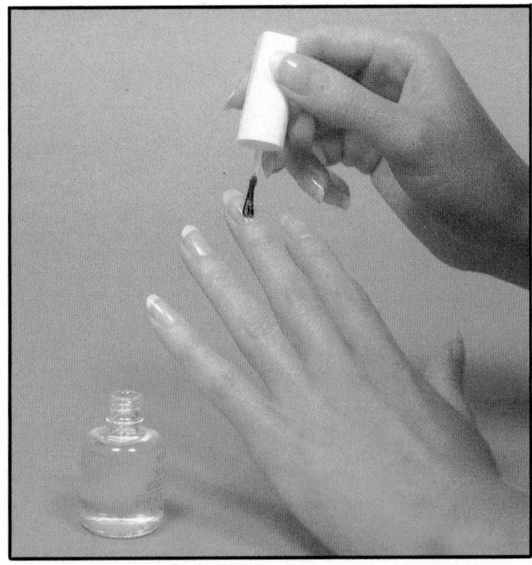

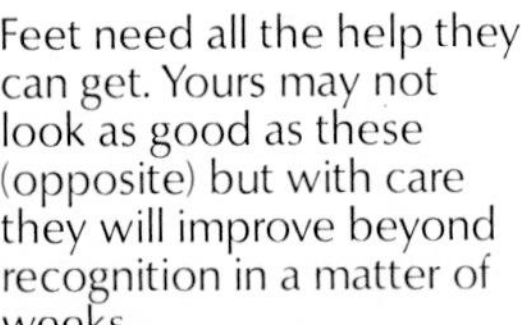

Feet need all the help they can get. Yours may not look as good as these (opposite) but with care they will improve beyond recognition in a matter of weeks.

8 Apply hand cream and massage into the skin, taking extra care around the nail area where the skin can be very dry, which in turn will make the nails dry also.

9 Wipe nails clear of any cream and apply base coat. If your nails are ridged choose a base coat that will smooth them out; there are several on the market.

10 When base coat is completely dry, apply colour polish in 1 or 2 coats, waiting in between for the coats to dry.

11 Finally, apply a clear top coat. This protects the polish and makes it last longer.

You will notice an improvement right away. Manicuring your hands is probably one of the most rewarding beauty routines as it can show instant improvement, and you won't often get that!

Feet Beautiful feet are very rare – if you have them you are extremely lucky, but if, like the majority of us you don't, we must start work now. For 9 months of the year we totally

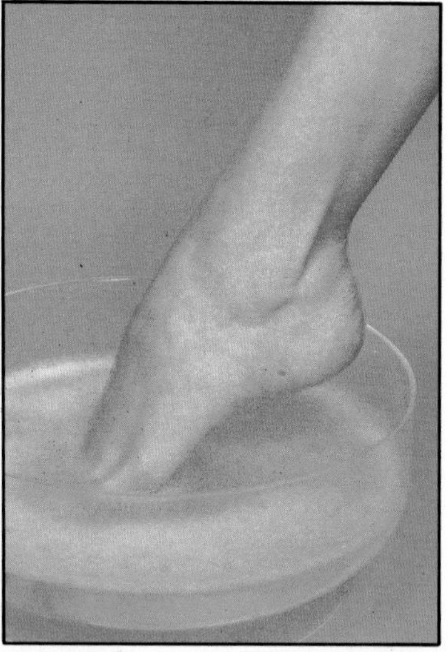

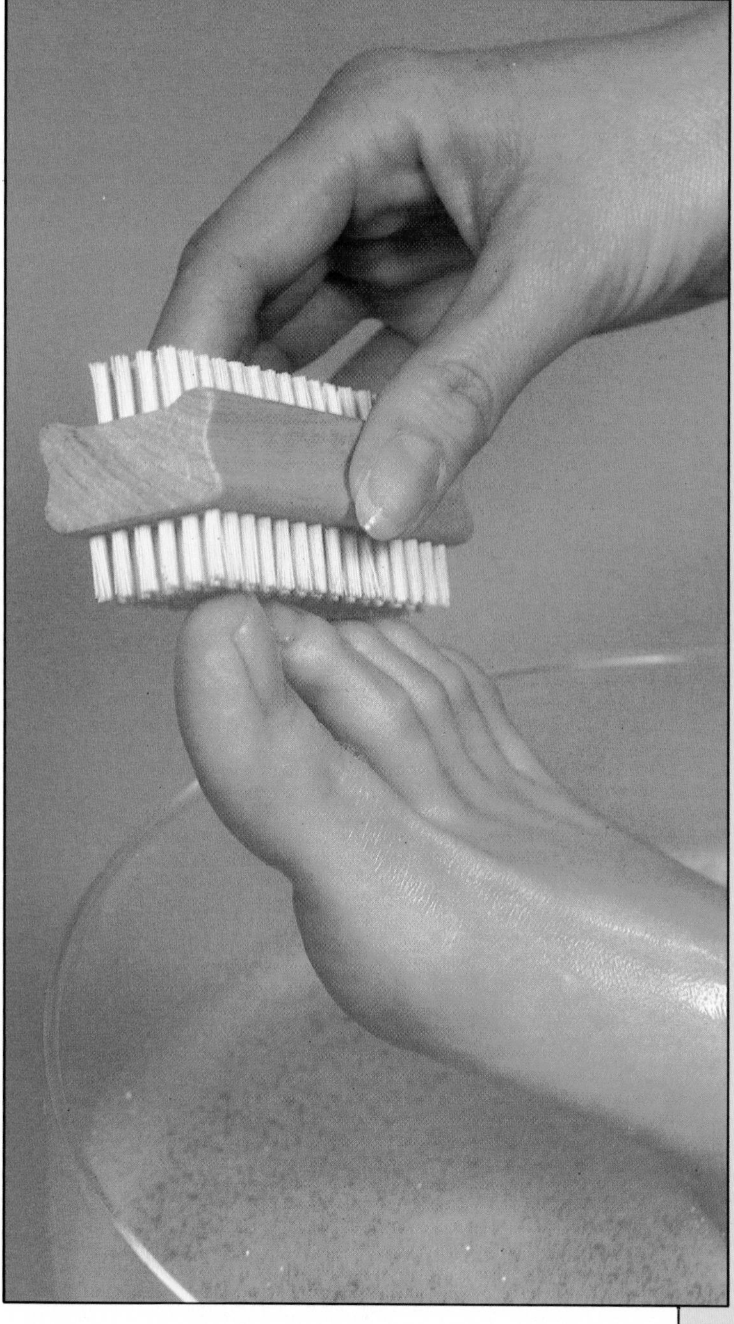

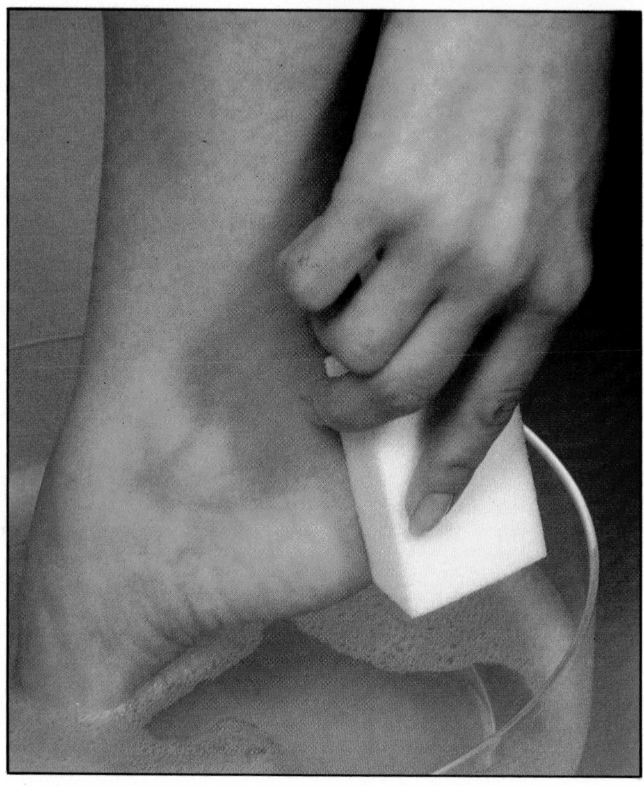

These six steps are well worth taking the trouble to follow precisely. Though they may seem very complicated, you will find, after a while, that they have become second nature to you.

ignore and disregard their existence, only in the summer do we prise them from our boots and shoes, and yes, we expect them to be beautiful.

Year-round care is essential: feet *are* seen, and at times we all must show our feet, even if it is only when buying a new pair of boots! Always be prepared to put your best toe forward. So, every week, when caring for your hands, don't forget the feet! Follow this easy routine.

1 Soak feet in a warm, soapy foot bath for 10-15 minutes. If feet are sore or rubbed, add a little disinfectant. Gently brush nails with a nail brush and rub away any hard skin with a special block or pumice stone. This can also be repeated daily at bath time.

2 Dry carefully with the towel. It is very important always to dry carefully between the toes, not only now, but generally after bathing or showering.

3 Trim the nails with scissors while soft. It's best to cut straight across the nail to give a square shape. File if necessary to finish off. (Cutting away the corners can cause ingrowing toe nails).

4 Very gently ease back cuticles with a cotton wool-covered orange stick, and clean under nails.

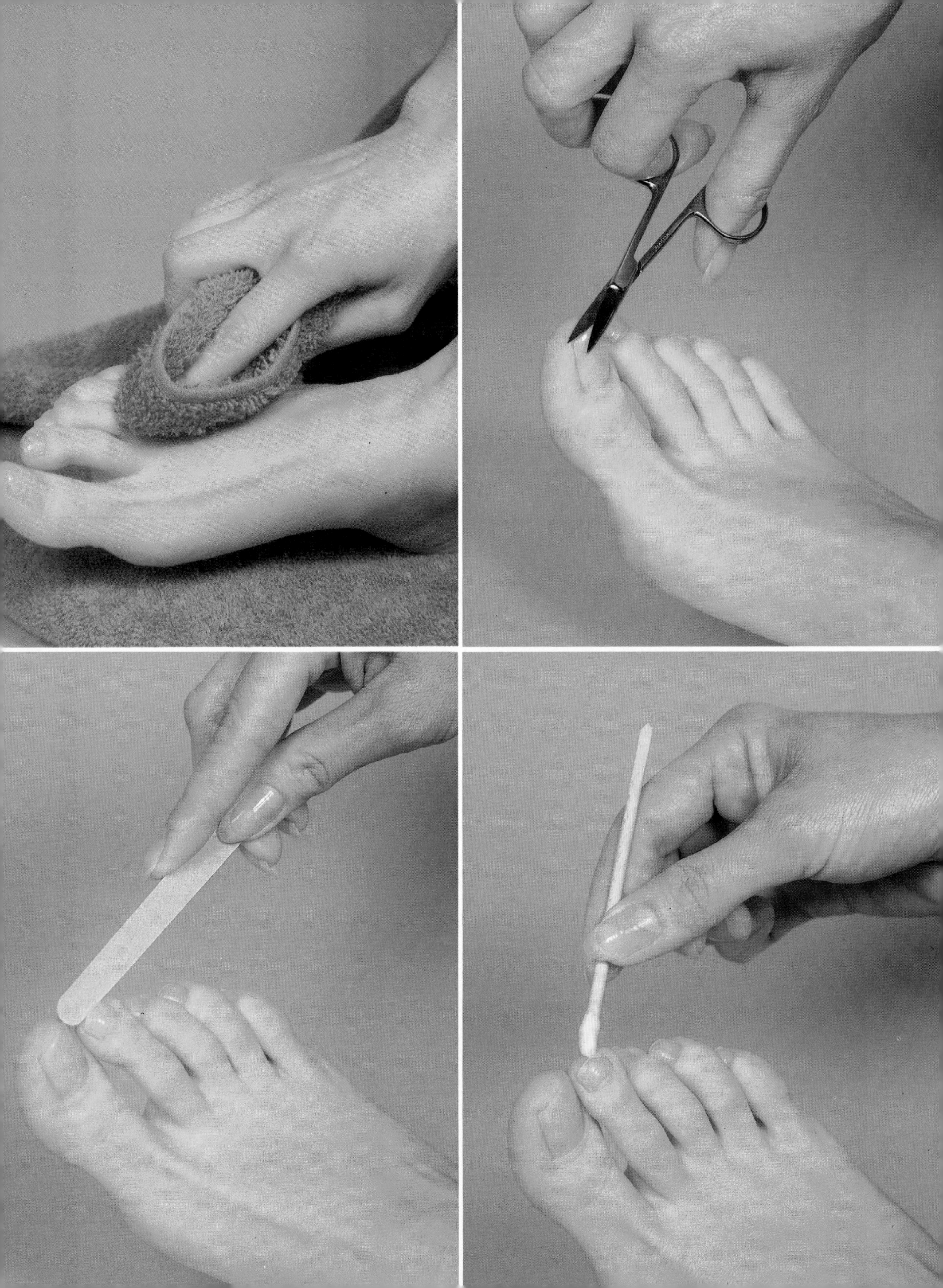

Put together a kit for hands and feet so that they are always together and handy when you need them. Keep all your polishes in the same place to avoid wasting time hunting for the colour you need. Inefficiency in organisation can make the whole job a drag. Tone the colour of toe nails with finger nails: darker colours are best for winter, fun colours for summer.

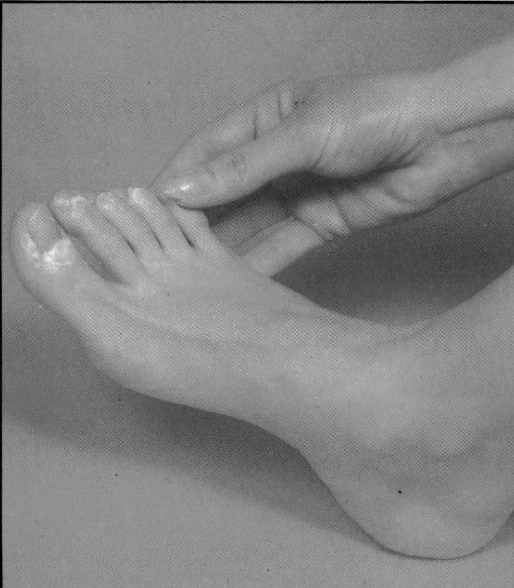

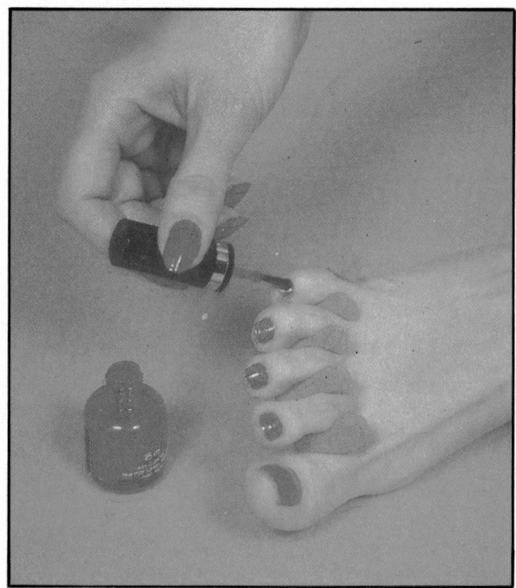

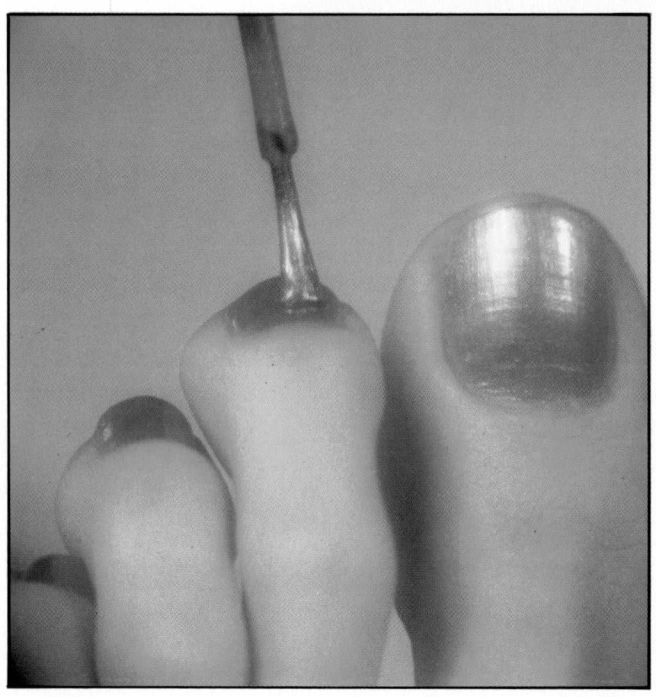

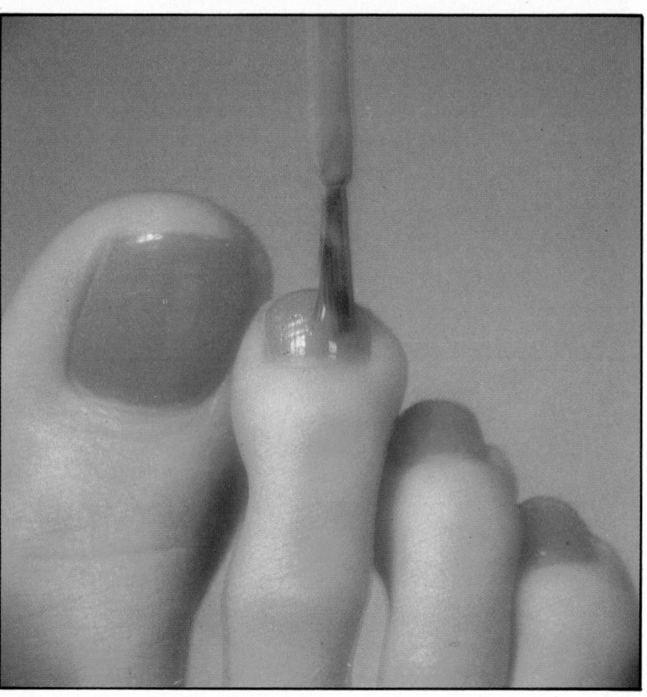

5 Apply moisture lotion or cream and massage into foot and ankle and each toe in turn.

6 Clean nails of cream and apply base coat, colour and top coat, letting each layer dry thoroughly. It may help to place something like pieces of cotton wool between the toes so that the polish is not smudged while it is drying. Smooth, pretty feet will make you feel glamorous from top to toe.

Hair Removal This may not be the prettiest of subjects but it is extremely important and something we all have to think about. Thick, luscious hair is great if it is on your head but, as with everything else, life is not always perfect and hair grows where we don't always want it! So first we must decide what exactly is the problem; it may be on your face, under your arms or on your legs. There are several alternative solutions, and some are better for some areas than others. On the face we can use special facial bleaches; these lighten the colour of the hair and in time weaken growth. Depilatory creams can also be used for this area but the only permanent and best answer is electrolysis, and one should seek professional advice on this. Waxing can be done, but in some cases this may increase the hair growth.

Eyebrows should only ever be plucked as described earlier.

Strappy summer shoes and evening sandals (right) can put the final, glamorous touch to a special outfit, but only if the feet in them come up to the mark. Plan ahead: get the right colour polish and make sure, as far as possible, that the feet and legs are smooth and silky.

Use a special depilatory cream – or consider shaving – to remove unpleasant hair from legs and underarms. What you use, and how, is not so important; it is the smooth, silky effect that matters. If you have fine, blonde hair on legs and arms it may be best to leave it untreated: you can afford to make your own choice.

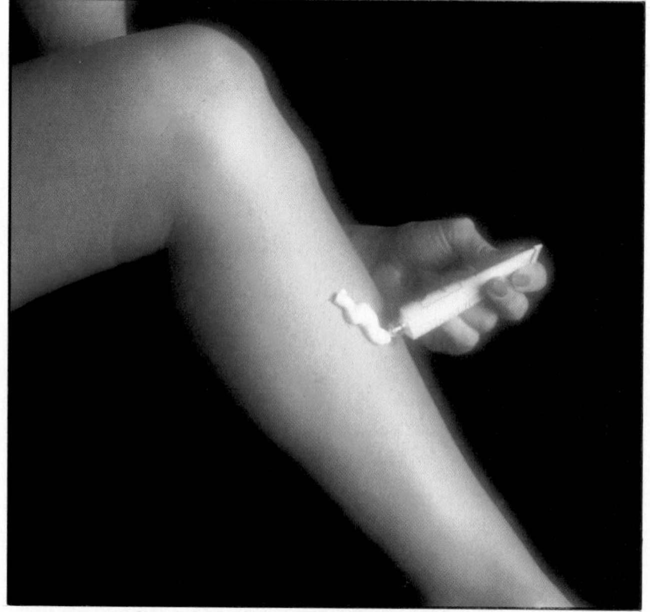

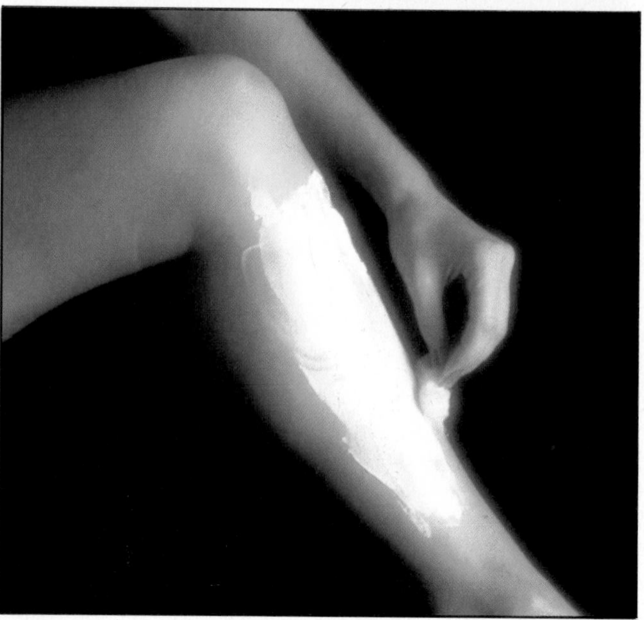

The Care of Hands, Feet and Legs

Naturally sexy legs need showing off, so if yours fall within this description, treat them with respect and make a fuss of them. The attention you command will more than repay every minute you spend on keeping them looking good.

Legs and underarms can be shaved, waxed, bleached or treated with a depilatory cream depending on the individual. I would suggest that underarms are best shaved, waxed or removed with depilatory cream. The same thing would be true of legs. Electrolysis is generally too time consuming and expensive for these areas.

The finished result should, however, be smooth, exciting skin. Finish all these treatments with a good, generous application of body lotion to soothe and smooth.

Legs Legs are one of the erotic parts of the body so the skin on them should be very important to us all. They should not be dry and hairy, althought naturally they probably are! So, where do we go from here?

Let's look at the possibilities. Good legs can be very sexy. We can wear beautiful stockings and tights which will put the finishing touches to a fantastic outfit, and there are so many wonderful colours and patterns to choose from that it seems a great pity to lose out. Winter can be fun too

TUNTURI PUCH
Watt
TUNTURI

– textured and patterned tights are such fun but they are not a cover up – you must be ready to 'show a leg' without the props later and the skin here needs to be smoth, sleek and totally touchable.

Hands and feet are often a trial but they can, once you have pulled them into line, be great fun. Colour is important and nowadays there are an incredible number of beautifully bright and vibrant or pale and muted polishes on the market and you have the great job of choosing. Match or tone your hands and feet, pick a colour to go with an outfit and paint away. In the summer, when toes show and feet are brown, show them in pretty sandals; well cared for feet can really put the finishing touches to a lovely outfit.

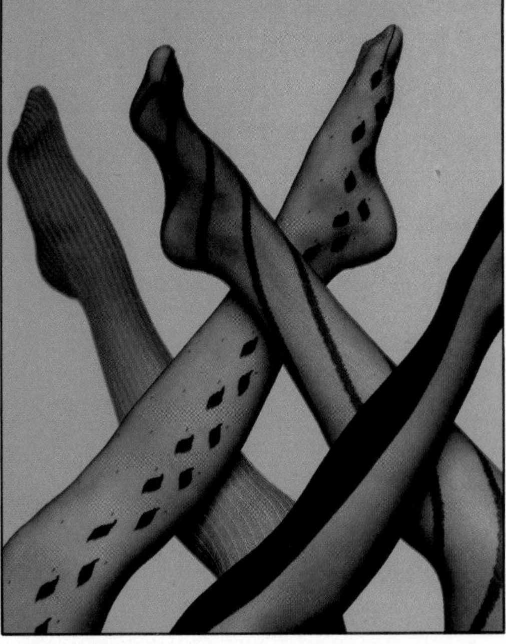

In recent years the fashions for legs have really hit the high street and there are more types and colours of tights than ever before. Be aware of them as an extremely important fashion accessory, and if your legs are a good feature, choose tights or stockings that will 'make' an outfit. Bright colours and patterns, fun textures to match and tone with the fabrics of your clothes – you can completely change the look of a simple dress or suit this way and it can be very inexpensive.

If your legs and ankles are not the best in the world, make them work for you: choose muted shades; avoid too dark or too bright colours; heavily textured tights may make legs look fatter so be careful when choosing and remember – a little time spent on leg and foot exercise when you plan your routine will help to trim and slim. Choose your shoes with care; the height of the heel and the cut of the shoe should give you a good line, which will create the illusion of a much more flattering shape. Good shoes can be a worthwhile investment here.

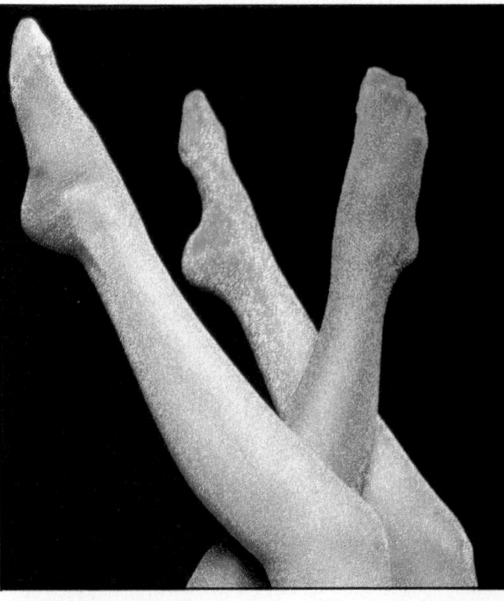

Recent years have seen an enormous increase in the range of stockings and tights available. Colours, textures and patterns offer all sorts of options for those who want to set off well-shaped legs, or who need to conceal unfortunate faults or blemishes in the most attractive yet inconspicious way. Discover as much as you can about latest developments – there is something in the shops for everybody.

Hair Care and Styles

Brushing your hair will do it good. Choose a brush that suits your type of hair, and brush it morning and night. This treatment takes away any knots or tangles and also stimulates the scalp. Getting the circulation going in the scalp will help lead to more healthy hair. Remember when you arrange your hair to use hair accessories that complement your outfit. There are a tremendous number available, and they can help change a plain style, adopted to get hair 'out of the way', into a fashion feature.

Looking after your hair is extremely important – no one's hair looks great left on its own – glossy, well behaved hair that you admire on others is never like that by chance.

Plan to wash your hair at least once a week, some of us need to do this more often, only with the help of your hairdresser can you work out the best routine.

A good cut, whether you hair is long or short, is vital – this will give you a head start, a basis to work on, then all you need do between visits to the salon is maintain the look. A good relationship with your hairdresser is essential as he will keep you up to date with new styles and products. Don't hesitate to ask for help and information – that is what he is there for. Ask about texture and condition, the possibilities of perms or colour, how to dry your hair at home, and tell him if you have any particular problems. A haircut is only a

Be aware of all the possibilities. Products for the hair, probably more than anything else, seem to change weekly, bringing new ideas and fashions. Learn what is available from your hairdresser and, with practice, you can soon acquire competence to use your dryer, brush and comb to create different effects for your different moods.

Condition Use a conditioner after shampooing; this will help keep the hair in good condition, shiny and easy to manage. Again, choose from a wide range to suit your particular needs. Wet hair will be much easier to comb after washing when conditioner is applied. Permed and coloured hair can be stretched and harmed if it is tangled after washing and difficult to comb through. Don't make life hard for yourself when help is at hand.

Drying Blow drying hair correctly is vital and it can completely change the look of your style. You can create different looks just by drying your hair a different way: you can control the curl and volume, make it spiky or smooth, lift the roots to give height, or smooth them down to achieve a sleek effect. There are also blow-drying lotions

good investment if it works and suits you, both as a style that flatters your features and as one that is easy to care for.

Shampoo Choose a shampoo that suits the condition of your hair. There are even special ones for damaged, coloured and permed hair. It is a good idea to ask your hairdresser which is best for your type. If you wash your hair every day you only really need one quick wash, if not, then two applications may be necessary.

which will add volume, and mousse can help you achieve a more spiky effect.

Using your dryer and hands you can encourage the wave and curl as you dry, or take it away – watch how your hairdresser works and learn these tricks.

Great Hair Beautiful hair is more important today than it has ever been. It shows off your face and skin to best advantage by providing a perfect frame. A clean, shiny, well controlled look is what we all aim for –

MADE IN ENGLAND

(Above and opposite) a full hairstyle, with length and width in a stunning combination which complements a well-considered skin make-up.

but be aware of shape and style. Your hair can create an illusion of width or height, balancing with your face shape: a long face can be softened and shortened, a round face can be slimmed. Never compromise – if long hair does nothing for you don't keep it; a new, fashionable short style could change your whole image.

Think about your hair as an accessory; change it with your mood and your outfit. Have an easy, more practical style for daytime, and then change it for parties or evenings. Put it up with combs, curl it, make it part of your look. Long, straight hair may be great with jeans but it might not go with a beautiful evening dress that needs to show the line of your neck. Long hair on frilly collars very rarely works well. Link up the colour of combs or ribbons with your outfit.

Think about hair colour. Today, almost anything is possible in this area and a new tone or highlights can give you a great lift, helping to make you and your skin look wonderful.

Ribbons and clips are no longer only for schoolgirls and will keep you young at heart if used to good effect.

Some Tips for Your Hair Hair is for everyone a never-ending problem: when it is clean it can have a will of its own; when it is in need of washing is can be difficult to control. Don't just leave your hair to fend for itself: take positive action.

1 Plait long hair to give a groomed, tidy look; add a ribbon which tones and complements your outfit – if hair is fly away, spray with water before braiding.

2 Take shorter, layered hair away from the face by using coloured clamps –

These sophisticated styles (this page) may take time, but clearly repay the effort. When time is short, however, a quick application of mousse or gel, dried with a hair dryer, gives an almost cheeky insouciance, as well as the appearance of having been carefully worked.

choose them to match or tone with your outfit.

3 Long hair, if it is greasy and needs a wash, doesn't have to look a mess: tie it back in two sections with toning or matching ribbons. You can actually create an interesting fashion look by choosing patterned ribbons to contrast with a chic, classic outift.

4 Hair that is layered and lacking in bounce the day before washing can be slicked into place with coloured combs; spray or gel the front for a spiky effect.

5 If all else fails, apply mousse or gel through the hair and dry with a hand drier to spike up. This look works well after a long day at the office or a stint in the gym or at dance class, when your usual style will not work; this works better on layered cuts.

Styles A good haircut, whether you have long hair or short, is a very good investment – once you have a good basis to work on you can change and experiment with your look.

1 Layered hair can be either tonged or dried with a round brush and brushed through to give a curly, groomed effect. This is a good look for naturally curly hair. You may not need to curl, but rather to finger dry with a dryer.

2 Shortish hair can be dried straight with brush or fingers to give a very soft, slightly spiky effect. After drying separate or 'break-up' hair with gel or mousse, bringing down soft, spiky bits in front of hair.

Long, fine hair complementing a fair complexion is always worth taking pains over. Natural drying is preferable to drying by tongs or heated rollers.

3 Long, one length hair can be tricky to look after – shampoo and condition gently and well – heated rollers and tongs to curl long hair can be very damaging so when you wash, dry off till almost dry and then set in rollers, rags or tissues. Wind the hair on any of these three and let it dry completely and naturally, which is good for hair condition and effective.

4 When curl drops from long hair or when it becomes a bit greasy, take the front section and twist and roll away from the face and fix in place with combs or pins. Soften the look by placing short, curly ends around hair line, this gives a soft but elegant look and is so much better than straggly, long hair getting in your way and looking untidy. Make your hair work for you by understanding its condition and needs from day to day.

CHAPTER 20

A Healthy Skin for Life

Peace of mind, total relaxation and calm are extremely important for you now. Take it day by day; see how you feel and do just what you feel able to. Don't feel guilty about just sitting, thinking or reading. So many things are changing at the moment that you need time to yourself to adjust. Make use of these quiet moments; don't waste them.

Pregnancy You may well ask what have babies to do with skin? The answer must be that babies are to do with you and you have to do with skin!

Having a baby is one of the most important decisions of a life-time and nowadays more and more people believe that we should really prepare, both mentally and physically, for this event.

Being healthy before you conceive is the answer. People have produced children in the worst of conditions, but why should we when we have the choice of being in 'peak condition'. Why take anything less?

Plan ahead for pregnancy as you would for anything else. Gain your strength by exercise, watch your diet, make sure you are getting all the right vitamins, try and be relaxed and calm. Some specialists believe that, from a very early time, the growing baby knows how you are feeling! The body will take from itself all it needs for the growth of your child but may leave you short, so make sure this cannot happen – and I don't mean use it as an excuse to eat everything in sight! Good, balanced meals are all that is required, and if this is your normal regime then no change is necessary. Watch what you drink: alcohol is not good for you in excess anytime, and smoking should really be out of the question. Generally, people who lead an active and balanced life tend to sail through pregnancy. There are exceptions of course

Spend time together: it's always important – not just when there are things to be done. Take a few moments to play, and enjoy the idea of just the two of you being together. Start to build your all-important relationship, experiencing moods and feeling together.

– but it can only be to your advantage that, if a problem arises, you are in top condition so that you can cope as well as possible.

Skin and hair also seem to take on a new life during pregnancy. You need to check for changes of skin, and act accordingly; as the body goes through so many different phases at this time, all will show in your skin, so be ready. Get plenty of rest; stress and tiredness will only lead to irritability and spoil what should be a very exciting time.

Young Mum When you have had your baby don't think it is all over; it has only just begun; the sleepless nights and the little uncertainties and worries, so try to steer away from stress and tension more than ever. You can't do everything on your own, so try sharing the trials and worries with others; it's not just your baby, it's your partner's as well. Involve them in caring – dads can feel very left out at this time – and try and get some time to yourself by letting them cope for a while so that you can do

Don't forget to make play fun: a trip to the swings or a day at the zoo can be good for you, too. Exercise and fresh air help to counteract the pressures of day-to-day chores. If you and three other mums get together to do this once a month with all the kids, you get three spare days either just for you, or for special times with a very new baby. Your children learn from you, so don't stint on the time you give them.

some exercises or relax, have a massage, get your hair done; do all the things that were important to you before. You haven't changed totally as a person – you've had a baby! And you still want to look good.

One of the best tips for looking good with a tiny baby actually came from a man! He said that the only rule to follow is to sleep when the baby sleeps – good advice if the new baby won't conform to your pattern of life. To begin with you must try and fit in with the new baby – difficult if you have other young children, I know, but worth thinking about. As sleep is so important to our looks and well-being, when you are exhausted you will feel it much harder to cope. A final word: if you need help or a little 'space' don't be too proud to ask, even if a friend just has your other children for an afternoon; it can take

Teenage skin can be difficult, so help and advice from mum – to cope with skin care, diet and emotions – is essential. Your parental support and understanding through this time will make you good friends with your children for life. Remember the relief when you discovered 'spot cover'? We don't change. We all need help from time to time.

the pressure away just when you need it most. The new addition, while asleep, won't know if you are doing exercises, or putting a face pack on; as long as you are there to care that's all that matters!

Early Start If you have teenage children, it can be difficult to control their eating habits – and getting them to wash can be a nightmare! What they do is very much what they are shown and accept as 'normal', and if they see you eating all the wrong things they will follow – because to them you are grown up and they

desperately want to be also, so imitating you is how they begin to do this.

Involve them in your routines, explain how you watch your weight and take exercise, and they may well join in. Share your knowledge, make it fun, and please note – boys are not excluded, health matters for them just as much. Help your children to be proud of their appearance, show them the importance of tooth care, hair care and skin care. It is amazing the difference it can make to have a mum and dad who take care and are proud of their bodies – apart from anything else you will look and act younger.

Young Routine Cleansing and toning are the important things to remember. Keeping the skin clean and fresh will help to reduce problems of spots and bad skin. Involve boys and girls in this; neither of them really want spots. You may have to provide the products or share yours. If I remember rightly, at that age pocket money was not for buying soap or cleansers in my book, so watch their skins

Start as you mean to go on. To help your children, you need to take part – they will respect you if you are active and interested in the same sports. You may not agree on every count – no one does – but understanding the problems is more than half the battle.

as you watch yours and help where you can. Hair also needs to be looked after. It is easier for a youngster to manage it if the cut is good, and nowadays they really do care how they look. Individual style is very important to them, so encourage it. You may not like or understand their look but it's their way of growing up. It's much easier to have a way-out or modern look if your skin is O.K. So maybe our job is to keep the basics healthy so they can have fun and experiment.

If there is an odd blemish, help to cover and hide it. I can remember not wanting to venture out of the front door if I had a spot but eventually I learnt about cover creams, so all was well. These are the ways you, with your own knowledge, can help. You may also learn from them new ideas and new ways of doing things.

Encourage a sport or hobby; as children we start off well, and then as we grow older we lose interest. Sports give kids a great boost; they can either be part of a team or work on their own, but it can only help them to keep fit, and things like ballet or judo will help them with posture and mental control, all very useful things to help them cope with everyday life. Some sports the whole family can take part in, so get-togethers at the weekend can be fun. Swimming, for example, is probably the best exercise there is for everyone.

As far as diet is concerned, you will never stop youngsters from eating 'fun' foods – remember, we did, so let them, but watch what you prepare. Milk shakes and hamburgers are not that bad as long as they get plenty of fresh fruit and vegetables as well, and remember, don't overfeed; the overwhelming desire to care for your children may actually do them harm. We are back again to my balance theory – they will not thank you for starting them on a career of spare tyres – so respect their diet as you do yours. Most children will not know or care what you put into food, so this way you can control the calorie intake. It is not unknown these days for children not to eat meat and if this is their decision let them do it. It just means they have the capability at a very young age to think for themselves, something we may not have had as kids ourselves; respect their choice and adapt your menus.

As the Years Go By Enjoy your children, and don't be afraid of them. Share and enjoy their company; they are the next generation and we can learn from them. There is nothing quite like the enthusiasm of youth so encourage them to look good in their own style; this way they will keep you on your toes and up to date with things. Buy clothes together, discuss your individual problems and needs, this is the only way answers will be found. Let dad help the boys while you help the girls. It is important to talk; you with your parents, your children with you. If you look good they will respect this. A young looking mum and dad is always a bonus, and caring for your skin, body and looks will be

As you get older, don't be tempted to play safe. Styles and colours you used to use may do you no favours. (Right) a safe, plain hairstyle and neutral lip colour can become boring and dated. You can still be subtle; using warm tones enhances the skin and emphasises the strong colour of lips and nails for a bit of excitement. (Opposite) strong, positive colours in classic styles are often best worn with the confidence we acquire over the years, and a touch of glamour is always acceptable.

appreciated. Even if nothing is said, they will want to be proud of you in exactly the same way you are proud of them.

As you get older it becomes more and more important to take great care in what you wear, your hair, clothes and make-up. Be subtle; choose good, fashionable shapes that are elegant and suit you. Make-up should be flattering and soft, making the best of good points and softening and playing down the features you know are not the best.

Choose colours you know you look great in. Whatever fashion dictates, there is always something up-to-the-minute that you can adapt to your look. I personally find that classic shapes always work for me and I just change odd things: square shoulders, the shape of the sleeves, higher heels on shoes, as these things can date you. Accessories will update your clothes in the most subtle way. As you get older, cheap clothes are not always a bargain; care is needed to get your image just right. Look at magazines and they will help you to identify shapes and new ideas with clothes, skin care and make-up.

This is the time you will really be pleased you took care of yourself over the years. Good skin is your best bonus for looking really great, and a good figure is irreplaceable. Growing older gracefully may be a cliché, but it is terribly important; cool elegance is always acceptable at any age.

The Finishing Touch

There is nothing more exciting than the memory of a special person and the perfume he or she uses. There is no mistaking a loved one's fragrance, and we should all use perfume that can be totally feminine or completely masculine – yet again, a part of the beauty world enjoyed as much by men as by women. Fragrances first for you, and secondly for others – hopefully provided by them, but if not, don't lose out. Treat yourself: it's the final touch that really counts.

Perfume You have managed to 'put yourself together' and you look great, so why not put the finishing touches to your look. Give some thought to perfume. The memory of a certain perfume, be it of a person, place or flower, can take you right back to the very first time you smelt it. I still remember the perfume of the first lipstick I ever used, and certain perfumes and after shaves remind me of times and people so clearly.

Even at a very young age we should be aware of perfume. Light, fresh smells are best to start with and we should very early on feel undressed without it. Marilyn Monroe once, when asked what she wore in bed, answered – 'my perfume'. What better answer? Judging by the incredible sales, and the cost of some perfumes, they are a luxury a great many people enjoy. Like flowers, perfume should ideally be bought for you, but if not, I strongly believe you should still wear it. It is something you provide for others to enjoy, so experiment till you find one you really love, but don't be overpowering; one can overdo a good thing. If you don't like anything too strong just use toilette water or flower water; bath products and body lotion can sometimes

The Finishing Touch

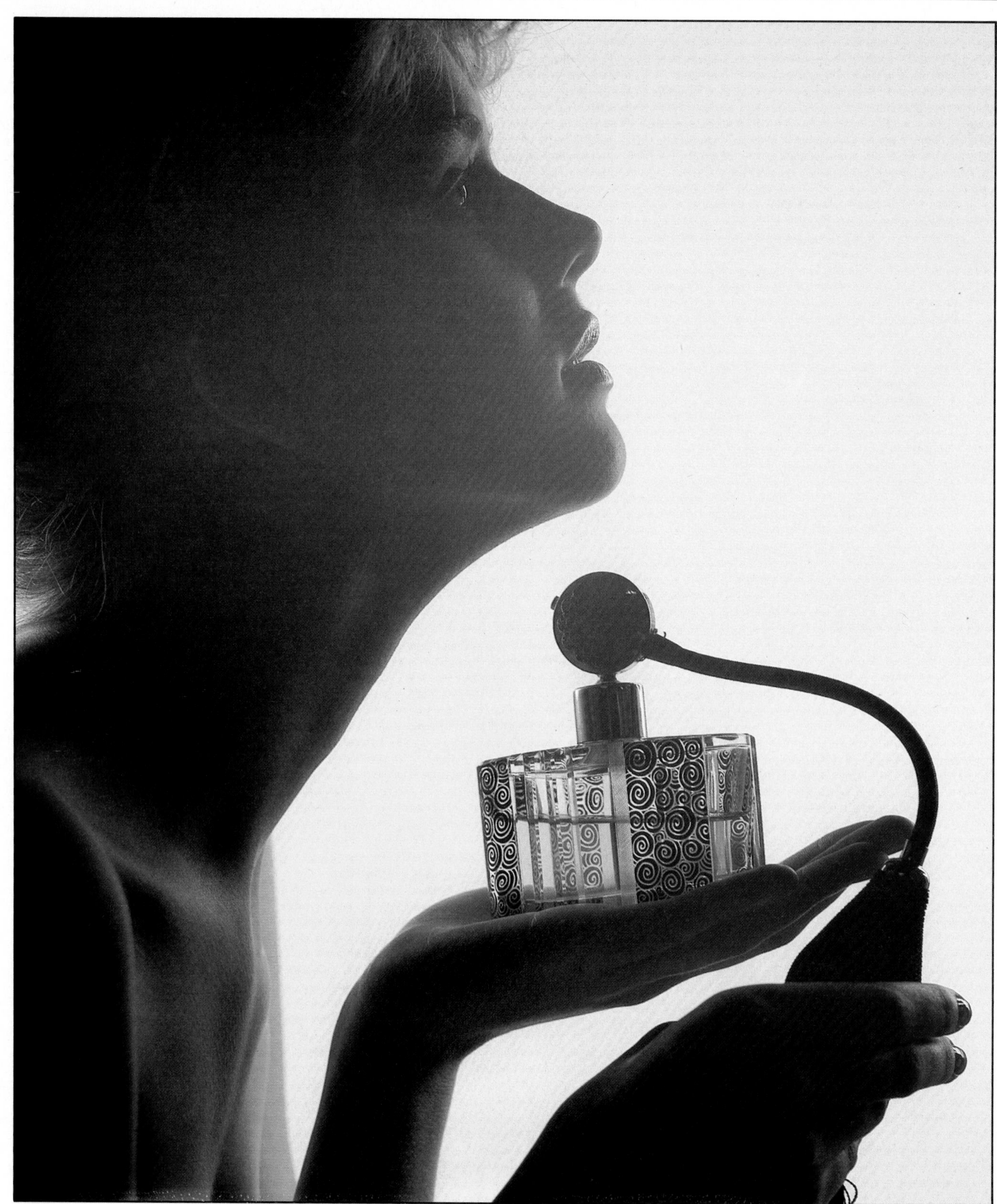

Perfume is a luxury for the skin, so use it as such. It will create not only the right aroma but also the right mood or appeal. Seductiveness and vulnerability are within your reach.

be enough to give a fresh perfume. A perfume sachet in your underwear drawer can be lovely. I even know people who spray their rooms with their perfume. It is one of the most important parts of being individual, so don't miss out.

Apply your perfume for maximum effect on the pressure points of your body; this is where they will warm to the body's temperature and give off a gentle aroma: behind the ears, wrists and back of knees. Don't spray straight onto the skin, this may

Try to vary your perfume to suit the effect you have created in your make-up, hair care, skin care and the clothes you have chosen. Avoid sticking slavishly to 'favourite' perfumes if there are others on the market which could suit you. The vast majority are available in small quantities for experimentation at comparatively little outlay.

upset the skin if it is sensitive. Spray onto clothes and hair, or if onto the skin, at a distance.

Remember, for birthdays and Christmas, men love perfume as well. There are far more men's products bought by women than men, so don't let yours lose out.

Perfume can be expensive but it need not be. Choose something within your budget – let it be fun, enjoy using it, not only for special occasions but every day: it's your treat.

HAIR CARE

Hair Care Contents

Introduction
pages 262-265

Hair – The Fundamentals
pages 266-275

From Babe to Junior Miss
pages 276-287

Teens to Twenties
pages 288-297

Curly versus Straight
pages 298-309

Your Hair During Pregnancy
pages 310-313

Colour Wise
pages 314-335

The Era of Change
pages 336-347

Long and Lustrous
pages 348-357

The Elegant Fifties
pages 358-363

True or False
pages 364-369

The Portfolio
pages 370-384

Introduction

Healthy, shiny hair looks so good whether it's cut short and sassy or left long and flowing. Hair styles today range from the outrageous to the classically elegant; literally anything goes as long as it complements the wearer, fits in with her lifestyle and reflects her personality.
With the modern styling techniques and products that are available today, women can become as adaptable as the chameleon, changing looks at will (whatever the length of their hair) to suit different moods, clothes and occasions.

Beautiful hair is the body's greatest natural fashion accessory. It can be curled or coaxed into the most incredible shapes to enhance your appearance and complement your clothes. Few fashion accessories are as pliable or as versatile and yet how many of us really appreciate it?

Well here is the opportunity to show your hair a little care and consideration. All it takes is just these ten easy steps and you are on your way to beautiful hair.

Step **1.** A healthy, balanced diet. For super hair and a clear skin.

Step **2.** Stimulate that circulation. After all it's the blood that supplies your hair with nourishment.

Step **3.** Learn to relax. You're more likely to keep your hair if you do.

Step **4.** Cleanliness. This means hair, brushes, combs and rollers too.

Step **5.** Condition. A must after every shampoo.

Versatile styles are the order of the day. Right: hair in poor condition, unevenly coloured and out of shape will not respond well or look attractive when styled. But when those faults have been corrected a new woman emerges.
Subtle, temporary changes in shade can be achieved with coloured mousse, while a simple, long, layered cut is extremely adaptable and can be worn straight, gently waved or curly.

Step **6.** The cut. A good cut is an investment and the foundation for any hairstyling service.

Step **7.** Products. Choose with care, seek professional advice or select well-known brand names.

Step **8.** Styling Equipment. The right tools for the job makes all the difference.

Step **9.** Curls. Perms and relaxers require special care: you'll need to adjust your conditioning routine for these.

Step **10.** Colour. Make it a colourful year. Whether it's outrageous or very discreet, colour can add new dimensions to your hair.

As you read through the book you will find more and more information relating to these ten easy steps. Quite simply, it's the how, why and when to beautiful hair.

Hair - The Fundamentals

Healthy hair looks and feels so good. To keep it that way it's important to choose and use high quality shampoos and conditioners that will gently cleanse and protect each strand.

What or who do you blame or bless for the texture, condition, colour of your hair: products? the hairdresser? your parents? Natural hair colour and texture tend to be hereditary, as does the colour of our eyes and skin, but condition; now that's a different matter altogether. The condition and appearance of your hair can be greatly enhanced by the way you and your hairdresser treat it. Badly permed, relaxed, tinted or bleached and it will look lifeless, dull or frizzy, and if the worst happens it may split or break off at the scalp. Correctly treated and conditioned and its appearance plus manageability should improve, even though the shine and general condition are purely cosmetic.

Manufacturers have spent thousands of pounds in the last decade or so developing products to colour and curl our hair in the gentlest possible way. A good, modern shampoo no longer strips the hair of all its natural oils, leaving it dry and flyaway, and conditioners have forged ahead, progressing from a purely cosmetic coating of the hair shaft – for smoothness

and shine – to complex restructurants which have a variety of uses. Some are designed to replace moisture and reduce brittleness, others actually penetrate into the hair, where they help temporarily to repair and strengthen the damaged internal structure.

Healthy hair growth depends a great deal on how well our bodies function. Regular exercise helps to keep muscles toned and stimulates the circulation. When combined with a nourishing, well balanced diet your hair and skin can't fail to reap the benefits.

Even so, with all these wonderful products around, the responsibility for the condition of our hair still rests squarely on our own shoulders or, to be more correct, in our mouths. "You are what you eat" could not more aptly describe our hair in relation to our diet. Most of us are b now – thanks to the media – familiar with what constitutes a healthy diet and healthy lifestyle. A balanced diet keeps the body functioning correctly, keeps the skin clear, prevents nails from splitting and helps teeth and gums stay healthy. All these facts are thrust in front of us every day, from early breakfast TV to the last high-fibre cereal advertisement at night. But did you realise that it's equally important for the hair? You only have to think back to your last cold or stomach upset to know how quickly your hair reacts to physical illness. Consequently, the result of a poor diet will soon manifest itself in the state of your hair. No, I am not about to launch the special 'S' Plan Diet that will save your hair and rock the nation: basic dietary common sense is all that's required.

Perhaps you are wondering how what you eat can affect your hair, especially as the hair we see and spend so much time, money and effort on is dead. Yes, I'm afraid that's true: once it appears above the scalp your hair is dead. Hair does not contain any blood vessels or nerve endings, which is why it doesn't bleed or hurt when we cut it.

Hair grows from an indentation or pocket in the skin called the follicle. At the bottom of the follicle is the hair papilla and this is where all the action takes place. The papilla is continually producing cells; these cells are pushed up and out of the follicle and as they move upwards they harden until they emerge as hard keratin, a protein we recognize as hair.

To ensure that the cells continue to reproduce, the papilla has a rich blood supply busily conveying the essential amino acids and nutrients for the hair's production. The papilla also has its own complex system of nerves, hence the reason for pain when your hair is tugged or pulled out.

From this simplified version of hair growth it's easy to deduce that if your blood lacks a reasonable supply of essential amino acids and nutrients then you hair will react, and if your diet is very poor, as with anorexics, excessive hair loss could result.

Stress and tension can also take their toll, so it's a good idea to take up some form of light exercise to help you relax and unwind. Energetic aerobics seems to be going out of favour, but swimming, cycling, walking and badminton are excellent ways to increase your oxygen intake and stimulate the circulation; all of which will benefit your hair.

From the hair inside to the hair outside. Everyone's hair is as individual as a fingerprint, and yet its basic structure is always the same. The outer layer, or cuticle, helps to protect the more complex, delicate cortex. The cuticle resembles the overlapping scales of a fish, and when hair is in good condition these scales lie flat and

act as a mirror, reflecting light that enhances hair colour and gloss. The cortex is more complicated as it's here that the hair's strength, texture and elasticity, as well as the melanin which gives hair its natural colour can be found. The bonds that are affected by any hairstyling process or chemical treatment are found in the cortex: this is why the state of the cuticle is so important, as it acts like a protective overcoat. The medulla runs through the centre of the hair and is not always present, its function is still unknown and whether you have one or not seems to have little affect on hairstyling services.

Cleanliness is the next stage to hair health. Shampooing: to many this is a simple process but it's often carried out incorrectly to the detriment of both hair and scalp.

Top: many would envy Sue's naturally wavy, red hair, and yet hair of this texture and colour has its problems, with a tendency to look dry and dull. An acid-balanced shampoo will help, but to encourage a more visible sheen we applied a moisturising protein treatment. This counteracts the dryness, strengthens the hair and closes the cuticle.
Bottom: finally a cut – to remove any dry, split ends – and an application of hair mousse to add body, control the curl and enhance the shine.

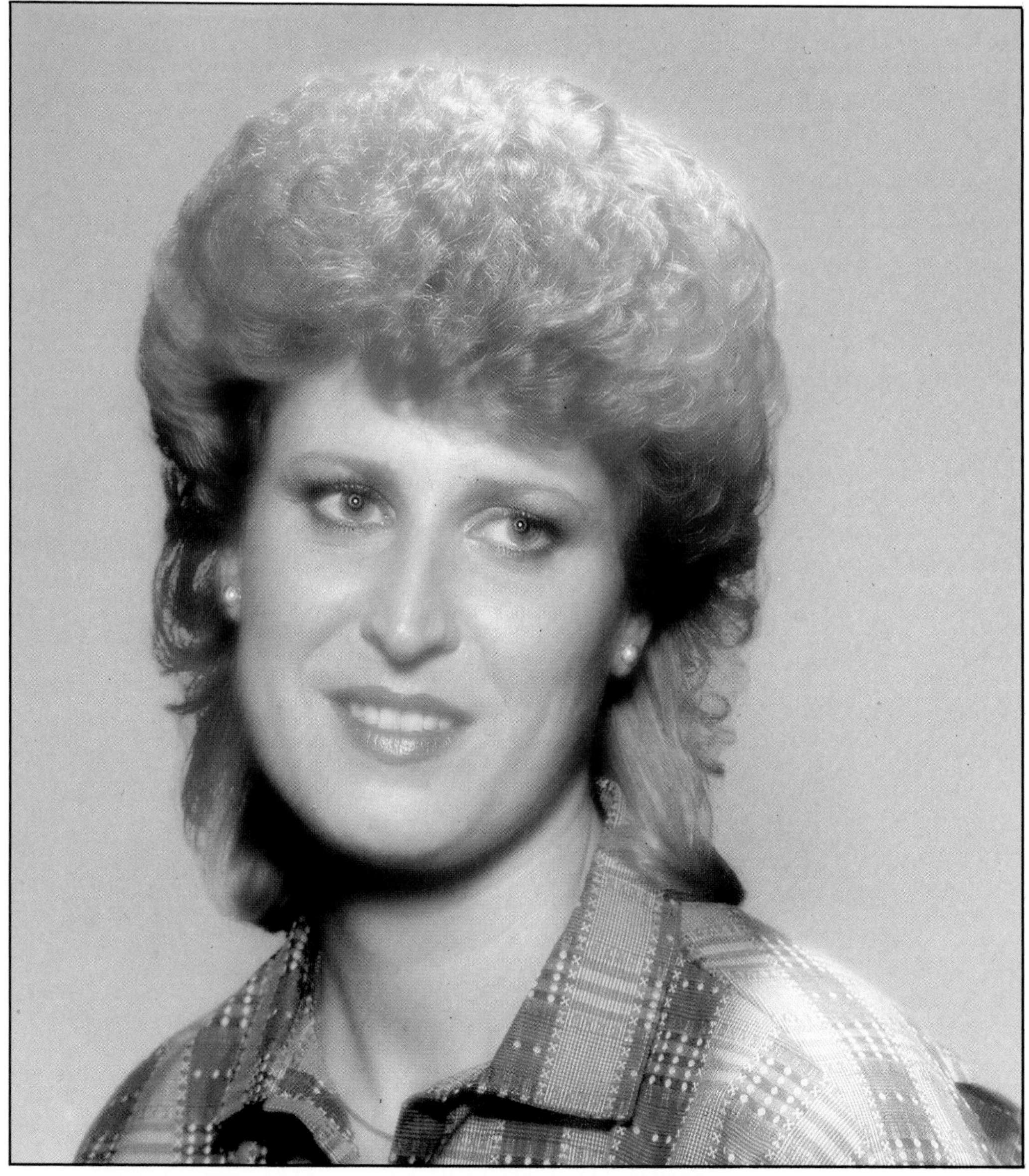

Choosing a shampoo is the first step, and whenever possible seek your hairdresser's advice as he may retail a line which is eminently suitable for your hair. Without assistance you face the daunting prospect of selecting from row on row of shampoos on display at the chemist's. Before you purchase, assess your hair type: is it dry, greasy or normal? Read labels carefully; for dry hair choose a cream or oil type shampoo, for greasy hair a lemon or liquid type and for normal hair a cream. Check that it's pH balanced – slightly acidic – this makes it more compatible with the hair and scalp, which are also acidic. If you shampoo daily because of your job, sports or overactive oil (sebaceous) glands, or greasy hair, select one of the gentle shampoos recommended for daily use.

To shampoo, assemble towels, brushes, combs, shampoo and shampoo spray. Dilute a good tablespoon of the shampoo you are going to use in warm water; this will prevent you from using excessive amounts and help the shampoo spread more evenly through the hair. Brush your hair thoroughly, removing any tangles or back-combing, wet the hair with warm water, pour the diluted shampoo over it and gently massage the hair and scalp, then rinse thoroughly. Often, it is not necessary to give a second shampoo but if it is then repeat the procedure. If you suffer from a greasy scalp then shampoo with tepid water and massage gently to avoid stimulating the oil-producing glands.

After shampooing, it's time to condition. All hair benefits from a conditioner. The cosmetic types are surface conditioners which will make combing easier because they encourage the cuticle to lie flat, therefore promoting a healthy, shiny look.

As I mentioned previously, restructurants penetrate into the cortex, attaching themselves to the broken or damaged bonds, and basically they help to strengthen the hair. This makes them ideal for those of us who overdo the blow-drying or chemical processes. Made from hydrolised protein, they are able to penetrate because their molecular size and makeup is very similar to that of your hair. Moisturisers and hot oil treatments are great for those with very dry hair and scalp, particularly black hair which tends to be naturally dry and brittle. Today's modern oils are light and penetrating, far better than the thick grease and hair dressings that are still around which clog the pores of the scalp, often giving rise to more serious scalp problems.

With any form of conditioner or treatment, follow the directions. After shampooing, towel blot out the excess water (do not rub), apply the product, massage or comb through with a wide-toothed comb and leave for the specified time, then remove as directed. If your hair is in really poor condition don't expect miracles with just one treatment as it will take a regular course of restructants to improve badly damaged hair, just as it takes a full course of antibiotics to relieve an infection. Once your hair is in reasonable condition you can switch to a maintenance programme. Usually, this will entail a light conditioner after every shampoo with a restructuranat treatment once a month.

Finally, lets take a look at hair types, texture and density. Texture refers to the diameter of each individual strand; density to the amount of hair on your head.

Inset: dry, naturally curly, almost frizzy hair like Christine's is often thought to be of a coarse, wiry texture when in fact it can be quite the opposite – baby fine.
Facing page: a damson semi-permanent colour puts some 'oomph' back into Christine's hair and improves the general condition. The balanced cut retains the length, but alters the shape of the style, adding width to a rather long face.

Fine hair can be fairly dense but, unfortunately, it is usually thin as well. An additional problem can be that it is often soft and fly-away: this can be controlled with the use of setting lotions, mousses, etc. As a rule this hair type is best kept short and simple. One length bobs to the jaw-line work well if the hair is straight; shorter bobs and layered designs if it's curly or wavy. A soft perm adds body but it must be done carefully to avoid hair breakage.

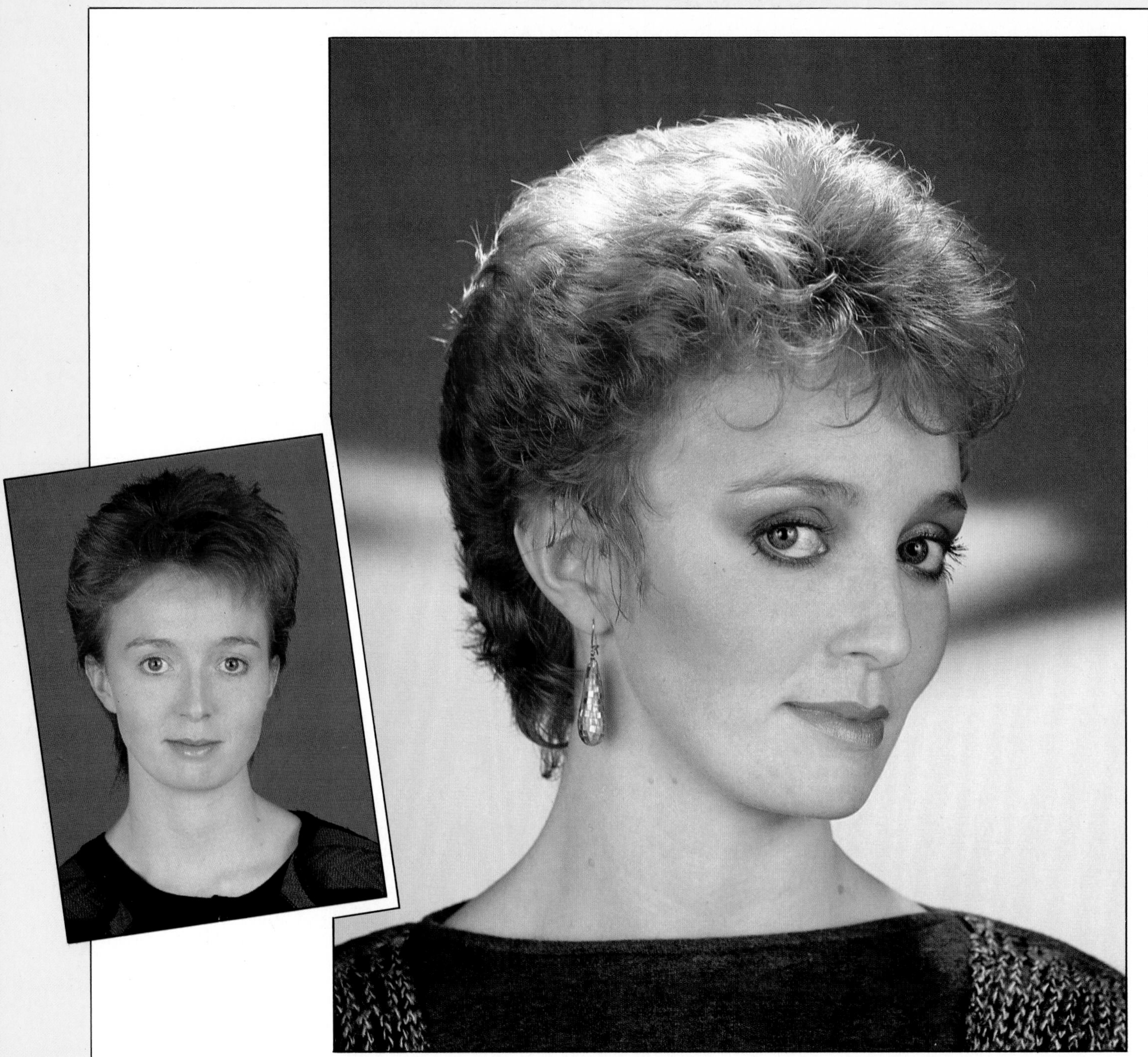

Above: what do you do if your hair is very short, straight, coarse and you are impatient for a new look? Answer: try a support perm (above right and facing page), providing, of course, that your hair is long enough to wind around a perm curler. The result: a lovely, soft, gamine look that suits Sue's facial features to a 'T'.

Medium/normal hair can be worn any way depending on what suits the individual. Although this type of hair is good tempered, it may still require a perm when a full or bouncy style is desired. If your hair is naturally curly or wavy make the most of it; have it cut to enhance the natural movement.

Coarse hair feels thick and dense and requires regular cutting. Although initially more difficult to style, the results can be superb. Short or long will depend on your physical characteristics. Sharp geometrics look stunning on straight hair, whilst wavy or curly hair can be worn in short or very long layers. This type of hair responds well to perming and colouring.

Knowing your hair and how it grows will help you to make the most of your crowning glory besides giving you a better understanding of the problems your hairdresser has to cope with. Manufacturers and hairdressers would love to work miracles, but the hair type sets its own limitations. If you know your hair you will appreciate what will and will not work. It won't stop you yearning for long, blonde, straight hair when yours is red and curly, but it will help.

From Babe to Junior Miss

Never pour neat shampoo straight onto the baby's head, spread it onto your hands first, then transfer to the hair. Rinse very thoroughly, remembering to support the baby's head throughout.

Facing page: clean from head to toe; just the finishing touches to Jemma's coiffure with a soft, baby brush. Mind you, at this age, obviously a thumb is far more interesting.

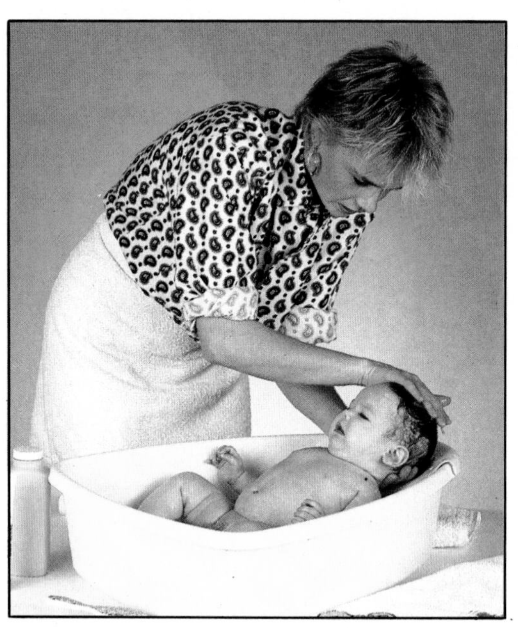

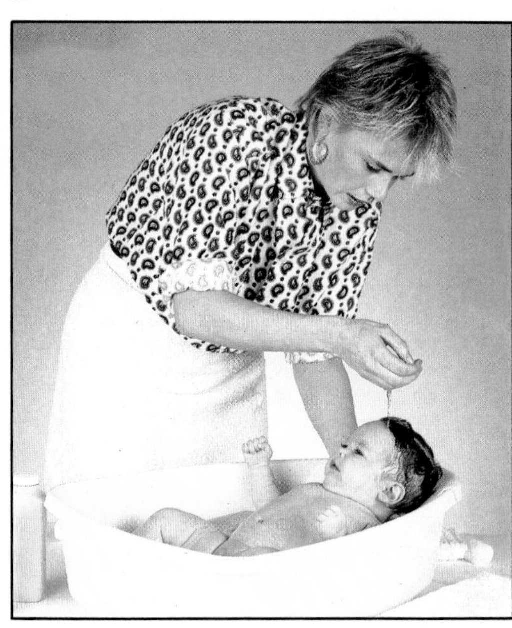

From a babe in arms to the ages of five or six are the years when you can expect your preferences about your child's hairstyle to be adhered to, but from then on you can expect it to be an uphill struggle. It is surprising how aware very young children become of hairstyles and clothes, and this can be for a variety of reasons. One of the most common of these occurs when the child starts playing with other children or going to play-school, where she will come into contact with lots of little girls. Suddenly she has lots of best friends and really wants to "have a slide like Claire" or "long hair like Diana". Fashion is not so important as a desire to be like one of her friends. This is where it can get tricky, but let's go back to that calm before the storm when she is still a little baby and your decision is final.

The amount of hair we have, its type and texture, is decided before we are born (see chapter on "Your Hair During Pregnancy"). At birth the baby's head may be covered with a fine, downy hair – lanugo – or she may be completely bald. Normally, any fine hair will disappear over the next few weeks, and the hair colour and texture at birth, therefore, cannot be taken as a clear indication of the child's eventual hair type.

Children are not all programmed to start growing hair at the same age, and those with fair hair may appear to have far less than their dark-haired playmates purely because the hair tends to be finer and the fairness creates an optical illusion of less hair. Personally, I can well remember photographs of myself which at a quick glance make me look almost bald, but on closer inspection the odd whitish curly tendril can be seen. So don't panic if the little girl next door has more hair than your baby; by the time they are both three or four things should have levelled out and the hair will be indicative of what her adult hair is going to be like.

Caring for a baby's hair and scalp should be a part of the bathing routine. Many mothers are frightened to wash a baby's head because of the soft spot on the top of the head – the fontanelle. Obviously you must take great care until

Above: A budding beauty queen! Pretty hair left to curl naturally; by far the best way to handle this kind of hair.

the bones of the skull knit (usually by eighteen months), but the scalp should be washed. Left untended there is a risk that "cradle cap" could develop. Cradle cap is brown in colour and can start as a small scalp patch which may spread. Normally, it is treated with a little warm – NOT HOT – olive oil on a pad of cotton wool. The warm oil is patted gently over the scalp and washed off with baby shampoo or baby soap. If you notice this condition developing do check at your clinic as it can also be caused by the baby's diet.

Hopefully, your baby will not have any problems, enjoy bathtime and get used to having her hair washed. Make sure that bathtime is fun time, so use an all-over bodywash and shampoo that does not

1

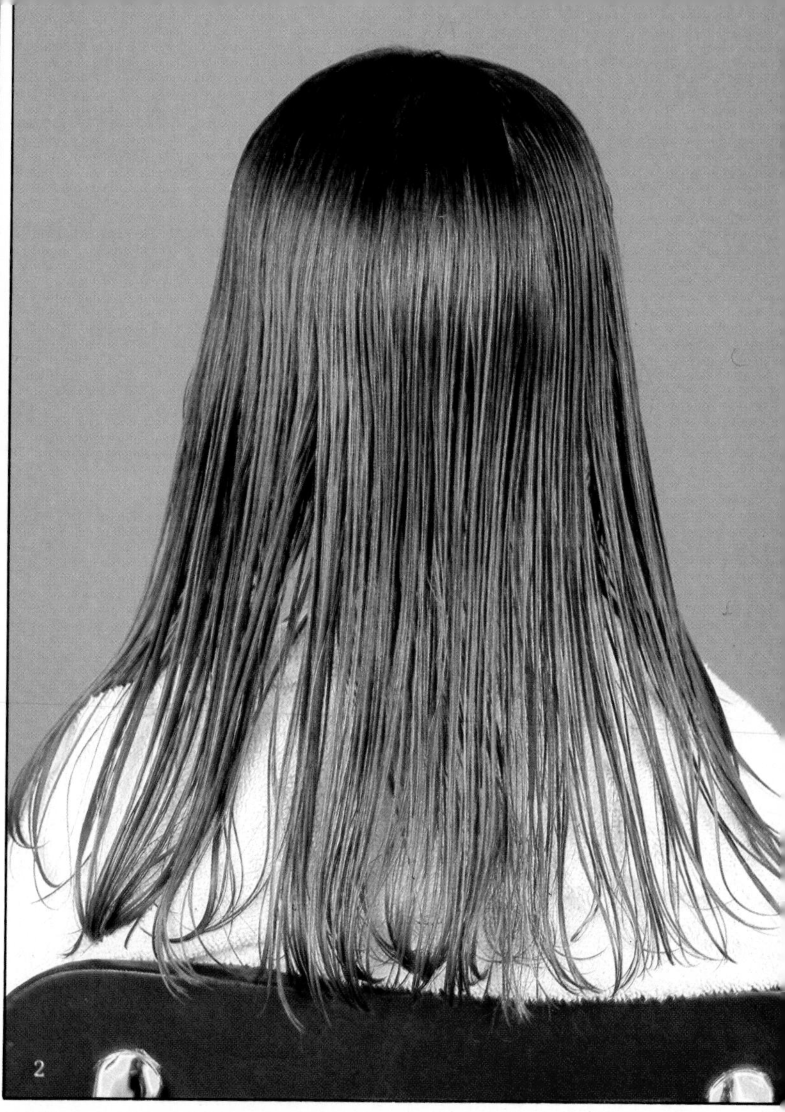

2

Previous page:
1 Maria is nearly seven; for her and other active little girls the following bob haircut is perfect.
2 Shampoo and condition the hair. Comb through and distribute the hair evenly from the natural parting.
3 Divide the back in two, down the centre. Part a small mesh of hair at the nape. The section is created by taking a diagonal parting either side of the centre. With the head forward, hold the hair firmly between your fingers and cut to the desired length.
4 Continue taking sections up to the crown. Ensure that you comb the hair smooth and hold it firmly before cutting.

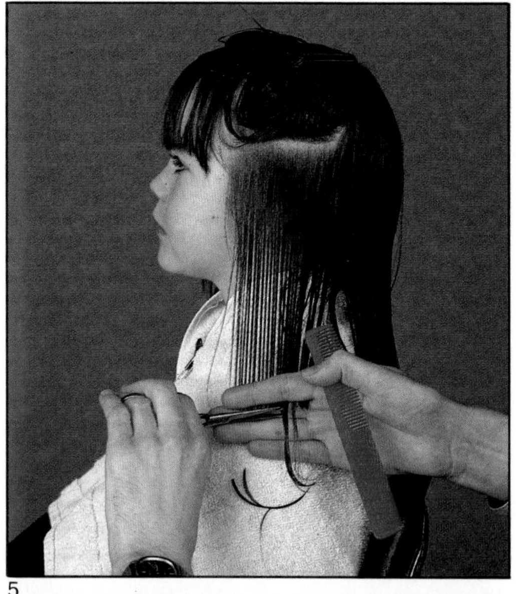
5

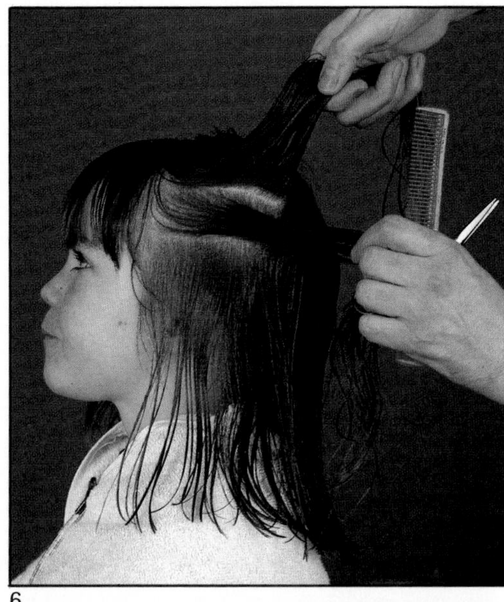
6

5 For the sides: take horizontal partings from the front hairline into the back hair. Hold the hair down with your fingers parallel to the parting. Blend with the back hair.
6 Work up to the natural parting, bringing down uncut hair and cutting to the same length as the first mesh.
7 Completed sides and back.
8 For the fringe: comb all the long hair back and pin out of the way. Take a small shaped section centre front. Hold the hair down carefully between fingers and cut.
9 Work out from the centre to the sides of the fringe only cutting a small mesh of hair each time. Do protect the child's face as you cut, and be prepared for sudden movements.
10 The finished cut professionally executed. If you do try this at home, use scissors with rounded points for the sake of safety.
11 Simple but effective style. Dried to just turn under at shoulder level. The perfect compromise for those who love long hair and mothers who have other ideas.

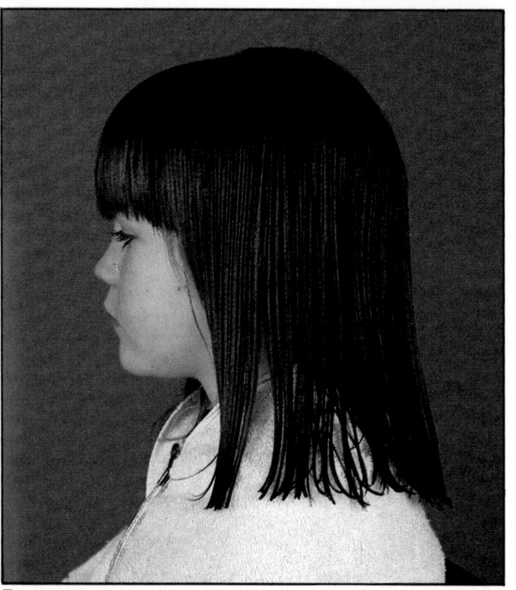
7

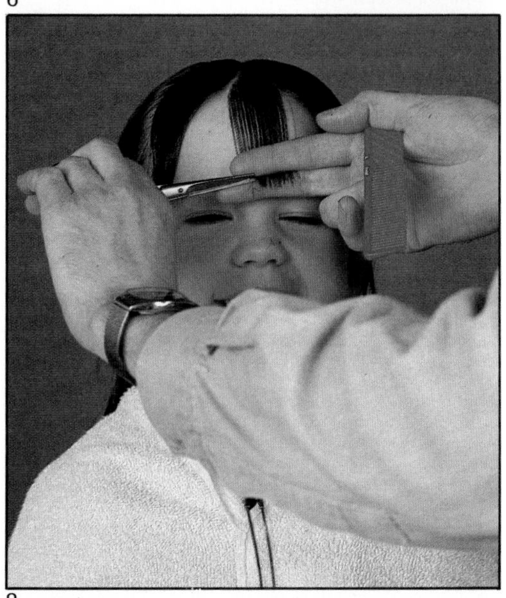
8

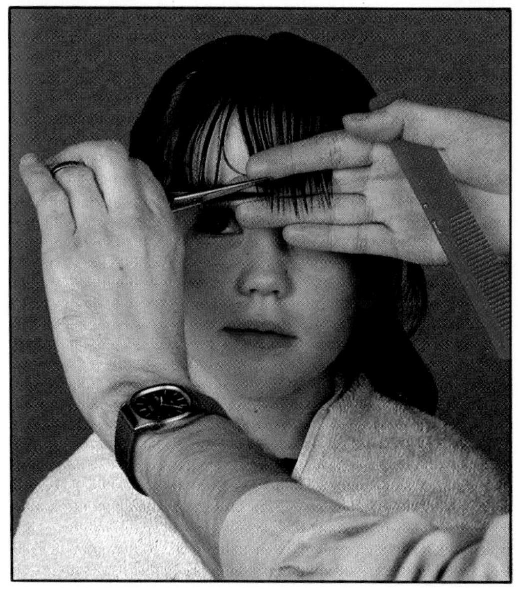
9

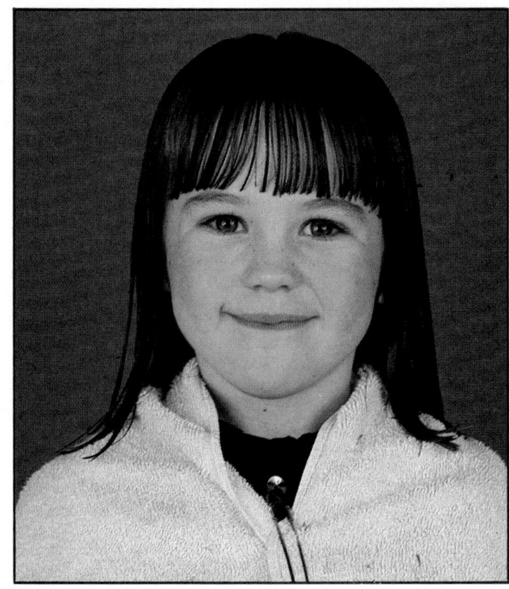
10

11

From Babe to Junior Miss

1 Five year old Naami has fabulous, long wavy hair, but for play or school it is not very practical to leave it loose.
2 Getting all that hair into a ponytail can be agony. Brush well and then use a wide-spaced comb as you start to gather the hair up. The hand holding the hair should be positioned where the ponytail is to be placed.

1

couple of times to get them used to the unfamiliar environment, then when the appointment comes around it will be a treat rather than something strange and frightening. Discuss with the stylist what you would like and what would be most suitable; keep it simple for the child's and stylist's sake. Children don't like sitting still and the more complex the haircut the longer it will take. You may be asked to hold your child or keep her attention, so be prepared and take along a favourite toy or game. Should your daughter rebel and become distraught try not to force her and don't be embarrassed: it can't be helped, just go home and try another day.

If you decide to snip at home, do be careful; use only rounded scissors and have someone to help you. Above all, try not to shout at the child; after all, how would you like a giant looming over you with what must look like a pair of hedge-cutting shears in their hands.

Getting a child used to the hairdressers will make life much easier for you and, hopefully, will not equate in their minds on the same level as a trip to the dentist.

As your child's hair starts to grow you will start to think about styles. I'm all in favour of keeping children's hair fairly short until they can manage to brush it properly themselves, but I will admit that little girls with long hair look very cute. As a general rule keep hair which is curly or very wavy short, as it tends to tangle very easily and every brushing session becomes agony time for both mother and daughter. Straight hair does not have the same tendency and can be grown longer without too much anguish.

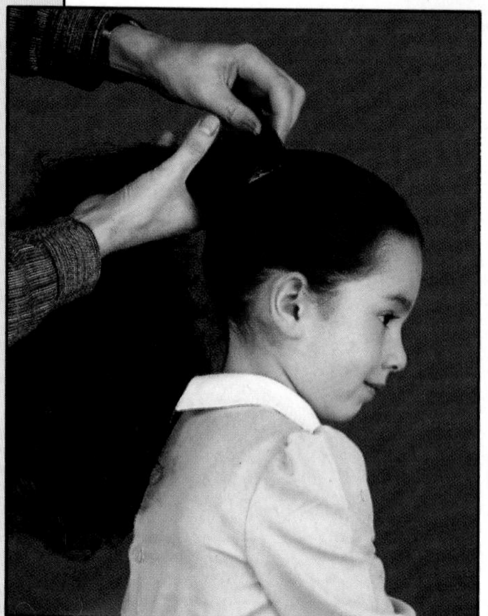
2

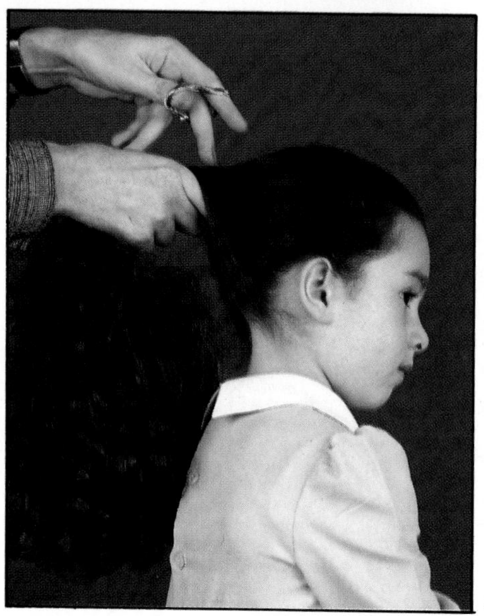
3

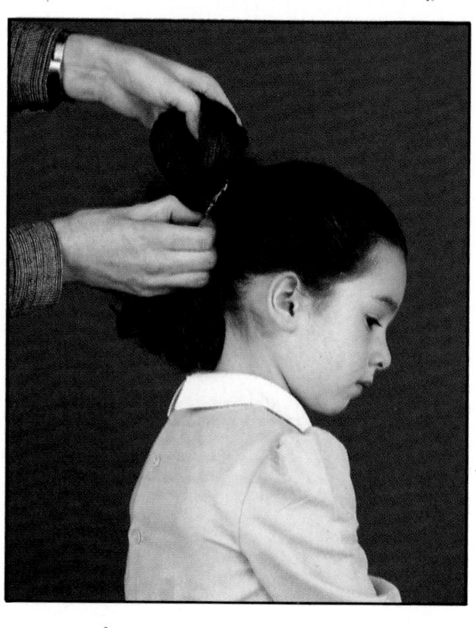
4

3 Use a covered band held open with your thumb, middle and index finger. Take hold of the hair with these three fingers.
4 Draw the hair through the band. The hand originally holding the hair is now free to hold the band close to the scalp as the ends are drawn through.
5 A simple ponytail which can be left as it is or used as the foundation for various styles.

sting the eyes. Nothing will make a child rebel more in later years than memories of sore, stinging eyes.

Once the hair has grown, try to select a shampoo and conditioner especially for her. Write her name prettily on the bottles so that they become her special things which nobody else uses. Avoid using general, all-purpose family shampoos as these are usually too strong.

Once a reasonable amount of hair has grown, and she is at a fairly controllable age, it's time to start thinking about the first proper haircut. It is important to get children used to the hairdresser at an early age. Some salons specalise in children's hair, with lovely toys and games to keep them amused. Don't worry if your salon does not offer the facilities to entertain children, simply take them to the salon a

5

1 Twisted three strand plait. Divide the ponytail into three equal sections.
2 Hold each section separately, close to the scalp. Take the right section over into the centre. For a firmer, neater plait twist this section before proceeding.
3 Bring the left hand section over into the centre and twist.
4 Continue working from side to side, remembering to alternate right then left sections into the centre. Don't forget to twist each section as you bring it over.
5 Secure the ends of the plait with another covered band.
6 A pretty, colour-coordinated slide completes the plait. For a special occasion little silk flowers can be pinned around the base and end of the plait.
7 As a variation, the plait can be hoisted into a bun or simply gripped under as shown.
8 For an attractive, alternative way to keep the hair off the face, twist the front hair up and back (like a roll), and secure with hair grips which can be covered with a slide or comb.

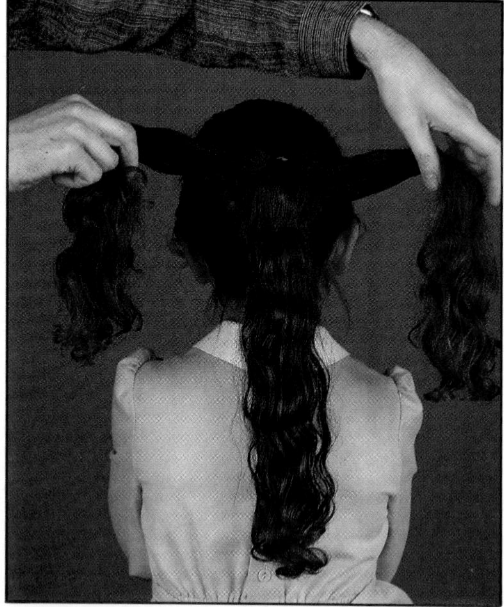
1

2

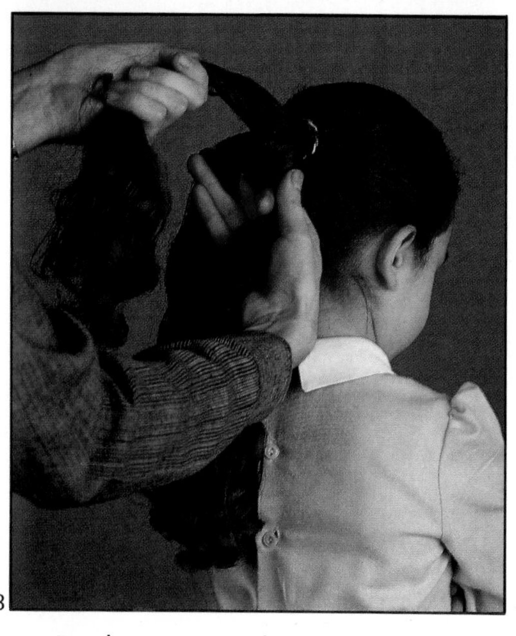
3

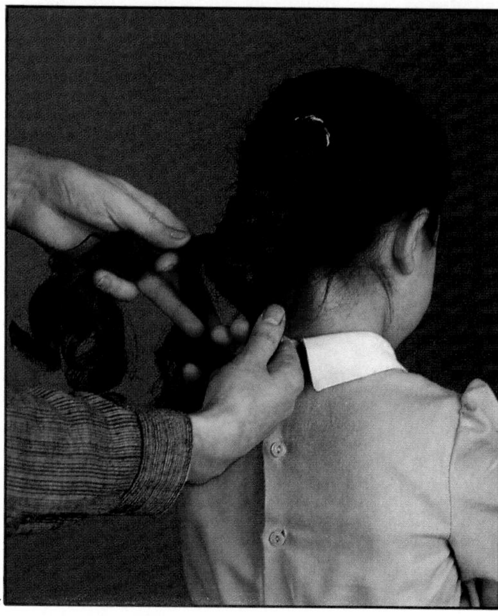
4

Purchase a good quality brush and comb and always remove all tangles night and morning and, of course, prior to shampooing. Always begin combing at the nape, working from the points to the roots as this is far less painful. For shampooing, follow the directions in the previous chapter, but once conditioner has been applied comb through with a wide-toothed comb before rinsing: this reduces the risk of tangles after the final rinse. Try to dry your child's hair naturally or with a blow dryer on a cool setting, and, as children's hair seems prone to tangles it's a good idea not to rub or tug too much.

Simple hairstyles always work best for children. Fringes should be kept short so as not to obscure vision and long hair should be tied or gripped back. A word on securing long hair: slides are fine but beware of elastic bands; use only the covered type available from most stores and chemists. Plaits and ponytails keep hair neat and tidy but try not to pull them too tight, your child's hair and scalp are still developing and the results of your efforts could be traction alopecia; "hair loss due to undue strain placed on the hair and roots". Would-be little ballet dancers are most susceptible to this condition as their hair is often scraped back into a tight bun. If you must tie it back, tie loosely and not in the same way every day.

Avoid perms at this age however much your eight year old may want curls. I feel that perms and colours should wait until

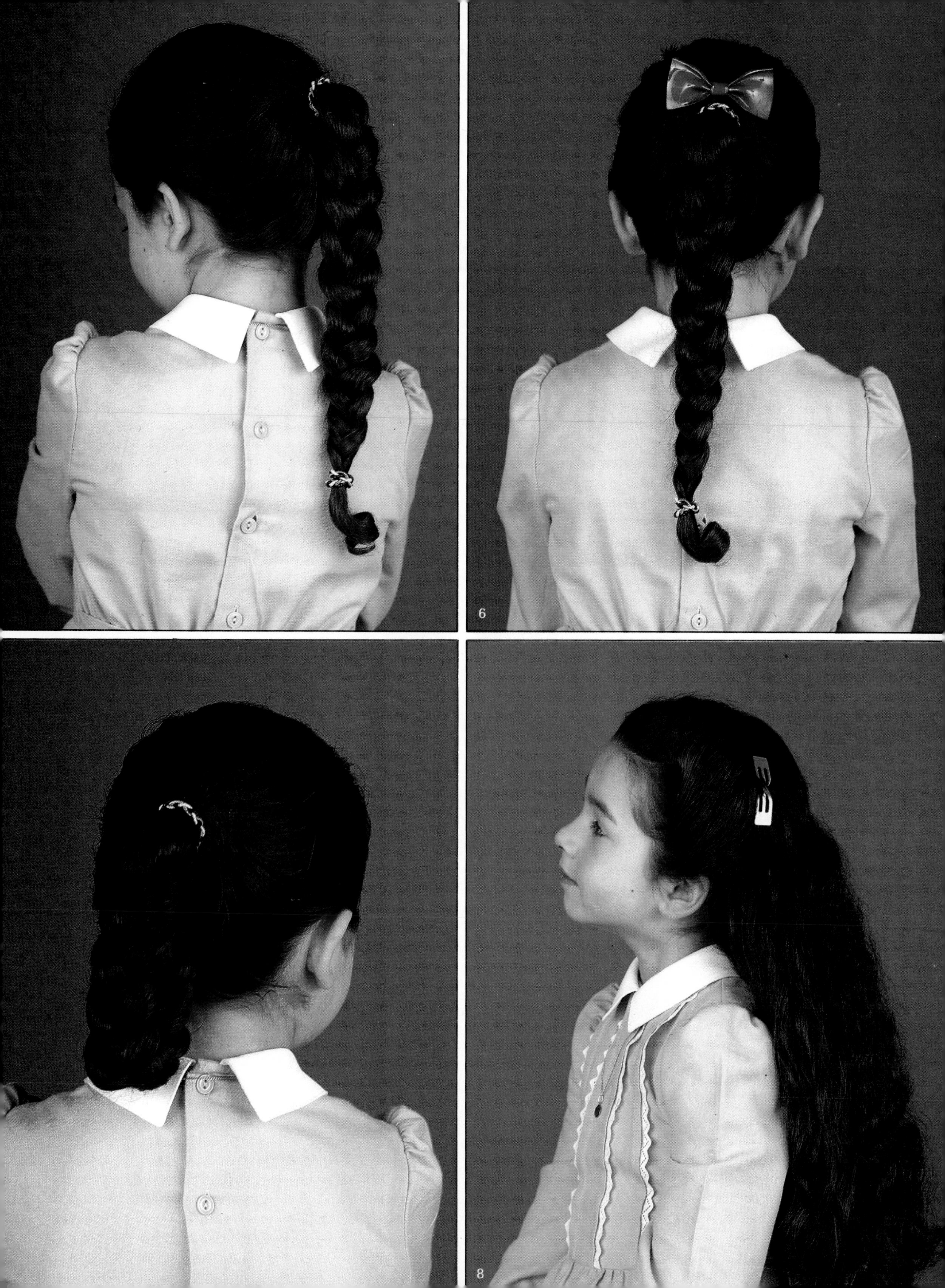

6

8

the fourteenth or fifteenth year, when they can cope with the additional attention chemically processed hair demands. The hair and scalp go through quite a few chanages in the intervening years, so it's as well to wait.

chemist and they must be used promptly. The shampoos and lotions are easy to apply and will help loosen the nits (eggs) from the hair, but you will have to do the final stage yourself and comb the hair, section by section, with a special, fine-

1

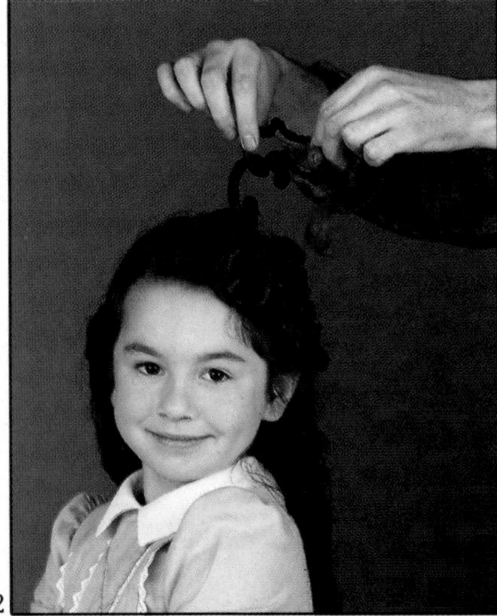
2

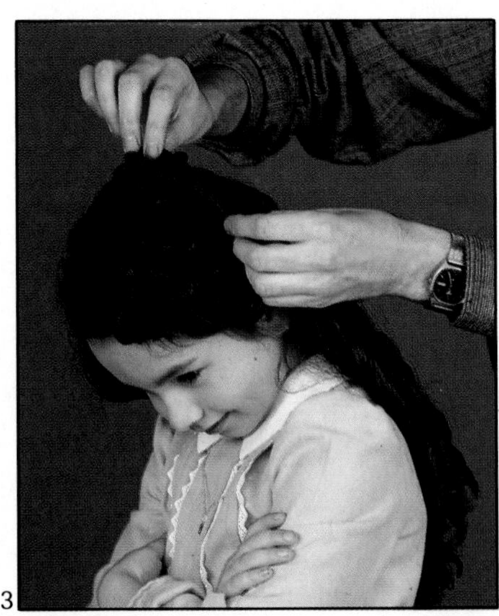
3

1 The easy way to curls without tears. Work with the hair clean and slightly damp. Part off a small mesh of hair, comb through and begin twisting from roots to points.
2 Keep twisting until the hair coils back on itself.
3 Secure the coil with thick hair pins or grips, close to the scalp. Work all round the head in this manner. Depending on natural curl, leave the coils in for fifteen to thirty minutes.
4 Starting at the nape, remove all grips and pins.
5 Do not brush, but use an Afro-type comb to relax the waves (brushing will result in tangles). Begin at the nape, working from the points of the hair to the roots.

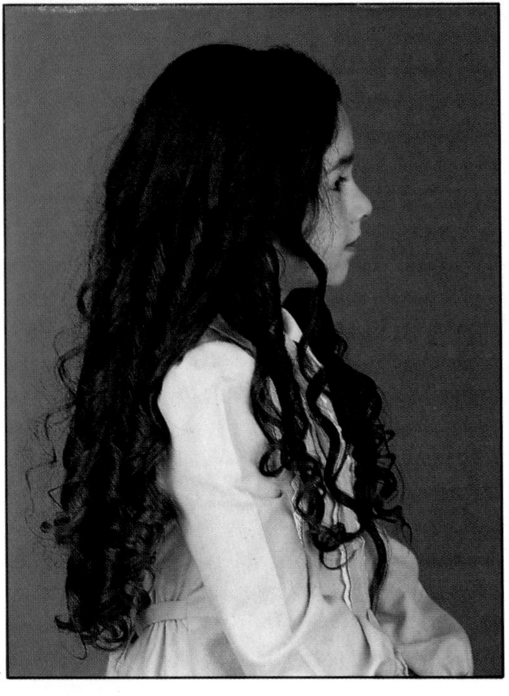
4

5

Facing page: pretty dress, pretty girl and an enchanting hairstyle that's quick, easy and painless to achieve.

Keep an eye on children's hair and scalp at all times, particularly if they start to scratch. Nits and lice are all too common and once a child starts school they can spread like wildfire. Naturally, it's upsetting to think of your child being infested, but don't start blaming yourself or your child for being dirty. Nits have little respect for cleanliness and can be found on the most scrupulously-clean children. Treatments can be obtained from your doctor or the toothed comb until not a trace of the nits remains. *Pediculosis capitis* is the correct term for this condition and it can return again and again, so be on your guard.

It won't be long before your daughter's idea of hairstyle and yours part company, so to avoid problems early on, try to compromise about length and style, in this way everyone stays happy and your nerves remain intact.

CHAPTER 24

Teens to Twenties

1 Toni's face shape and hair texture suit this square, graduated bob, but like many people she needed some tips on blow drying.
2 After shampooing and conditioning, blow-dry lotion is applied to add body and reduce static.

Coping with the psychological and physical changes at puberty can be problematic for both parents and children. For some, the transition from little girl to young lady is relatively smooth, whilst for others it's a battle, when nothing is right and the entire adult world is against you. Understanding what is happening and learning to compromise will help.

1

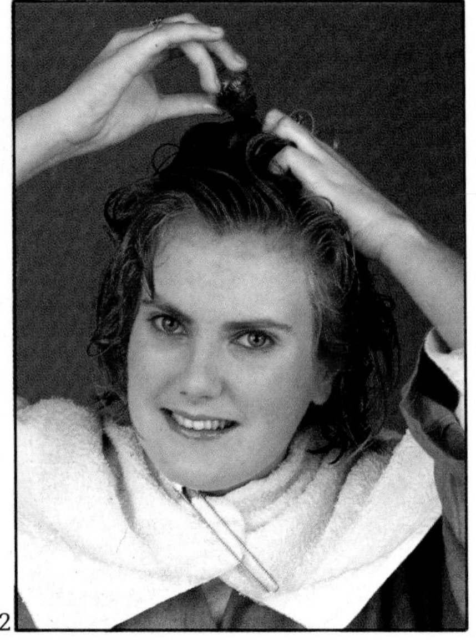

2

3

3 Rough-dry hair to remove excess water.
4 Section hair across from ear to ear, beginning at the nape.
5 Using a radial bristle brush, dry the hair section by section, aiming warm air down the hair shaft.
6 Dry crown hair down, turning just the ends under.
7 To dry the sides, take horizontal partings and keep rotating brush up and down, still maintaining the downward flow of air.

Hormonal changes become apparent as the body shape changes, underarm and pubic hair develops and menstruation begins. Alongside physical development come the fluctuations in mood, swinging from rational behaviour to irrational tantrums so rapidly that it's hard to keep up. This is all normal and we all go through it to a greater or lesser degree.

One of the side effects of this surge in hormonal activity can be the dramatic effect it has on your hair. More often than not hair and skin will become greasy. As the entire glandular system goes into overdrive the sebaceous (oil producing) glands are stimulated, resulting in greasy, lank hair. The skin may also react, becoming very spotty, particularly on the forehead, nose, chin and back. All this can be very trying when you're so conscious of your appearance and endeavouring to look your best.

If greasy hair is your problem then here are one or two tips that will help:

1. Keep your hair clean: wash every day with a mild shampoo if need be. Follow the advice in chapter 1 for shampooing greasy hair. If your hair is long, then apply conditioner to the middle lengths and ends, do not massage it into the scalp. Don't be put off using conditioner; if long hair is washed frequently the ends will soon become very dry and split.

2. Greasy hair often gives off an unpleasant odour, another reason for keeping hair scrupulously clean, but a change in your diet will also help. Avoid oily, fatty and highly spiced foods; eat as much fresh fruit and vegetables as you can as this will not only help your hair but your skin as well; and say goodbye to junk food, at least until your body has adjusted.

During this time it's a good idea to keep your hairstyle simple and easy to care for; it may be boring but its better to look fairly nice than a total wreck, and you'll soon be

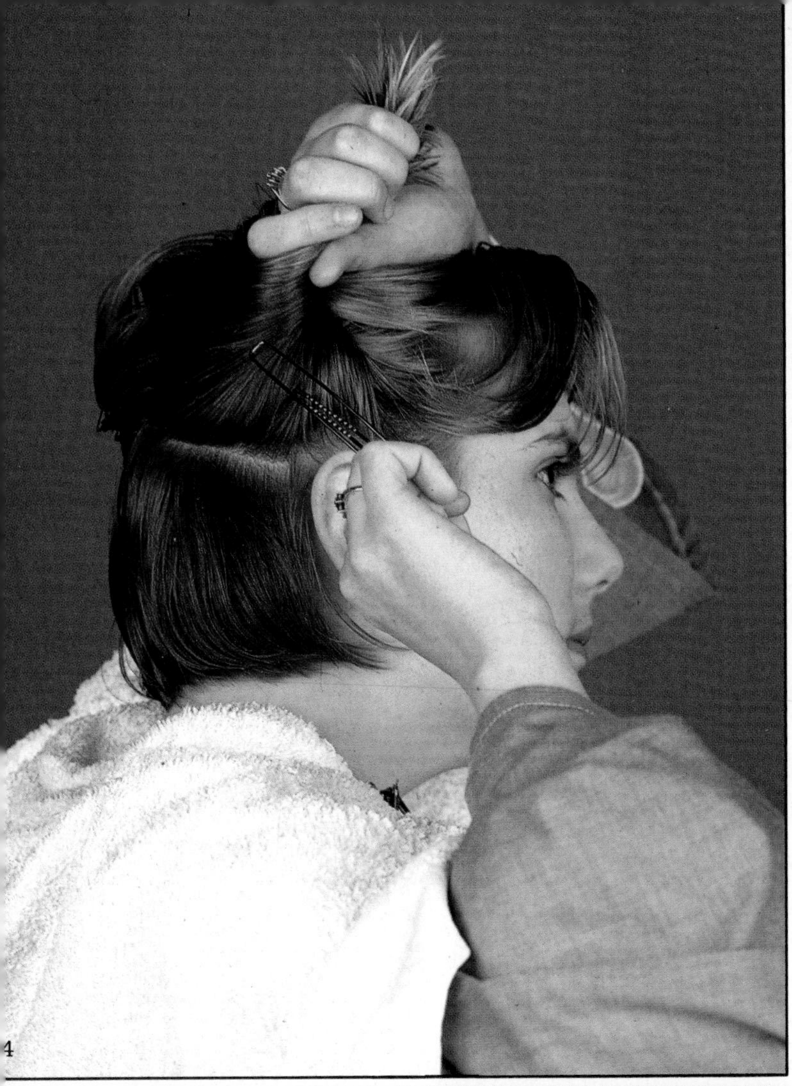

4

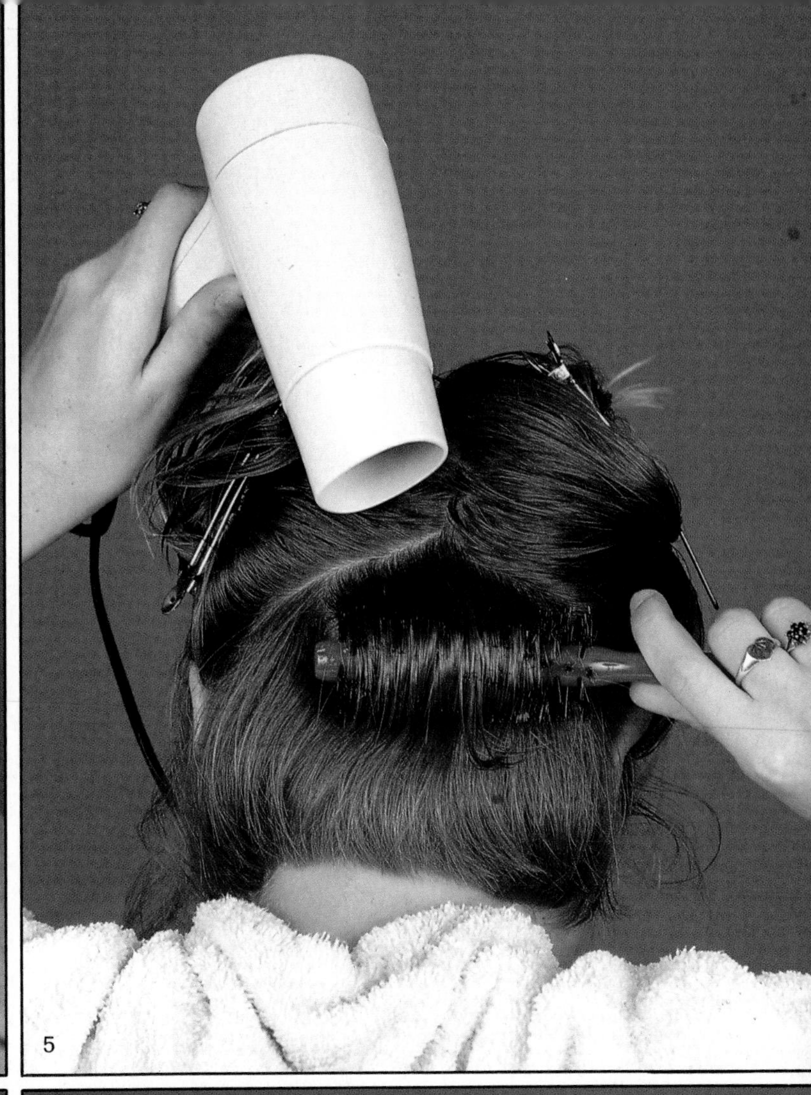

5

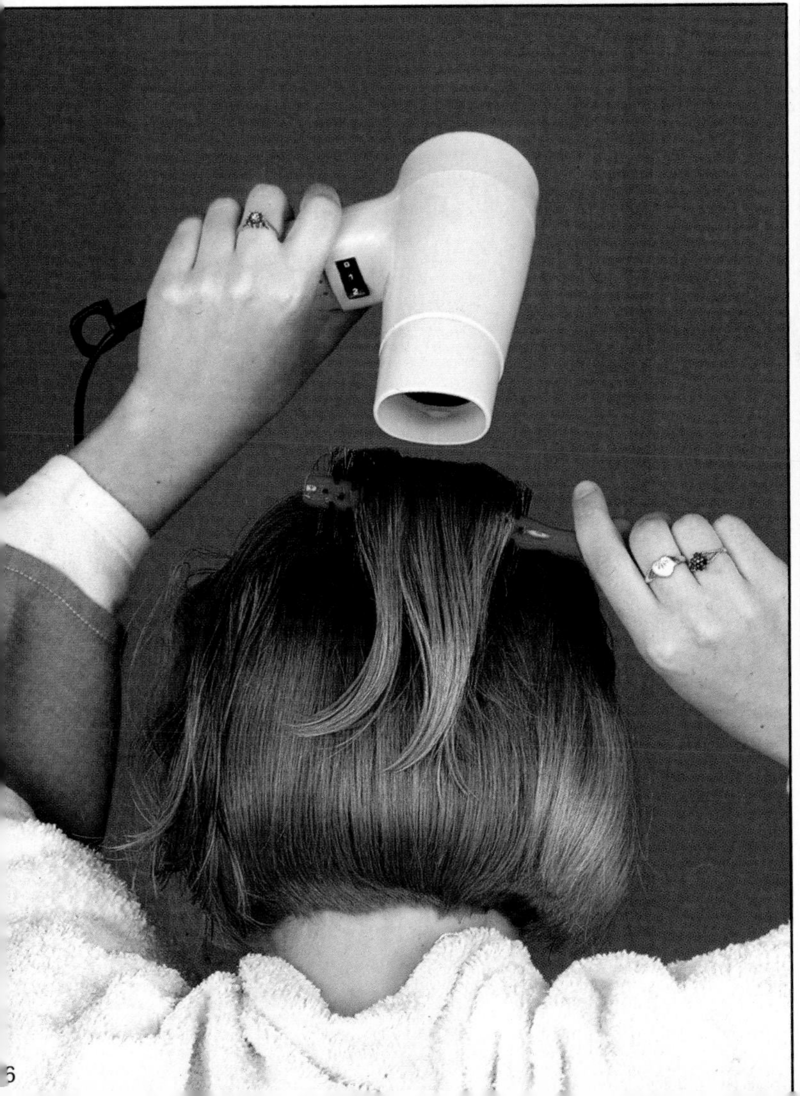

6

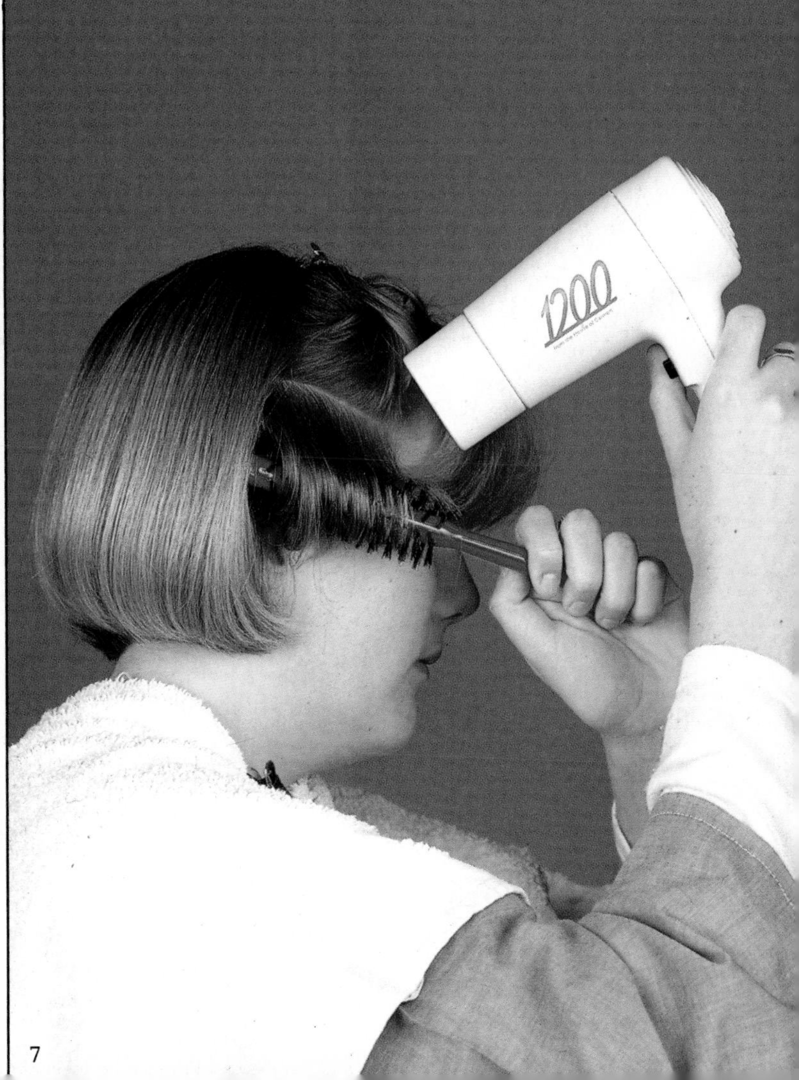

7

8 Try to ensure that the ends of the hair lie smoothly around the bristle of the brush. Continue up to centre parting.
9 Blow-dry the fringe forward and under. Brush thoroughly to blend all sections.
10 Combination of correct brush control and air flow direction helps to keep the hair smooth and bouncy.

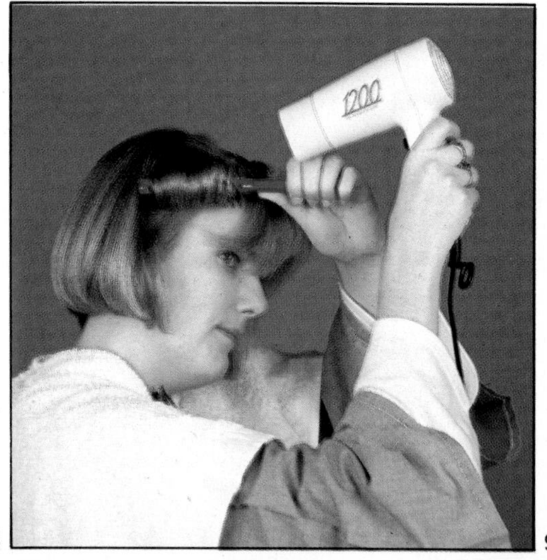

8

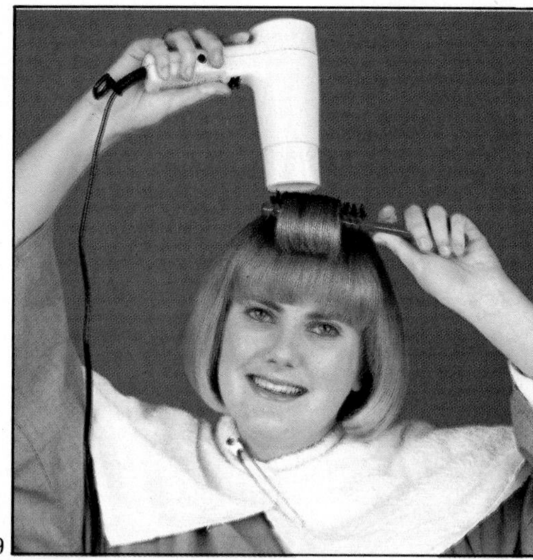
9

10

11

11 A lovely style which is perfect for college, work or leisure.
12 A transformation that you too can try. Take a small ponytail just behind the fringe, bind with thick picture hanging wire. Backcomb fringe and ends of ponytail, spray, mould the hair up into shape while sticky and spray again. Emphasise your creation with strategically-placed fluorescent gel. Simple but very effective bob creation.

able to experiment with more adventurous designs. Whenever possible, try to let your hair dry naturally. If you must blow dry then keep the heat down to a minimum; a hot dryer will only stimulate the oil glands further and rigorous brushing spreads the oil through the hair. Unless you're going somewhere special keep greasy hair off your face (especially if you're just lounging around at home), so as not to encourage a spotty skin.

For those still at school there are three main problems you may have to contend with: 1 The hairstyle that you want. 2 The hairstyle that your parents think suitable. 3 What your school will allow.

Combining all three shouldn't be too difficult: remember, a good haircut is a versatile one. For school and parents your hair can be worn casually but neatly dressed. There is no need for shocking colours that result in suspension, and avant-garde haircuts can wait a while. However, in the evening the simplest style can be transformed with just a little practice and, using gel, you can create outrageous shapes. Backcombed, a tame, innocent haircut can become wild and bold, and

12

when sprayed with vibrant colour your image changes completely. False swatches of colour or artificial plaits can be gripped in. A good hairdressing salon or chemist will retail coloured sprays and gels which brush or shampoo out, but be careful if your hair is fair as some of the stronger colours do stain the hair. When using coloured sprays it's wise to cover your clothes and stay well away from the furnishings, just in case your aim is not too good. Temporary looks are far more fun, allowing you the flexibility to change your image and mood depending on the situation and clothes you are wearing.

Split ends are a big problem and the only answer is to have them cut off. Try to discourage split ends by going easy with electrical equipment, blow dryers, tongs etc., and do use a good hairbrush, either a bristle type or plastic one which is well finished, with all the quills properly rounded off and no rough edges to tear your hair.

From school to college or the first job is a time when ideas about fashion and image are still developing. The guidelines for the school years still apply, although at college or work the rules are more relaxed, and dress is entirely up to the individual. It's also a time to experiment, trying different clothes, hairstyles, hair colours and make-up, finding what suits and what doesn't. Try to co-ordinate clothes rather than buying lots of different bits and bobs that can only be worn individually: it saves money.

Be sensible about hairstyles, especially as far as your job is concerned, as there is no need to go out of your way to shock. Assess the kind of place you're going to work in and dress accordingly; save the way-out looks for the evening, you can establish two images – one for work and one for play. When jobs are thin on the ground it's ridiculous to put people off with a very punk hairdo.

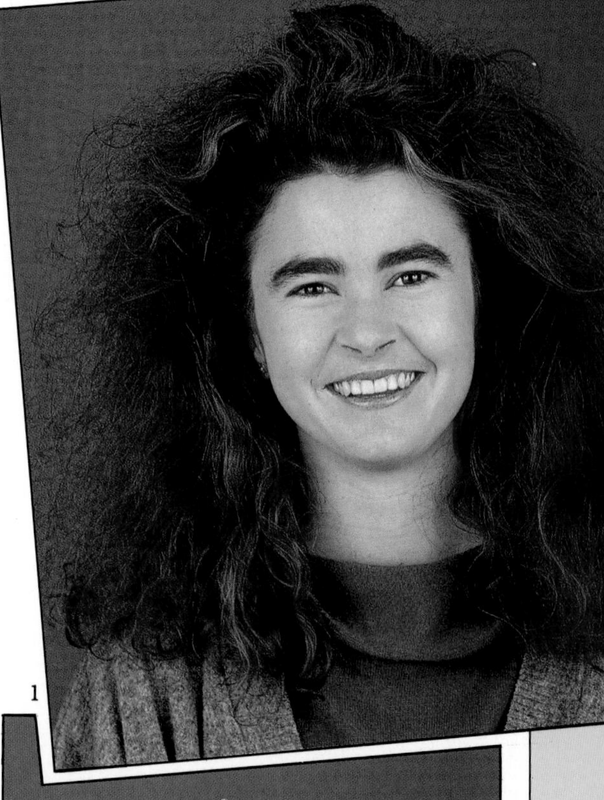

1

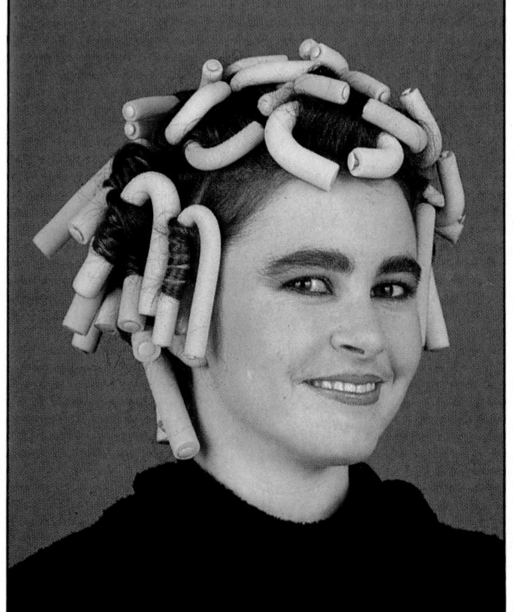

2

3

1 If you have masses of fine, frizzy hair like Melissa, how about this fun way to make the most of it!
2 Pretty in pastels. Wella Molton Brown Stylers control and define the curl. Top hair is wound conventionally, side and back hair was twisted first for a more rippling wave.
3 No grips, no pins, but what a curl!
4 For a wild look remove Stylers and run your fingers through each curl. Leave loose or pile your hair on top, securing with a few grips or pretty combs.

Whilst establishing an image you'll also be deciding on the type of hairdressing salon you prefer. Initially, most people start by going to the same salon as their mothers, and if this still suits you, fine; if not then you will be looking around. One of the 4

1 Curly hair is not always the blessing most people imagine it to be and many people – Maria included – would prefer a sleeker, more sophisticated look.
2 Shampoo and condition. An application of hair mousse will help to control that strong curl.
3 Begin at the nape after pinning the rest of the hair well out of the way. Using a tufted, radial bristle brush for control, take a small section and wrap firmly around the brush. Keeping the hair smooth and taut, unwind the brush as you dry and roll up again. Repeat this procedure, following the brush with the dryer until mesh is dry. Work across nape.
4 & **5** Take the next section from ear to ear, across the back of the head, just below crown.
6 Starting at the centre back, take vertical partings and roll hair in towards middle.

best ways to find a good salon is through personal recommendation, so if you see someone whose hair you admire ask them where they had it done; everyone loves a compliment and they are bound to tell you. Otherwise, shop around for a salon that appeals to you from the outside, and go in: does it look as nice on the inside? Explain your requirements to the receptionist and ask for a consultation. A good hairdresser will discuss your hair, your likes and dislikes: take a picture along of a style you think might suit if it will help you to explain. While you're talking, the hairdresser can assess your personality, how you like to dress and whether you are an introvert or extrovert. If the stylist and staff are interested in your hair you will soon sense it, but if the attitude is one of indifference, leave and continue looking.

If you're continuing your education at college or university or are unemployed, money may be short. One way of getting your hair done cheaply is as a model for salon trainees. Look in the personal column of your local newspaper for advertisements. Good salons hold regular evening training sessions for juniors and stylists to learn and work out new styles or experiment with the latest looks and products. They are always looking for young people to act as models. The charges are minimal, sometimes free, but you must have plenty of time and be flexible about your style.

Regardless of how, when or where you have your hair done, do keep it clean, and well-cut by a professional. If colours and perms appeal to you then read the relevant chapters in this book to find out when it's safe for you to do it yourself and when you must seek professional help. Eat healthy foods and try to take some exercise: incidentally, dancing is a great form of exercise and fun. You want your hair to last a lifetime so treat it with respect.

1

2

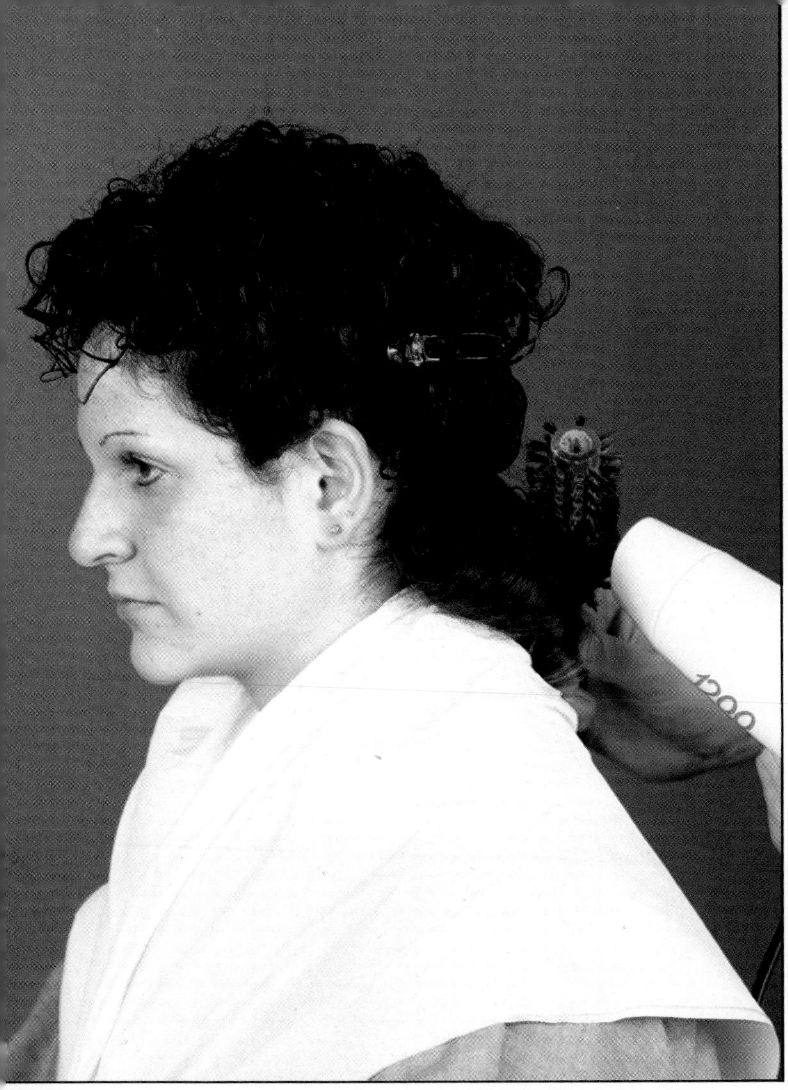

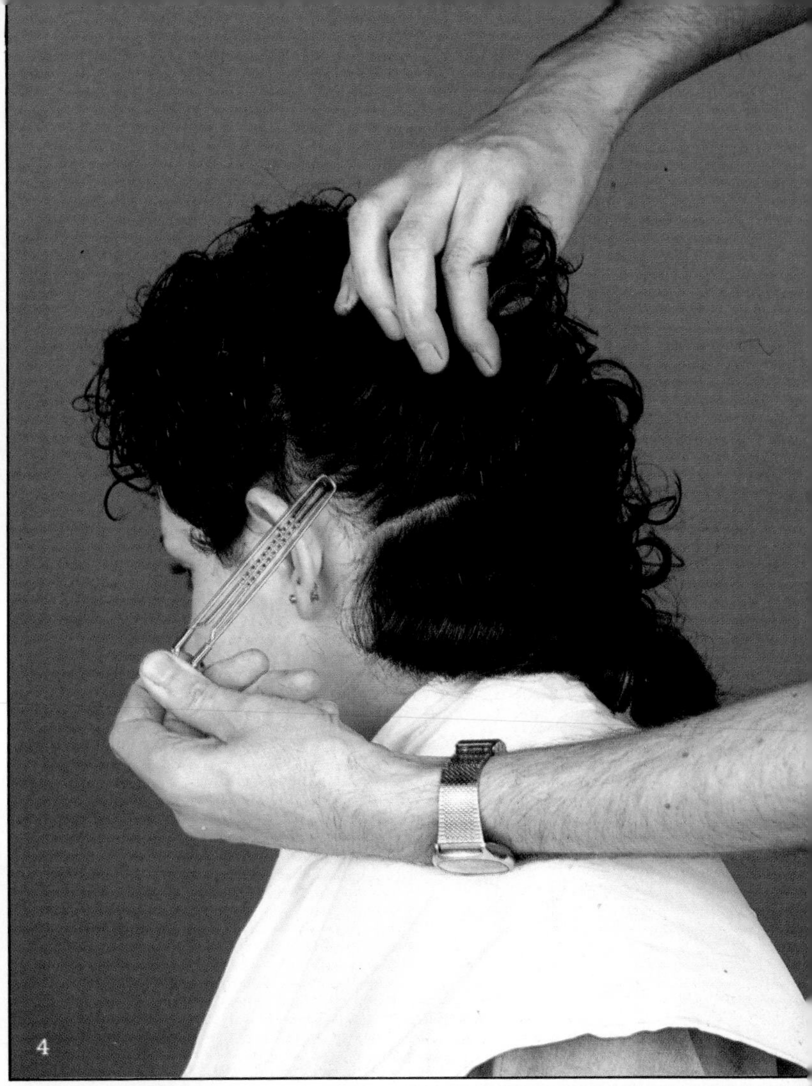

4

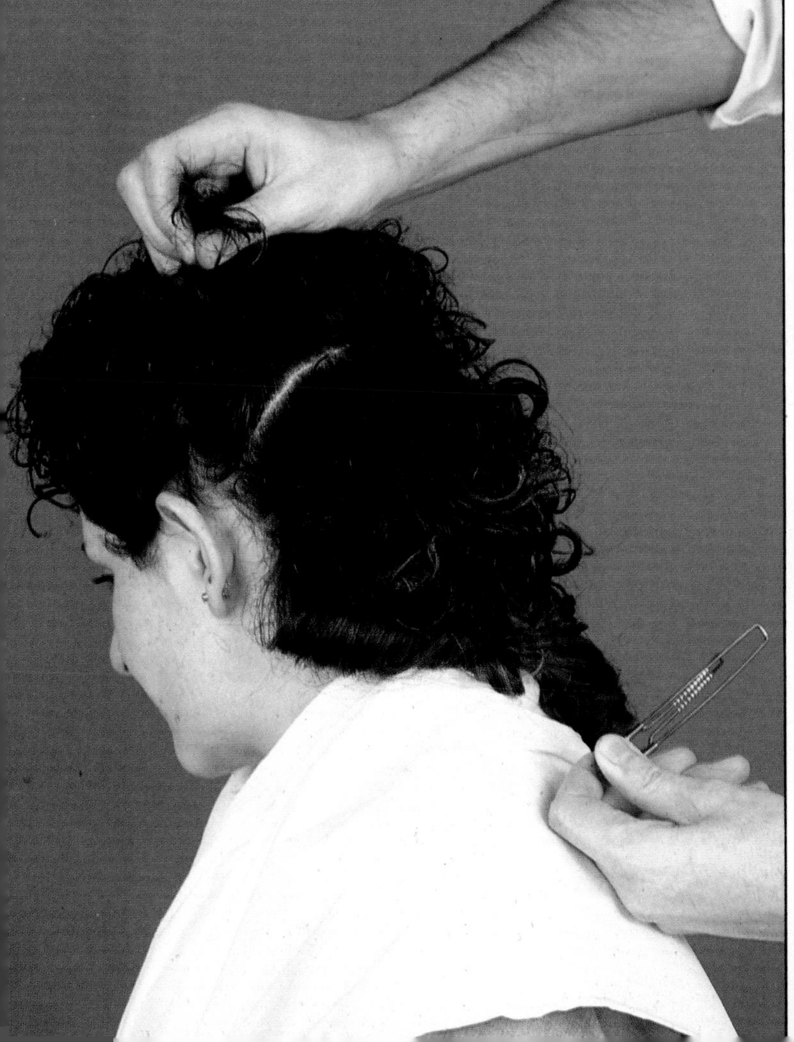

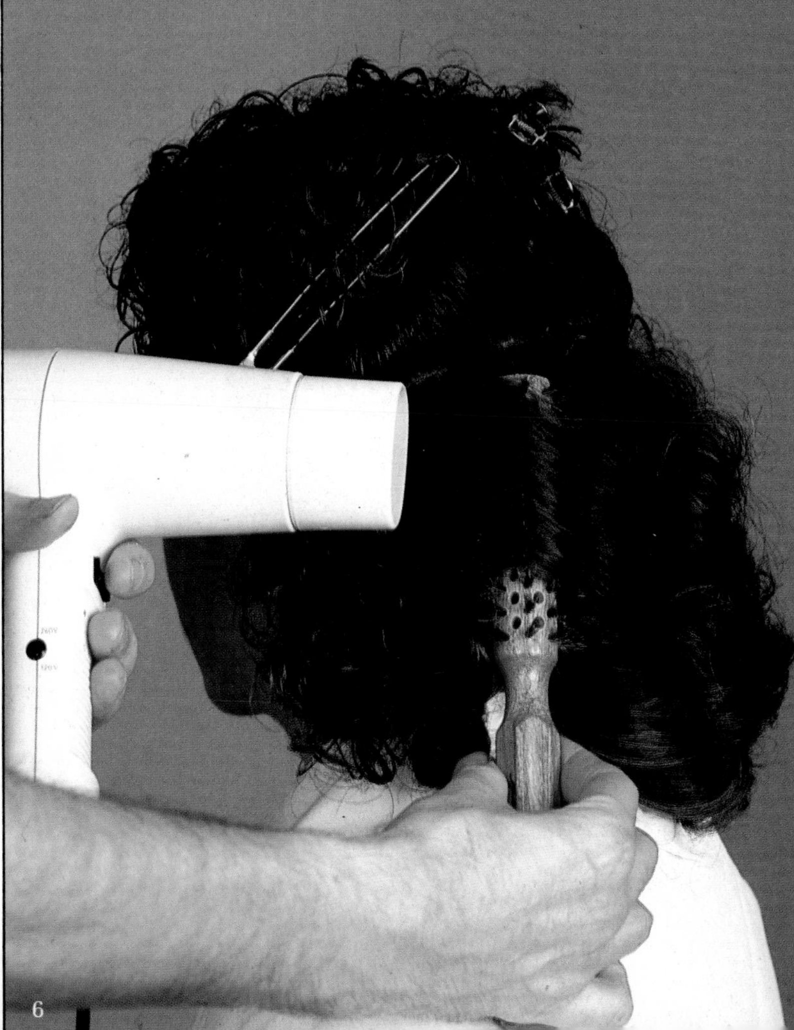

6

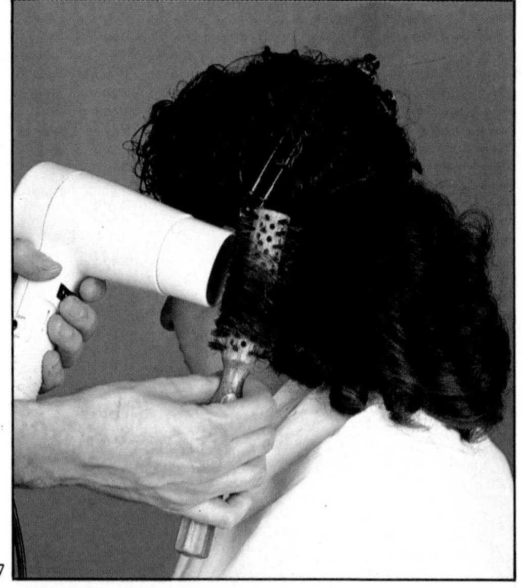
7

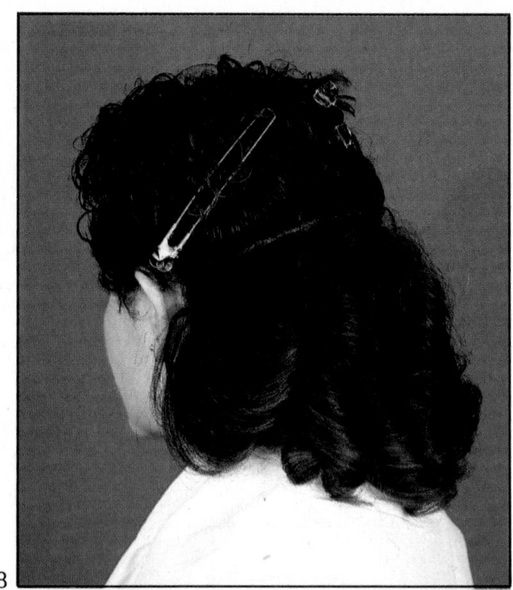
8

7 Work outwards – small section by section – towards the ear. Try to keep hair smooth and taut over the brush. Remember not to overheat the hair.
8 Return to centre back and repeat for the right half, reversing directions. Completed lower back.
9 Section off the top and crown.
10 Dry the top and lower crown hair towards back.
11 For the sides: take diagonal partings and roll the sides up and back, pulling the hair back ever further as you unwind the brush.
12 Front hair is dried over to the side rather than straight back. This will elongate the profile shape and create softness across the forehead.
13 Thoroughly brushed through, and then sprayed lightly with hairspray to protect the hair from moisture. Curls are fun, but it's nice to know that with a little help you, like Maria, can have a more elegant hairstyle.

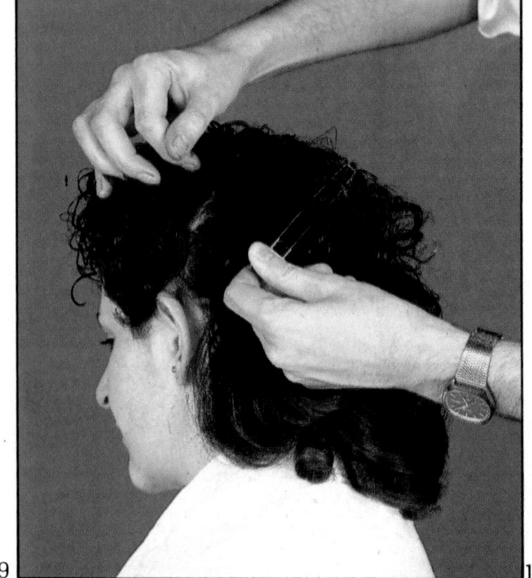
9

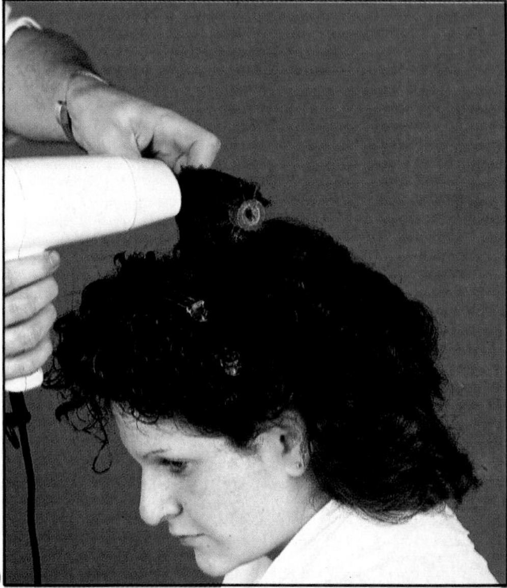
10

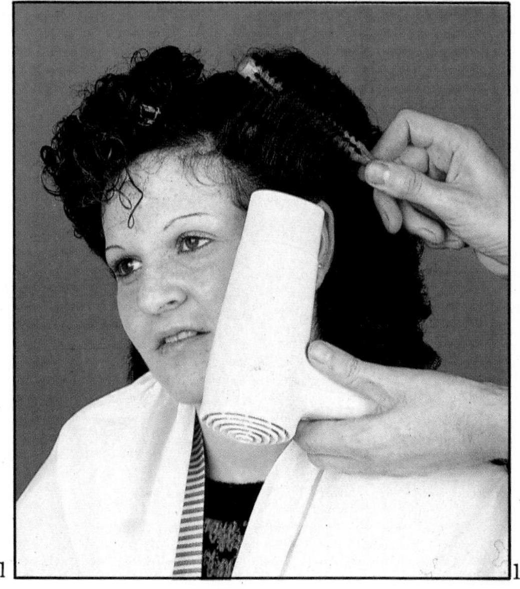
11

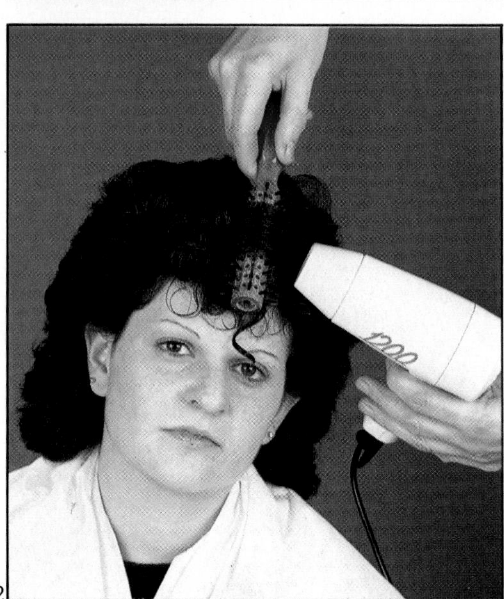

12

13

CHAPTER 25

Curly versus Straight

1 A long face, high forehead and fine, thin hair are three problems Laura has to contend with. Professional help and advice are a must in this case.

Whether our hair is curly or straight it is a paradox of human nature that we will always want the opposite. How well I recall relatives congratulating me on my good fortune at being blessed with curly hair, and my chagrin as a teenager in the late sixties and seventies, when straight hair was "in" and curly hair "out".

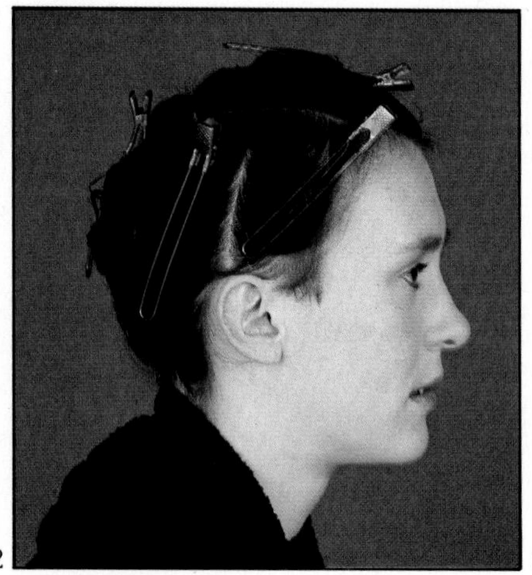

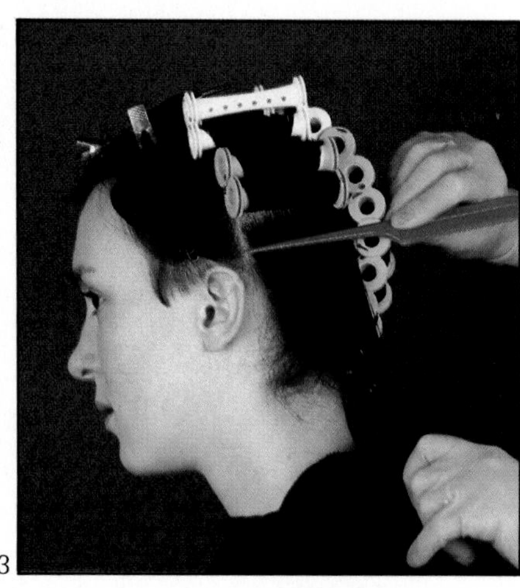

2 After consultation and a haircut, a special pre-perm lotion was applied to protect the hair. Sectioning the hair enables the permer to work methodically.
3 Centre back is wound first, followed by the side sections. Here, the comb indicates the size of the mesh to be parted off.
4 The long back hair is pre-damped with permanent waving lotion, mesh by mesh.
5 End papers protect the points of the hair.
6 The hair is then placed around a large perm curler.
7 The curler is carefully wound down.

Nowadays, hair fashions are far more flexible, with no "in" and "out": the style depends on what suits you and your lifestyle. The majority of people decide that what suits them is a soft, flattering, versatile hairstyle which is easy to manage and will stay looking good from morning until night. For their hair to fulfil these requirements a permanent wave is essential.

Today's permanent waves are many and varied; this applies to both professional products and home perm kits. Some are designed to be used when only a soft result is desired, others for a more conventional curl. Even though they are much safer and more reliable than the perms of old, it must be remembered that the chemicals involved can still cause severe internal structural damage to the hair if misused. Therefore, it is important that the quality of the hair to be permed is correctly assessed and the person doing the perm is competent.

Perming your own hair can be a tricky business, and whenever possible I would advise you to seek professional advice. However, economy measures sometimes have to be taken and a home perm is the only answer.

There are certain instances when a professional permanent wave is a must. When your hair is for example:

a Dry or in bad condition
b Tinted
c Bleached
d Highlighted
e Still has the remains of a previous perm in it
f Is one length, or longer than collar length.

In the salon, a good perm technician will take into account any of the above conditions and discuss with you and the stylist the type of perm and degree of curl required to enhance your haircut.

Providing your hair is in a suitable condition to perm, the next step is gently to shampoo and then restyle if necessary. The application of a pre-perm prior to winding will help to protect your hair and act as a buffer to the lotion. Now we come to the

4

5

7

8 On completion, each curler is carefully post-damped with waving lotion.
9 The head is covered with a plastic bag while processing takes place. Once a satisfactory curl can be seen, the hair is rinsed, neutralised and conditioned.

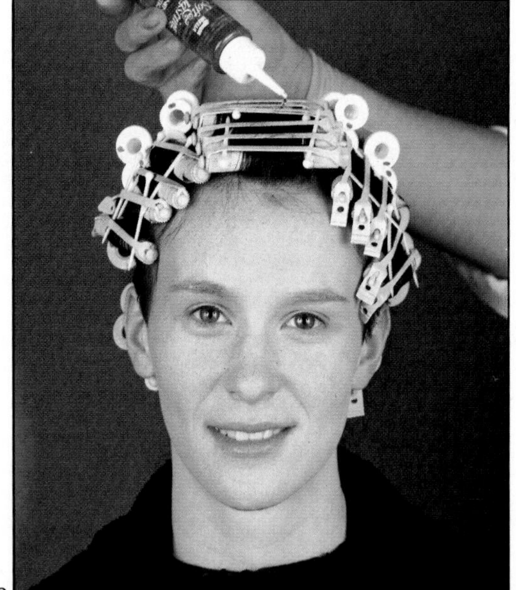
8

Once all the hair is wound onto curlers and the solution applied, the hair is covered with a plastic cap and left to process. When the desired degree of curl has been reached every curler must be thoroughly rinsed and then blotted with a towel to remove as much water as possible. Now the neutralizer can be applied; this will help to reform the bonds in the cortex into their new wave pattern. After approximately five minutes the curlers are gently removed and more neutralizer sponged onto the ends to ensure all the hair has been properly treated. Rinsing and conditioning complete the process.

For certain styles the hair is also cut after perming, but don't be alarmed that all your curls are going into the dustpan; your hair has been permed from the scalp, and post cutting is used for very short styles, when the finished length would be far too short

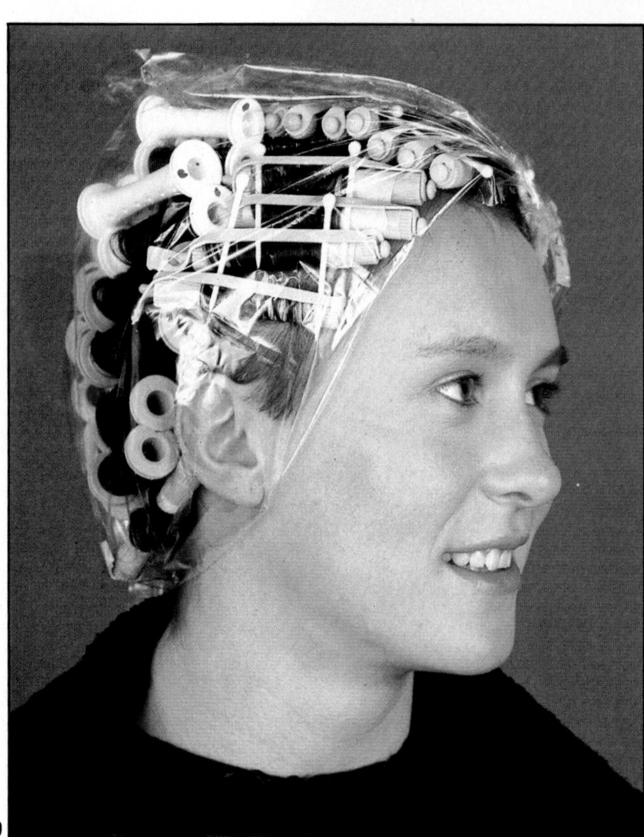
9

10

10 The finished perm. The wet curl is bouncy, round and uniform.
11 Gently blow dried to avoid stretching the hair. From fine, limp hair to soft, flattering movement; a professional perm is worth every penny.

serious business: after sectioning, your hair is wound by mesh around the perm rods/ curlers, perm solution may be applied as the hair is wound up (pre-damping) or to each perm curler on completion (post-damping).

The choice of a) the lotion and b) the curler is critical; a) relates to the texture and condition of your hair b) to the size of curl required.

to perm, or when a certain effect is required.

As your hair is styled watch the hairdresser and try to pick up some tips. What brushes do they use? Is a styling aid like mousse or gel applied? Can you buy the same product in the salon? Ask questions about home maintenance, what shampoo to use etc.: do you need to damp your hair down every morning (you do with

11

Curly versus Straight

1 To update the bob, perms are almost de-rigeur. For example, Caroline's hair is flat and ordinary.
2 A little movement is introduced with a support perm, wound on Wella's Molton Brown Permers.
3 The wind is directional to complement the finished style. Processing and neutralising follow as before.
4 A scrunch dry encourages the asymmetric shape without distorting the curl. Perfect easycare wash-and-wear style for the modern girl.

some styles), how often should you have your hair cut? This information should be volunteered but if it isn't, ASK.

Thinking of a home perm? Then think of your hair first. If it falls into any of the categories previously mentioned, then "don't". Only if you have virgin hair (untreated) in good condition and a fairly short, layered cut should you attempt a home perm.

Choose your home perm kit carefully, read the labels and select one suitable for your hair type and style. It's also preferable to go for a well-known brand name, to have your hair professionally cut beforehand and if your hairdresser is fairly understanding discuss the home perm with him or her.

Before you start, assemble everything you will need and read the directions carefully, at least three times. Enlist the aid of a friend to help you wind the perm, especially the back hair. Follow the directions implicitly. They are the result of years of research and not to be disregarded. If you're at all doubtful about the result, carry out a test curl: you will find instructions on how to do this in the pack.

1

2

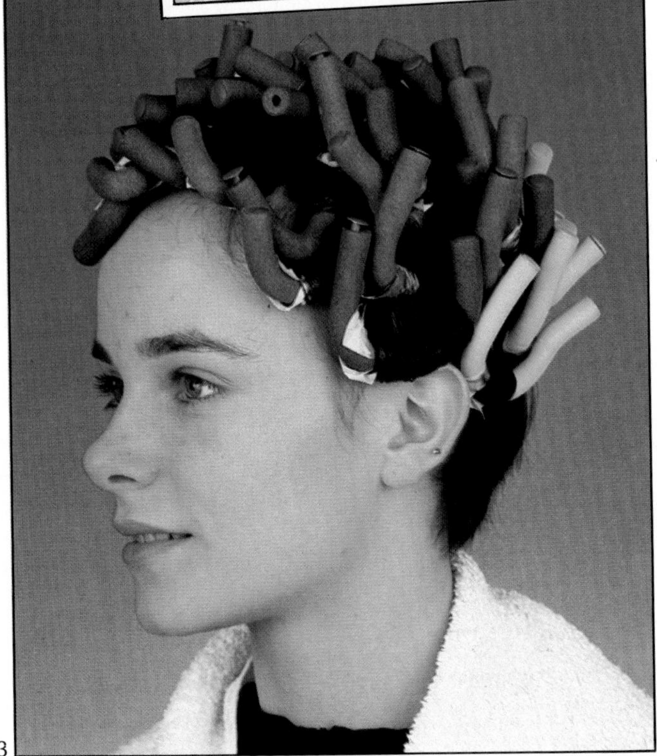

3

WARNING – do remember to keep these products away from children and, once you have finished, dispose of any left-over lotions safely.

Drying: the perfect way to dry freshly permed hair is naturally, as the less tension and strain put on the hair the better, but, if you prefer to blow dry do so gently; don't pull, stretch or overheat each strand. Give your hair a chance to settle down first, you'll find the perm will last longer.

In the unfortunate event that something goes wrong, go back to your

4

Curly versus Straight

1 Short, straight hair that lacks style and shape, Jenny's hair is perfect for the bodywave.
2 As the hair was so short only the top was permed, employing a weaving technique for a very natural result. To ensure a good blend with straight hair, side and back curls were positioned vertically.
3 Nape and sides cropped after perming. Top is dried with the fingers, and a little gel accentuates the feathery fringe.
4 A simple but very effective short hair design.

1

hairdresser and tell them everything you have done to your hair. Unless they are completely in the picture, repairing the damage could be difficult.

Whether you have a home or salon perm, the hair must be carefully treated, regularly conditioned and cut to keep the curl at its best. Avoid permanent colours for ten to fourteen days before and after perming. A good, normal perm should last until it is cut out of the hair, although it will start to loosen close to the scalp as the hair grows through. You may feel like hanging onto your perm and avoid haircuts, but the longer and tattier it gets the more the extra length and weight will pull your hair flat. Cutting every four to six weeks will prolong the life of your perm rather than decrease it.

In the salon you will hear lots of different terms bandied about to describe various perming techniques. These

2

3

4

1 Chemical relaxing will make Sandra's frizzy hair more amenable to current popular styling methods.
2 First the hair and scalp are checked for breakage and abrasions. For protection, a special conditioning gel is applied to the hair and hairline.
3 Four sections make application easier and more efficient for the technician.
4 A small mesh is parted off at the nape and held down.

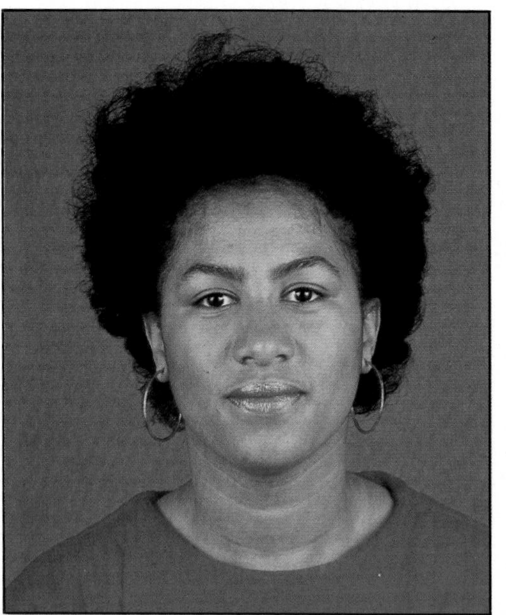

1

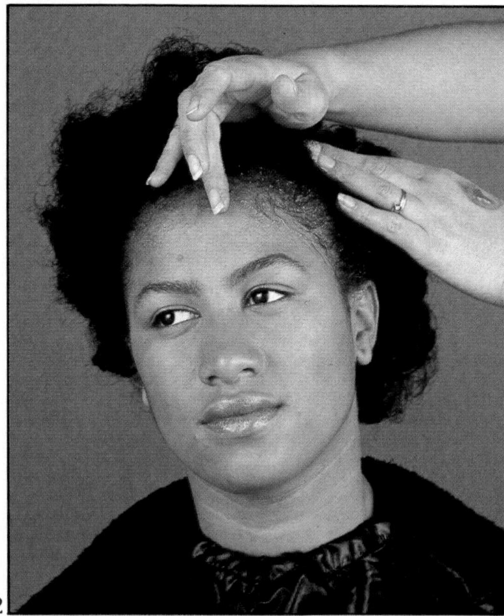

2

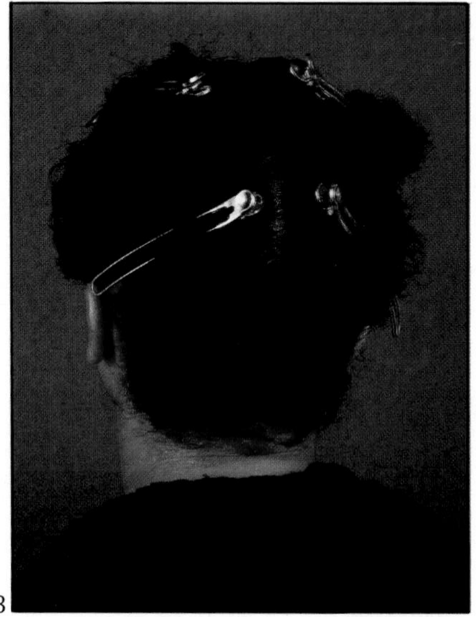

3

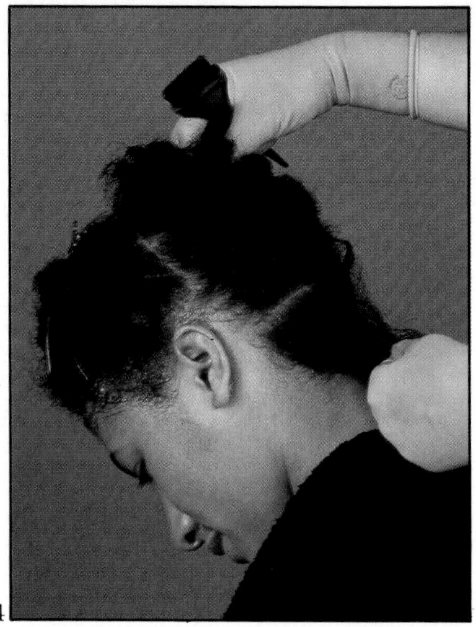

4

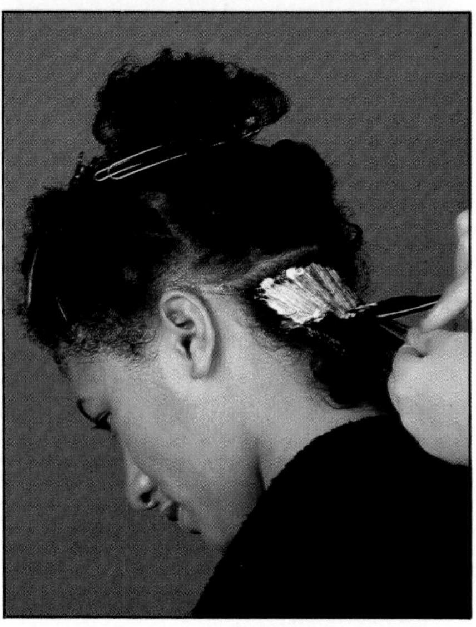

5

5 Relaxer is applied, with a brush, to the hair (not the scalp).
6 One back section complete.
7 Once both back sections have been treated it's time to move to the top. Application begins at the crown and works forward.
8 The front hairline is very delicate so it is treated last of all.
9 Finally, all the hair is gently smoothed mesh by mesh.

techniques are used to create certain effects. If one is to be used on your hair and you don't understand what they are talking about, try not to sink further into the chair whilst nodding your head sagely in agreement, speak up and ask for an explanation. It's so important that you and the permer are on the same wavelength. Here are just a few techniques that may sound familiar:

Perm wrap – another way to describe winding a perm.

Directional perm – instead of a conventional wrap the hair is permed to follow the lines of the finished style.

Root perm – normally used on fairly short hair. Hair at the roots is wound around the perm curler and the ends left straight. Very casual effect for root lift only.

Body/Support perms – very soft curl or bend is put into the hair. The result is very natural and easy to manage. This type may need doing more often than a conventional perm.

Partial perm – used when just part of the hair, like the top or back, requires perming. For example, the underneath nape hair could be permed to help a one length bob turn up or under.

Perm curler, Perm rod – one and the same thing.

Black Hair. Special perms for black hair are a fairly recent innovation, although many of us have been adapting conventional perming methods to suit very curly hair for some years. Since these perms first came onto the market there have been vast improvements and now the technique

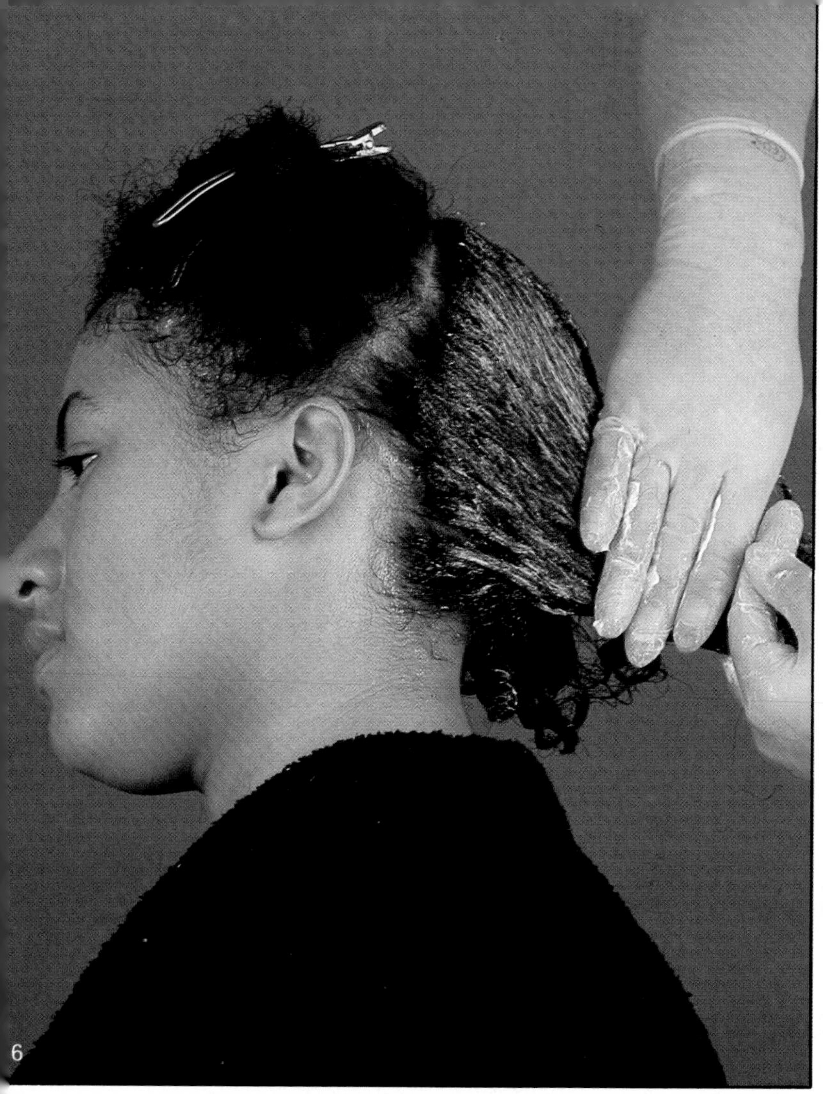

6

7

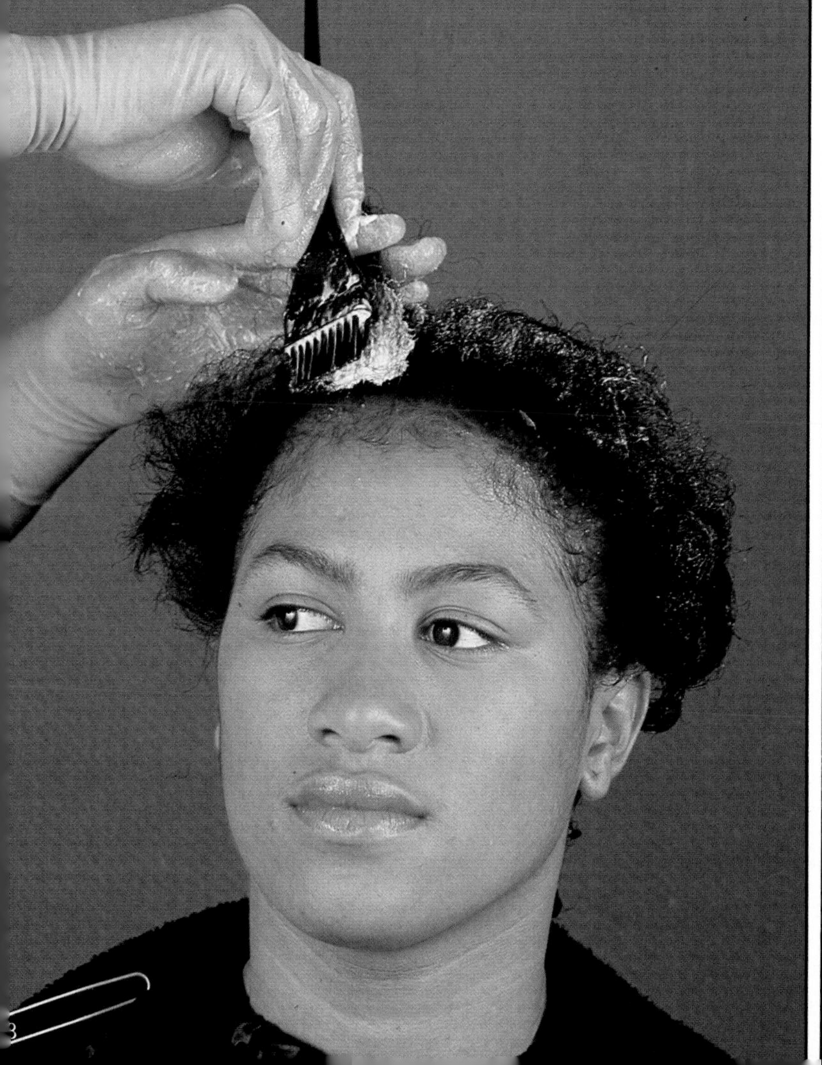

8

9

is very similar to that used for Caucasian hair, except that the very tight curl is being realigned into a soft, manageable curl that can be easily set, blow dried or left natural. For hairdressers and consumers this has been an extremely exciting time for black hair, and at last we have the versatility to change styles easily.

Relaxing is the modern term for straightening hair: we no longer try to get hair bone-straight as this can be detrimental. It is a process that I feel should only be carried out in the salon. New and better products are continually being developed, but the risk factor is still there, particularly as black hair is so very delicate and brittle. If you must relax your hair at home please be very careful and follow the directions.

It is a good idea to prepare your hair for any chemical process. Build up the condition by applying regular protein packs for three or four weeks prior to a perm or relaxer. This should also be continued afterwards to help repair and replace moisture and oils that may have removed by the process.

One of the biggest problems is a dry scalp and dry hair, so make sure you invest in a can of moisturising oil sheen spray. As a rule, salons specialising in black hair design carry a good range of professional hair care products for retail, and the stylists are only too happy to advise you on home maintenance.

After relaxing, Sandra's hair was neutralised (to fix in the sleeker pattern), conditioned and cut. It should be noted that this is a skilled professional service.
Facing page: a straightforward blow-dry, plus a little additional work with the curling tongs and 'Voila!', Sandra can now wear her hair in a variety of fashionable styles.
Right: backcombing and hair spray enlarges the shape for a more exaggerated style. Whatever your style preference, make sure your stylist explains the aftercare routine for relaxed or permed hair.

Finally, the female of our species is not the only one to reap the benefits of modern perming techniques; men have also jumped on the band-wagon. It began mostly with sportsmen, who found the idea of easy care "wash and wear" looks ideal. Others quickly followed suit, finding that soft perms made hair look thicker and also easier to blow dry. Perming a man's hair is no different to perming a woman's, except that the finished style is obviously more masculine.

Your Hair during Pregnancy

A healthy, pregnant woman has a beauty and serenity all of her own, whether it's from a sense of fulfillment or pride in the new life growing inside her is hard to define, but one thing is certain: mums-to-be do have a certain radiance.

Obviously, your health prior to conception, during pregnancy, and after, are the prime concerns of your doctor and gynaecologist. Your diet will be checked and revised if necessary; your general health monitored throughout the term, and it goes without saying that smoking, drinking and the taking of unprescribed drugs are taboo. But with all this advice, where is there anything but a passing reference to your hair? Do people assume that you are not going to bother about it for the next nine months, or that changes in the way your hair looks and feels at this time are not important?

Whilst hair will not be the number one priority it still plays a major psychological role in that the better it looks, the better you feel.

Right: in her seventh month of pregnancy, Norma's hair is in superb condition, although somewhat out of shape. Far right and facing page: restyled into clean, simple lines – the perfect hair to show off a classic cut.

From my own observations and discussions with other hairdressers I've found that very little advice is offered to people other than "its because you're pregnant" or, "wait until your body settles down". Such platitudes are fine, but a little more explanation would not go amiss.

The first trimester: most people will tell you that during pregnancy your hair and skin will be at their peak, with shining hair and glowing skin. In reality this could be quite the opposite for the first three months. Apart from morning sickness making you look and feel wretched, the sudden increase in hormone activity may also affect the sebaceous glands, resulting in a greasy skin and lank, oily hair. A mild, hypo-allergenic cleanser and toner should help the skin and, as for the hair, shampoo as often as required with a mild shampoo. Don't go mad and have all your hair cut off because you're fed up; the grease problem should soon abate.

The second trimester: by this stage your body should have adjusted and you will

feel at peace with yourself; people will begin to tell you how marvellous you look and your skin and hair will be smooth and manageable respectively. You may even notice that your hair seems thicker and grows more quickly; this is quite possible and once again it is influenced by the increase in hormone levels. Feeling as you do, the temptation will be to rush out and completely change your hair, but stop and think seriously before you do anything drastic. By all means experiment with new styles, but remember that as you get larger

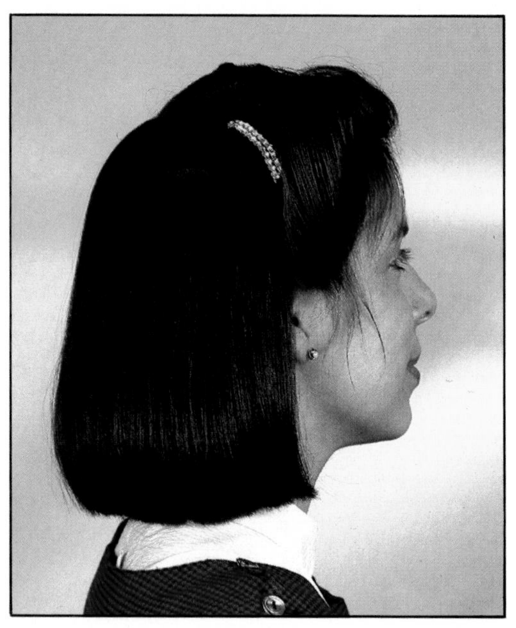

Right: no need to forego glamorous events when you're pregnant. Section hair from ear to ear over top of head. Sweep all the front hair to the right. Facing page: twist the ends together and turn the hair up, back on itself, and secure the ends with grips. Cover tell-tale pins with a diamante slide or two.

and your energy level decreases you will feel less inclined to fiddle with a complicated hairstyle that takes an hour a day to make it look presentable. Opt for a good, versatile haircut that can be dressed in different ways and is easy to manage. In the early stages, if your hair is in good condition a perm can be a blessing, but only have one if your hairdresser says it's OK. Many hairdressers prefer not to perm your hair during pregnancy, especially in the later months, so be guided by their advice.

Paradoxically, some people notice that their hair falls out more at this time. If you suspect you're losing excessive amounts, consult your doctor.

The third trimester: nearing the end of your term you will probably feel more tired, and this is normal. Prone to back ache, etc., you'll worry about your appearance but feel less inclined to spend a lot of time on your hair. It's crucial that you pamper yourself, so maintain your visits to the hairdresser, whether it's for a regular four to six weekly haircut or a weekly shampoo and blow dry.

Throughout your pregnancy ensure that you regularly shampoo and condition your hair, adjusting the products you use to suit your hair as it changes from greasy to normal or dry. Do not stick to the same products if your hair and scalp alter. If you shampoo at home get someone to help, leaning over a bath or basin is a tricky business in the later months and may make you feel dizzy so it's advisable to have a helping hand.

General advice: tell your hairdresser on your next visit to the salon that you are pregnant so that they can keep an eye on the condition of your hair. As I have already mentioned, be guided by them with regards to chemical processes such as perming and colouring. If your hair is already tinted, then obviously you must keep up regrowth applications or your hair will look unsightly.

The baby: believe it or not the amount of hair your baby will have is determined in the womb. The scalp of the unborn child is the centre of much activity as the epidermis indents to form the hair follicle, and at the same time cellular action is taking place to create the papilla. The first hairs will be of the lanugo type (fine downy hair), this will soon be shed, sometimes before birth or just after. Gradually, new, more recognisable hair will grow and those follicles will continue to produce hair after hair after hair, hopefully for a lifetime.

After pregnancy: hair grows in cycles. Basically there is a growing cycle and a resting cycle. During pregnancy the growth cycle is longer and normal hair loss during the resting stage decreases. Once the baby is born the pregnancy-induced hormones plummet, and this may result in a substantial increase in hair loss which can seem alarming. But really you are only shedding the normal amount plus the hair you should have lost during pregnancy. This will occur around three to six months after the birth, although it has been known to continue on and off for a couple of years. The hair and scalp will gradually return to normal, so just be patient. However, if you are worried ask your doctor for advice or go to a qualified trichologist.

As we have discussed in previous chapters, your diet and general health can have dramatic repercussions on your hair, now more than ever. Make sure that you eat properly and try to get plenty of rest in-between baby feeds and nappy changing. It won't be long before you're slipping back into your tightest jeans and thinking of a new hairstyle.

CHAPTER 27

Colour Wise

Top right: Haley would love to experiment with colour, but nothing too shocking or permanent. Below: mahogany coloured styling mousse will add warmth and interest. Below right: just a hint of red that attractively catches the light. Facing page: fashionable, high, spiky front that emphasises the colour even more.

Not so long ago, any woman who coloured her hair – unless she was a movie star – would be labelled a "scarlet woman". Perhaps this was due to the rather unsubtle colours available: red, blonde or black. Artificially-coloured hair looked just that, artificial. The results were unpredictable, as many young women found out to their cost. Fortunately, this is no longer the case and today, we can choose from a wide range of colours, all designed to give a natural result and leave the hair in good condition. Not only do we have natural-looking shades to choose from but also

some vivid, vibrant hues that nature never dreamed of: rich burgundies, bright reds, blues and fuchsias, to name but a few. In fact, anything goes, but before you reach for your coat and dash out to the nearest hairdresser or chemist let us consider a few important points.

Right: not only was Sharon's hair very out of shape, but an experiment with colour had left her with the legacy of a two inch regrowth.
Below: a semi-permanent colour, 'Black Cherry', helped to camouflage the regrowth. Applied like a shampoo, the colour has not only blended-in the regrowth but added a lovely rich tone and sheen to the hair.
Facing page: rainbow hues for artistic colouring.

1. Before you contemplate any form of colour, ensure that your hair is in good condition. Do not colour it yourself if it is dry, brittle or damaged in any way, but seek professional advice.

2. Do not attempt to bleach or recolour bleached hair to its natural shade yourself.

3. If your hair is permanently waved, relaxed or already tinted, once again you should go to the hairdresser.

4. If you are fed up with your present artificial colour do not attempt to remove/strip it yourself; go to the experts.

5. Do consider the cost before embarking on any form of colour change. Some colouring techniques are expensive and may require retouching every three to four weeks. Make sure you can afford the upkeep.

WELLA
effecton
Tönungsbalsam
spot light

1 Pale blonde hair requires a fair amount of maintenance. For example, Sonia regularly has to have her regrowth lightened.
2 Bleaching just the root area can be more tricky than treating the entire head. Great care must be taken not to overlap the bleach onto previously lightened hair.

1

complexion lightens, and going darker will only emphasize the ageing process, resulting in a harsh, unnatural look.

Colour Types Temporary colours, as the name implies, last from shampoo to shampoo. They coat the outside of the shaft and can be used to even out colour in salt-and-pepper hair, or to improve the appearance of white hair that has a yellow, dingy look to it. This type of colour will also enhance the natural glints in hair: for example, a mahogany temporary colour on a natural medium brown base will add rich, warm lights.

This type of colour is available from most chemists and hairdressers. Generally, it is sold in small, individual bottles as a temporary colour and setting lotion combined. The latest innovation of foam-type temporary colours are great for those of you who prefer naturally to dry or blow dry your hair. These can be purchased from some hairdressing salons.

2

3

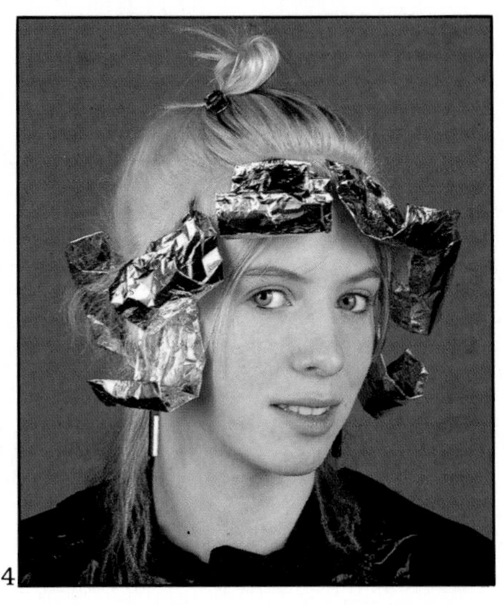

4

3 Bleach has been meticulously applied to the new growth. Previously bleached hair is lifted away from the head.
4 Once the roots have lifted the bleach is removed. The foil packs contain fine meshes of hair treated with black tint.
5 This process adds body and texture to Sonia's fine hair and once scrunch dried, the black meshes feather back for that extra flair.

Colour Choice If you are considering colouring your hair at home, keep it simple. It is advisable only to lighten or darken your hair one or two shades with a permanent tint, or use a semi-permanent colour to enhance the natural glints.

Colours should complement your skin: this includes how light or dark you are going and whether the tone, e.g. red, gold, ash or violet, is warm or cool.

A golden tone will add warmth to a pale skin. Florid complexioned? Then avoid warm tones and opt for more neutral or ashen shades. Olive skins can take very dark shades, but be careful of choosing a colour with a very red or gold tone as this can make the skin look sallow.

Mature gracefully if you're naturally dark and going grey, and resist the temptation to colour you hair back to its natural brunette. As we age, the skin tone changes, small facial lines appear and the

To apply, towel blot your hair after shampooing and, if using the liquid kind, sprinkle the contents of the bottle evenly over your hair whilst massaging the colour through with your free hand. Be careful not to tip the entire contents of the bottle onto the top of your head, especially if your hair is porous, as you could end up looking like a piebald pony.

For the foam variety, expell an orange-sized amount of the foam into the palm of your hand and massage it evenly through your hair: use a little more if your hair is fairly long.

Unfortunately, the drawback with this type of colour is that it rubs off on collars, brushes and pillowcases, and if you accidentally get caught in a shower without your brolly the colour may run.

5

Semi-Permanents Semi-permanents are a great way to introduce yourself to colour. Modern semi-permanents are a far cry from the sixties products; they last longer and the colour range is far greater. Lasting from six to eight shampoos, the conditioning agents in the colour leave the hair remarkably shiny and bouncy.

Above: if you can't make up your mind whether to go light or dark, compromise; like Sonia you can have the best of both worlds.
Facing page: a casual, upswept design that proves how stunning bleached hair can look.

The colour itself penetrates into the cuticle, unlike a temporary colour which merely coats the hair. Certain ranges of semi-permanents are specifically designed to cover grey hair and do so fairly successfully. Others are designed to produce fashion shades – rich reds, burgundies or golds. These should not be applied to white hair, which could turn very pink or yellow. One thing a semi-permanent will not do is lighten your hair; it can only enhance your natural shade, cover grey or make hair darker. Always check the manufacturers "colour choice guide" and don't be misled by the words "shampoo in colour". If it claims that it will make you hair lighter then it is a permanent tint. You can check inside the pack and if there are two bottles which have to be mixed together then, once again, it is a permanent colour.

If your hair is already tinted but fades in-between root retouches, a semi-colour of a similar tone can be used to boost the colour; do not attempt this yourself but ask your hairdresser. Before applying, carry out a strand and skin test: you will find instructions on how to do this in the directions enclosed in the packet.

Assemble everything you will need before you start and take the phone off the hook unless you want a coloured phone as well. You will need plenty of old towels and it's a good idea to cover the floor and work tops with paper, just in case things get messy. Wear gloves to apply to either clean, dry hair or shampooed, towel-dried hair (check instructions); massage evenly through the hair and cover with a plastic cap if necessary; allow to develop and remove as directed. If your skin is dry and porous it's a good idea to apply a thin layer of barrier cream or vaseline close to the hair line to prevent skin staining. After removal dry and style your hair as normal.

Permanent Colour Permanent colours are just that – permanent – and once in the hair they can only be removed by cutting the colour out as the hair grows. Professional colourists can remove artificial colour, but it is a long and expensive business.

Permanent colours can lighten, darken, cover grey and add a variety of tones to the hair. Permanent colours actually penetrate into the cortex of the hair, working on the natural colour molecules (melanocytes) and depositing colour.

Permanent colours for home use usually come in an oil form. In a pack you will find one bottle of colour and one bottle of hydrogen peroxide which, when mixed together, form an oil-like gel. Normally, I recommend that all permanent tints are carried out by a professional colourist, but if for economic reasons you prefer to colour at home, give considerable thought to colour selection and always choose a well-known, reputable brand.

You can go as dark as you like with a permanent colour as long as it suits you. When going lighter, choose a colour only one or two shades lighter than your natural hair. If you lighten any further, your natural tones will have a marked effect on the end result. If you are covering grey hair then stick to a fairly neutral colour: leave the fashion shades to the hairdresser.

Application: remember to carry out a strand and skin test as per the manufacturer's directions. Assemble everything you will need (see semi-

1 Pretty, dark brown hair, but rather dull and flat in colour; this is where henna comes in handy, especially if, like Clare, you have a sensitive scalp.
2 Protect clothes and surroundings and apply vaseline all around the hairline and ears to prevent staining. The person applying henna should always wear gloves.
3 Section the hair into four. Mix henna powder with hot water in a large bowl. Start at the nape and take a section ½ to 1 inch deep. Scoop up some henna from the bowl.
4 Apply to the hair, massaging it down the lengths. Twist the section to force the henna through onto each strand. Apply to the back sections then the front two. Use same method throughout: section, apply, massage, twist.
5 When all the hair has been treated, cut cotton wool into strips and press onto vaselined area.
6 A few final twists to ensure all the hair has been treated. Cover hennaed hair with a large sheet of foil – press edges onto the cotton wool strip. Clean up immediately. A hood dryer will speed up development time – approx 1 hour in Clare's case. Check directions on your kit first.
Facing page: rinsed and shampooed, Clare's hair emerges richer in colour and very glossy. After blow-drying, the hair was backcombed and sprayed, and the ends of the top hair bent over with curling tongs. The sides were slicked back with gel.

1

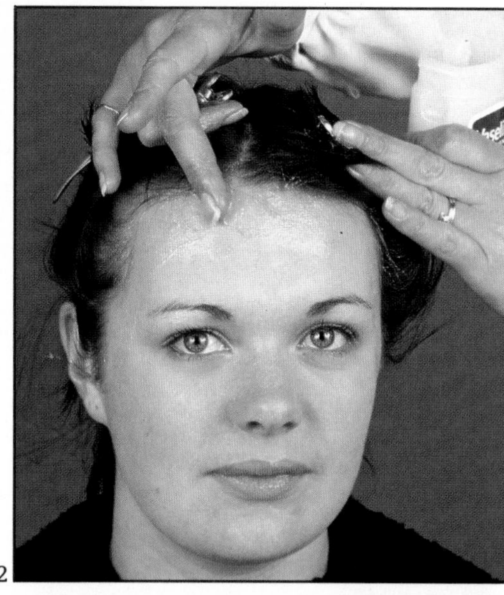
2

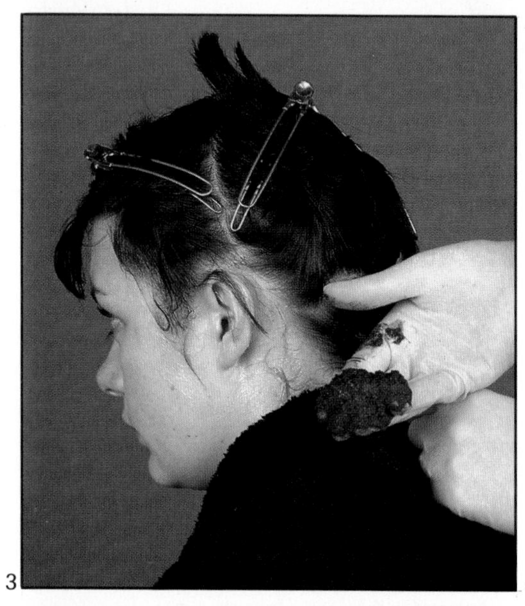
3

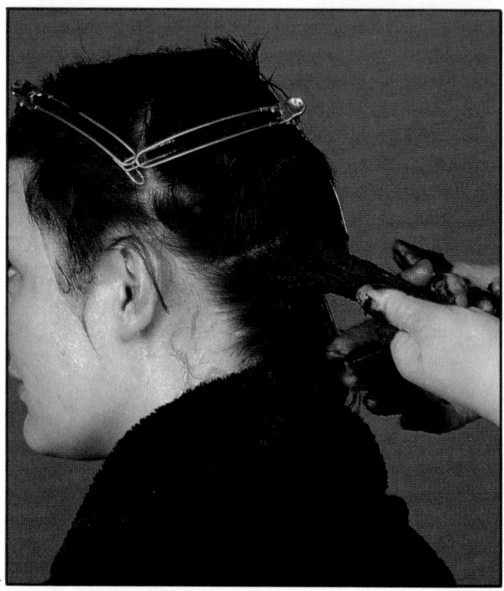
4

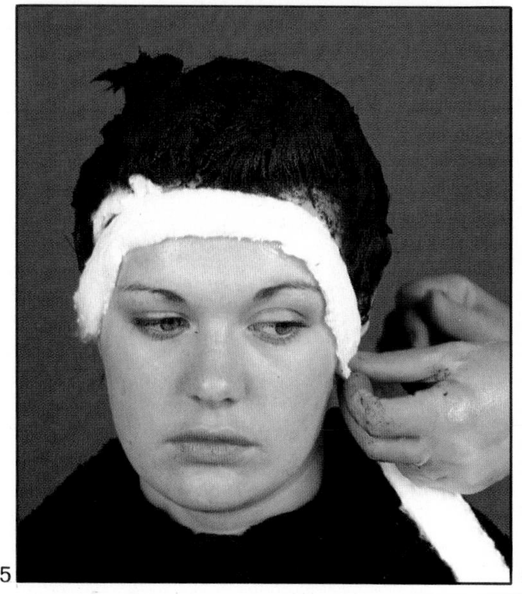
5

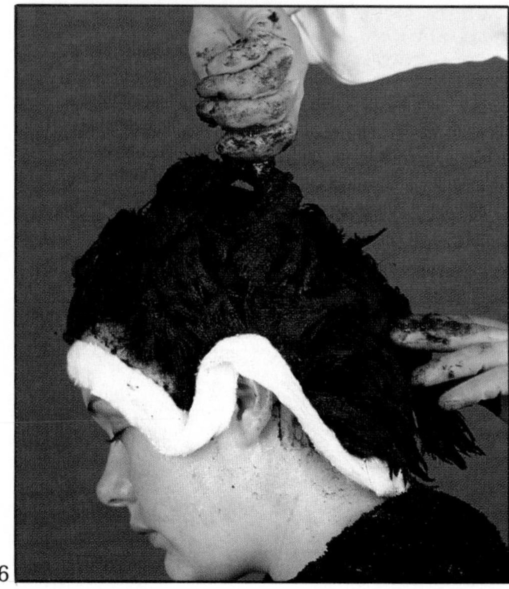
6

Right: and now for something completely different. Firstly, Imogen's hair was cut and blow-dried to style. Bleach was stippled onto the ends of the top hair and applied to the longer meshes behind the ears. With the bleach removed, a mid-burgundy tint was applied through top and back, omitting the long, bleached meshes. The sides and tips of fringe are tinted blue-black. Below and facing page: the incandescent effect of the bleach under the burgundy hair catches the light beautifully – a different and distinctive effect that shows just how well curling and colouring go together.

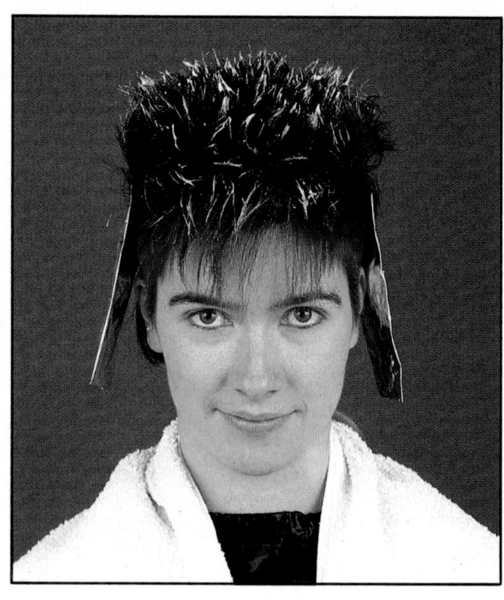

colours). Each manufacturer's directions will vary slightly, so read them carefully before you begin. Some will imply that for a first-time application the colour is massaged through the hair like a shampoo, allowed to develop and removed. This is fine if you're going darker, but going lighter requires a little more care.

To tint the hair lighter enlist the help of a friend. The prepared tint must be applied methodically, mesh by mesh, to the middle lengths and ends of the hair, approximately an inch from the root. This is because tint will take quicker on the hair closest to the scalp, partly because of body heat, and if the colour is applied to the root area first, an uneven colour will result. Once the middle lengths and ends begin to lift (about fifteen minutes), apply tint to the roots and ensure that all the hair is covered. Develop for the recommended time.

To remove, add water and lather up the tint as much as possible, rinse thoroughly, shampoo lightly, condition and style as normal. Do not try to keep any left-over tint: once mixed it cannot be kept and must be thrown away. Safety first: if any tint goes into the eyes rinse IMMEDIATELY with cold water. Seek medical advice if any irritation results. Keep all products away from children.

Regrowths Hair grows approximately half an inch a month. This new growth will require attention every four weeks, more often if there is a marked difference between your tinted and natural hair. Prepare as before – don't forget to carry out a skin test. Section and apply colour to the new growth only, and allow to develop. If the lengths and ends are faded, then

Facing page: bleached and toned highlights, styling gel and blow drying skilfully combined to create a stunning effect. Photograph courtesy of Wella.

massage the remaining colour through the hair for the last five minutes or so. Remove as before.

This guide to permanent tinting is very general: do read directions carefully and keep them handy as you work. If in doubt, go to the hairdressers and leave well alone.

Henna Henna has its pluses and minuses; on the plus side it is eminently suitable for people who are allergic to other forms of manufactured colour preparations, while on the minus side it can be messy to apply and the results unpredictable.

Henna is produced from the powdered leaves of *Lawsonia Inermis*, a native shrub of the Far East, Middle East and Asia. It has been in and out of favour since Cleopatra first dipped her dainty toe in the Nile. The sixties in particular heralded a rebirth for henna, when everyone went back to nature and natural products. Since then its popularity as a colour has waned somewhat, but henna shampoos and conditioners have remained a firm favourite.

Natural additives can vary the shades henna will produce, from indigo for black to woad for chestnut. The country of origin is also important as different growing conditions affect the quality of the henna.

Henna is a permanent vegetable colour and works by both penetrating and coating the hair; it will also leave hair very shiny. Never use henna on very dry, permed or tinted hair. For best results the base shade should be naturally medium to dark brown. To apply: follow the directions carefully and take care to protect yourself and your surroundings – remember, it can be messy. Apply barrier cream close to hairline. Mix the henna powder with hot water in a large mixing bowl. Section the hair and apply the henna with your fingers, massaging it thoroughly through each section. Work quickly and if the henna starts to dry out in the bowl add some more hot water. When all the hair has been treated, cover with foil and leave to develop. Development time can be halved by going under a warm hood dryer. Clear up as soon as you can – you don't want henna walked all over the house!

When you're ready to remove the colour, lean over a basin before removing the foil so that any loose powder falls into the bowl. Rinse and rinse again, shampoo and rinse once more, and repeat if hair still feels gritty. Be prepared for fifteen minutes of rinsing and shampooing before it's all gone. Style in your normal way; the finished result should be very, very shiny with a good, deep, rich colour.

Words of advice: do not use henna on fair hair. Do not henna over tinted or permed hair yourself, and do not attempt permanently to wave or permanently tint hennaed hair, but go to the hairdresser.

Bleaching To bleach the hair means removing all the natural colour pigment: it is a strong process and one which should only be undertaken by a professional colourist.

Bleached hair is showing signs of making a come-back, especially with young people into "street fashions". Some of the looks around are very strong, and bleached, pale blonde hair can certainly be dramatic.

For the more conservative among us, completely bleaching your hair should only be contemplated if you have naturally dark blonde or lighter hair and if your complexion can take it. At the same time you must consider the condition of your hair, the time it will consume (retouching every three weeks), and the cost.

If bleaching is for you then keep the style short, apply protein packs regularly and always use a cream rinse after shampooing to close the cuticle. Perming is OUT, sometimes it works on bleached hair and sometimes not, so concentrate instead on the three C's – cut, colour and condition.

Highlights: these are fine meshes of hair which are bleached or tinted to create a sunlightened effect.

Lowlights: fine meshes of hair which are tinted darker to add colour or introduce a warm tone to the hair.

Naturalising: once again fine meshes of hair are tinted, but this time three or four colours from, maybe, copper to mahogany are used. As the hair moves the colours catch the light, adding depth and interest.

These are just a sample of the technical terms you may come across. The methods employed are all similar; sometimes strands of hair will be pulled through a special self-sealing cap with a fine hook; these strands are then bleached or tinted, or the strands will be methodically and individually woven out, coloured, and wrapped in foil or cling film.

Other techniques include hairpainting: applying colour stratigically to emphasize the lines of a style; two or three tone effects where large area of hair are coloured, for example, from dark blonde at the nape, getting progressively lighter towards the

Contrasting styles, but both equally eye-catching. Right: a sleek, classic style subtly coloured for maximum effect and (facing page) dramatic blue-black colouring complements a chic, feathery bob style.

Overleaf, left: a light, bouncy bob, fanned with colour to emphasise its shape. Overleaf, right: warm-coloured streaks for that adventurous yet natural look.

Pages 76-79 a variety of styles, all achieved using Wella products. Photographs courtesy of Wella.

crown; finger or touch colours, where colours are applied with the tips of the fingers or comb to enhance a style, or you could go really mad and have a large mesh of hair bleached and then coloured turquoise, violet or brilliant, poppy red. Providing it's properly done, crazy colours can be great fun.

Whatever your colour choice, from the sublime to the ridiculous, make sure it suits you and your lifestyle. Choose with care and if you're in the salon make sure you fully understand what the colourist is going to do, how often it will need retouching and the cost.

The Era of Change

Facing page: a blaze of colour: fabulous, natural red hair cut to complement the natural curl. Nature at her best.

Thank goodness the days are fast disappearing when a woman was considered "over the hill" at thirty-five, or as soon as she had produced the required quota of children. Now, a woman in her forties can be as glamorous as her twenty-year-old daughter.

A higher standard of living, magazines, television and the economic climate have done much to bridge the age barrier. Let me expand on this theory. In the Western world our diet has improved considerably and those of us concerned about our looks and well-being have kicked the junk food habit and are into a more sensible, well-balanced diet. As I mentioned earlier, healthy hair and skin come from within.

Magazines and TV bombard us with features on apparently ageless women, and not just the rich and famous nor those who have undergone plastic surgery. We regularly read features about seemingly dowdy women of all ages who are transformed by a new hairdo, make-up and clothes. Admittedly they had expert advice, but with a little time and patience you too could present a different image to your family and friends.

More and more of us continue to work after marriage, and mothers pursue their careers whilst managing a home and children, or they return to work once children are of school age. In today's tough economic climate the majority of people have to work, but this need to work has gone some way towards encouraging us to take more care of ourselves. Hair, clothes and make-up are kept as stylish and fashionable as our purses will allow, and in the long run hair is, perhaps, one of the cheapest ways of keeping yourself up to date.

Staying "in vogue". One of the best ways of keeping a check on yourself at any age requires very little expense, just time, a good mirror and a few old photographs dating back over the last couple of years. Look at your hair, clothes and make-up in the pictures and then compare this with your reflected image. Clothes have probably changed according to fashion, but has you hair and make-up? Nothing dates you more than these two things. It is so easy and comfortable to stay with a hairstyle that suited you ten years ago, and to change your make-up requires experimentation and practice. Changing your hair and make-up first thing in the morning when you're dashing off to work is not the best time. We can all find a little time in the evenings to try something new.

Updating your hairstyle may mean nothing more than blowdrying instead of setting, or dressing your hair in a softer or sleeker way. Changes come more expensive if a restyle, permanent wave or colour are required, but presumably everyone has their hair cut regularly and a perm or colour won't need doing every week, so the extra expense can be budgeted for. The boost a new style can give you far out-weighs the financial outlay, especially when friends and loved ones start telling you how much younger you look. The only drawback to this is when you start to wonder what you have been looking like for the past few years if you look so much better now!

Remember, too, that a new hairdo is a great confidence and morale booster, so if you are searching for a new job, or returning to work, put a new hairstyle at the top of your list of things to do before interview day.

Twenties: by now you will have left the problems of puberty and adolescence behind you, but your hair and skin will continue to change as you age. In the twenties everything should be at its peak: hair, skin and general health. Hormonal disturbances at the onset of puberty will have levelled out, although your hair can still become unruly or greasy prior to menstruation. Unfortunately, the twenties can also be a time when we are so keen to do and try everything that we abuse our

1 Vivienne has pretty, dark golden blonde hair with masses of matural movement. Here we show how to make the most of wavy hair with a scrunch dry.
2 After shampooing and conditioning, hair gel is used to give body and bounce. Massage the gel well into the root area and then comb through to ends.

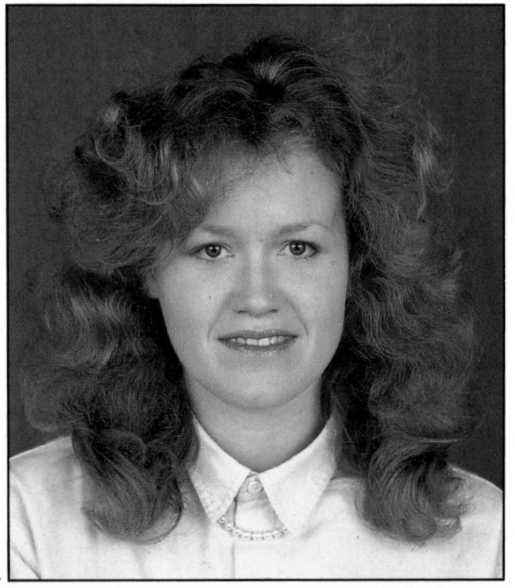
1

always protect your hair with a sunhat, scarf or a conditioner which blocks out the harmful rays of the sun. Shampoo and condition after swimming, and be especially careful if your hair is chemically processed in any way.

General care of your hair at this time should be simple. Shampoo as you feel necessary; if it is every day choose a mild shampoo. If your hair is permed, tinted or relaxed, choose one that is formulated for those conditions. Regular use of conditioners goes without saying.

Into the thirties: it's a sad fact that from now on everything is going into decline, your skin and muscle tone are not as elastic, your hair is not as bouncy or naturally shiny as it once was. But before you decide to leap off the nearest bridge – stop – think positively,

2

3

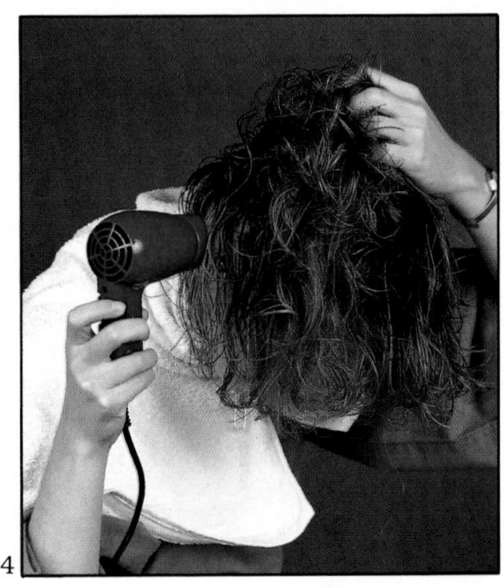
4

3 Rough-dry hair and push it all forward. Begin at the nape, opening your fingers like a claw.
4 Lift and scrunch the hair up with your fingers. Keep opening and closing your fist to allow the air to circulate.
5 Sides – dry roots upwards and then scrunch ends.
6 Slide the fingers into front hair, moving the hair up and to the side; scrunch ends.
7 Drying complete. Run fingers up through hair to ensure roots are dry. That's all there is to it.
8 Completed back view.

bodies with crash diets, lack of proper exercise and sleep, and our hair comes under attack as we experiment with hair colours, perms and tortuous hairstyles. Remember: all things in moderation.

Nervous disorders and high stress situations can also have dramatic repercussions on our hair and as the twenties can be a traumatic time in affairs of the heart you may experience some adverse hair reaction purely because of emotional stress. Getting married can be exciting but exhausting, so at this time be sensible and eat properly; don't crash diet, and get plenty of rest.

This is also a time when sunbathing is a must and the browner you are the better you look and feel. It seems hard to believe the effect that sun and sea can have on your hair and skin when you look so good, but think of the future; damage done now to the skin is irreparable, and the hair too must be protected. When sunbathing

you know you will have to exercise and maybe diet more strictly than before, but equally you should be more at ease with yourself, more self-assured and confident. The physical changes are gradual, which makes them easier to cope with. At the risk of repeating myself, healthy diet and exercise are a must, no matter how hectic your schedule. If you smoke or drink a lot cut down now; smoking only encourages the small lines around your eyes, deprives cells of oxygen and makes your hair smell terrible.

One thing you may notice about your hair is a tendency towards dryness, even if it was greasy in your teens. As with the skin, the sebaceous glands are not as active as they once were, therefore the hair and skin are not receiving as much natural oil and moisture. Indications may be dry, dull, flyaway hair, or a feeling of coarseness. Be aware of what is happening and adjust your shampoo and conditioning routine

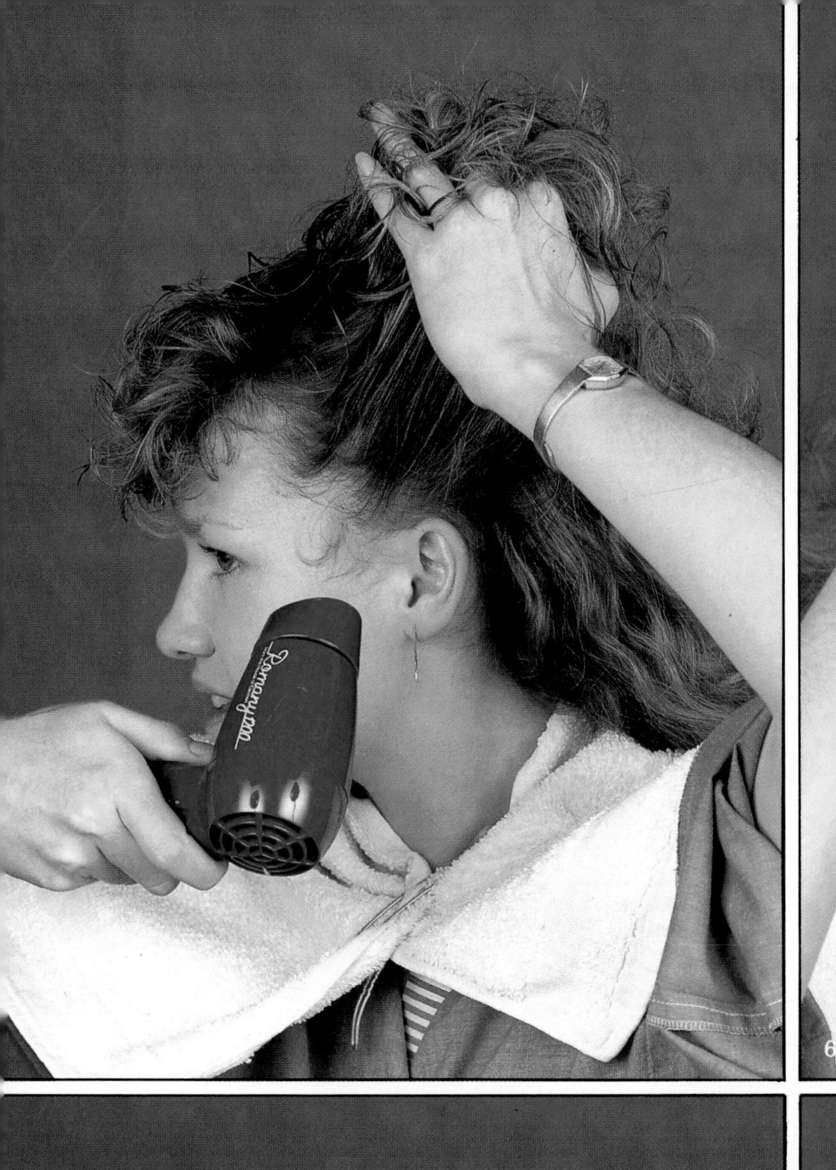

6

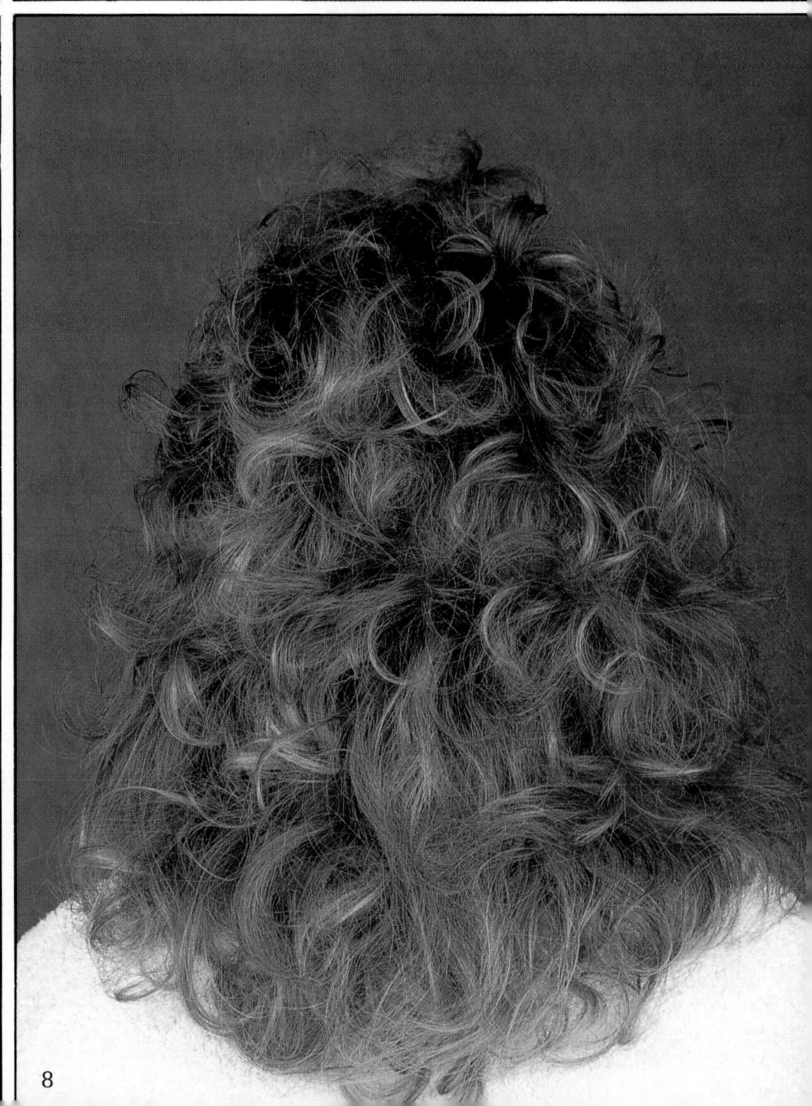

8

For more fullness the hair can be backcombed.
1 Beginning at the top, part off a small mesh of hair no wider than the teeth of your comb. Starting close to the scalp, slide comb up the hair approximately 1½ inches.
2 Slide comb down towards roots. Work up the lengths in this way, gradually forming a pad of backcombing at the scalp.
3 One firmly backcombed mesh of hair.
4 Once the entire head has been backcombed, smooth over lightly with a brush and pull curls into place with the fingers.
5 Should the curl have lost its definition, spray with a fine mist of water or use a tiny amount of mousse on the ends. The picture shows the stunning effect that can be attained simply by using gel and the correct drying technique.

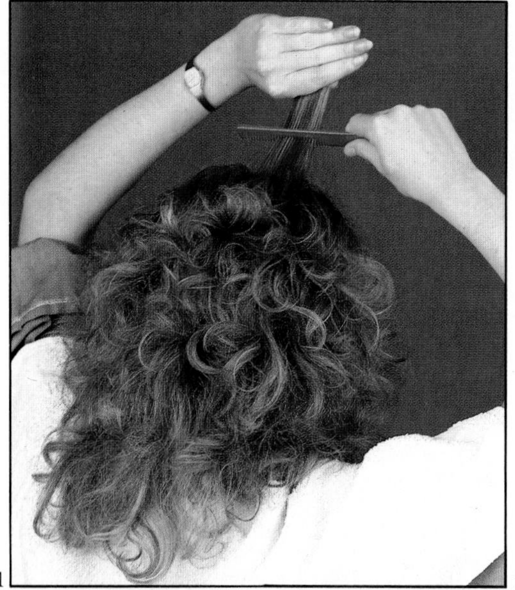
1

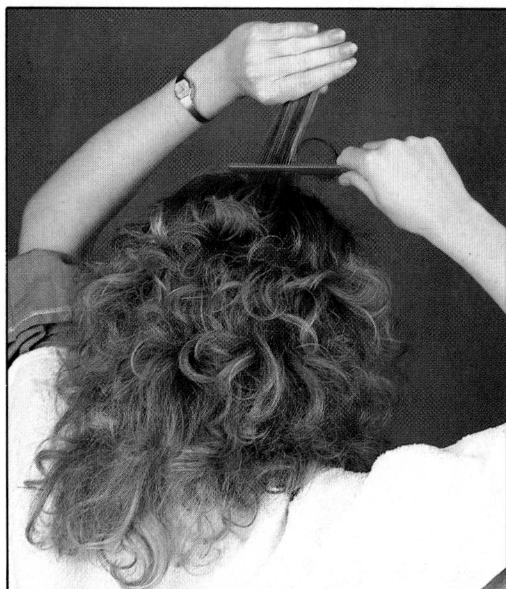
2

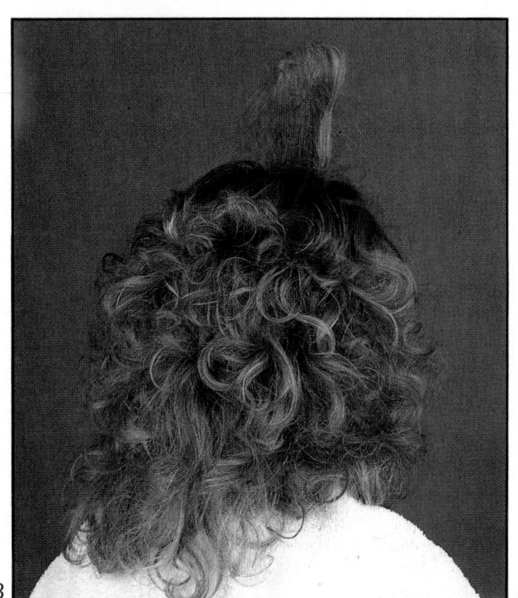
3

4

accordingly. Where once a light cream rinse was sufficient, a more penetrating moisture/protein pack may now be required, especially if your hair is permed or tinted.

Dryness in hair also means a dry scalp, and you will find that your scalp feels a little tighter and is more sensitive, so remember to have a skin test prior to a colour application, and do take care if you do a home perm.

Stress can affect us at any age, but the thirties can be high stress years. Holding down a full-time job, rearing children, running a home, divorce, marriage; all of these put a strain on our bodies and our minds. Help yourself as much as possible, trying to relax, etc., and at the first sign of problems consult your doctor.

Grey hair. Some people have always had the odd stray white hair, but for most of us they seem to creep up unannounced sometime in the thirties – not enough to give a glamorous, distinctive streak but enough to be annoying. White hair is really no different from your other hair, it is just that the melanocytes (colour producing cells) have stopped producing colour, but this does not affect hair growth. Grey hair is in fact white hair, it's only because coloured and white hairs are intermingled that we call it grey. A few stray white hairs can be blended in with a simple semi-permanent colour or highlights, but if you have a high percentage of white hair then you would get more satisfactory coverage from a permanent colour. For more advice on haircolouring see the appropriate chapter.

For a neater shape Vivienne sets her hair using heated rollers.
1 Starting at the front hairline, part off a section and comb forward.
2 Slide roller down to tips of hair; when the ends are smooth over the roller, wind up. Very uneven ends can be wrapped in tissue first to keep them smooth and together.
3 Secure with the pins provided.
4 Top hair is set in brickwork pattern. Sides move diagonally up and back on large rollers. Back hair down and under on jumbo rollers.
5 & **6** Wait until each roller has cooled down and then remove carefully and brush thoroughly with a vent brush. Push into shape with your fingers.
7 A more controlled style for those smart occasions.

1

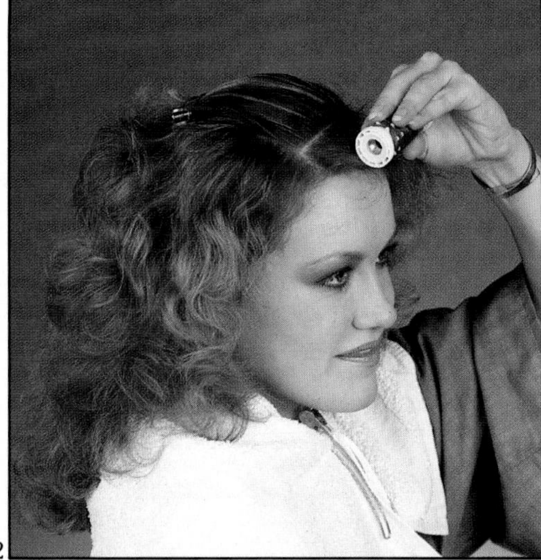
2

3

4

5

6

7

1 Eva is a busy housewife and prefers a short, no-fuss style that stays looking good all day.
2 After blow drying, Eva uses a steam styling brush; this type of styler is very easy to use. Work from the centre to the sides, progressing to the front.

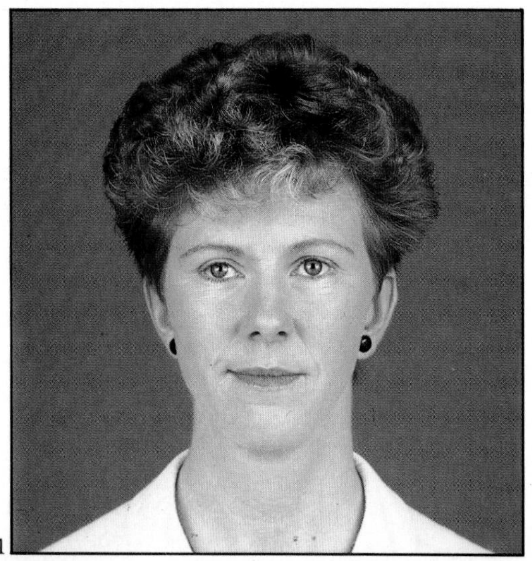

1

Life begins at forty. How we used to smile at the old adage from the safety of our teenage years. Forty: that seemed so very old. But the tables have turned, and look just how true it has become. Look around at the attractive, successful women in their forties, both housewives and career women.

Unfortunately, if you have abused your hair and skin over the years the problems you started all those years ago may now come home to roost. But fear not, a lot can be done with flattering hairstyles and clever, subtle make-up.

The problems of dry hair, scalp and skin intensify during the forties, so in the same way that you will be lavishing extra attention on your skin, spare a thought for your hair. Use a shampoo especially formulated for dry hair and apply a special moisture protein-enriched treatment once a week or fortnight. You may also find that your scalp is dry and flaky and the temptation will be to reach for a strong, medicated shampoo – don't. It's unlikely to be dandruff; just lack of natural oils. Treat the hair and scalp for dryness and the problem should abate. Seek professional advice before resorting to strong, medicated shampoos.

Hair colour and make-up should be adjusted as you age, particularly if you have gone very white. Never be tempted to tint your hair very dark, even if you were once a natural brunette, it will just look 'dyed'.

One problem you could face is full, lifeless looking hair, even though the style is perfect. Keep a can of spray hair tonic handy, style and spray as normal, and as a final touch spray very lightly with the tonic. The shine is instant and, providing you're not heavy handed, will not reduce your hair to a flat, oily mess.

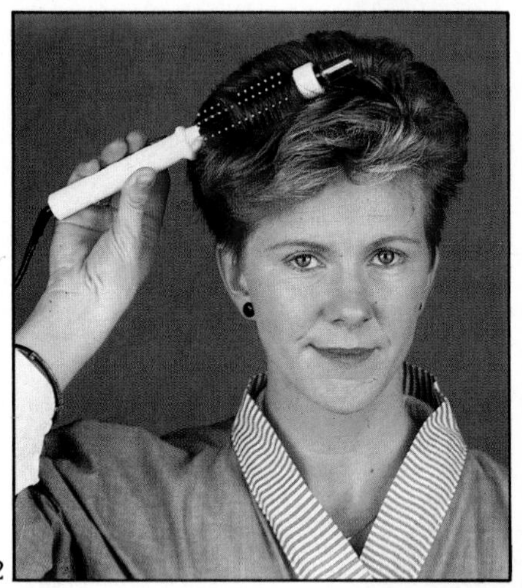

2

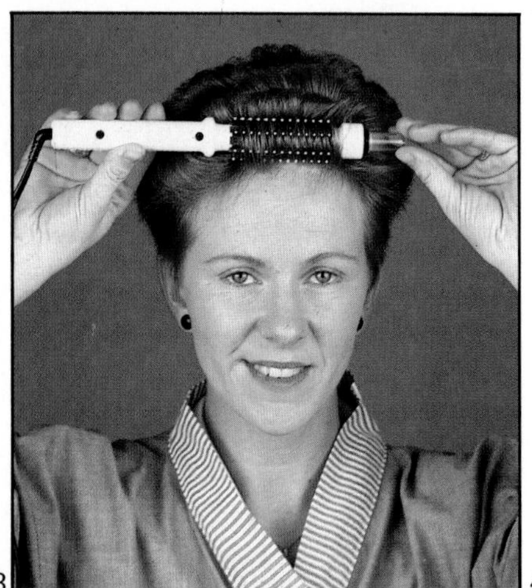

3

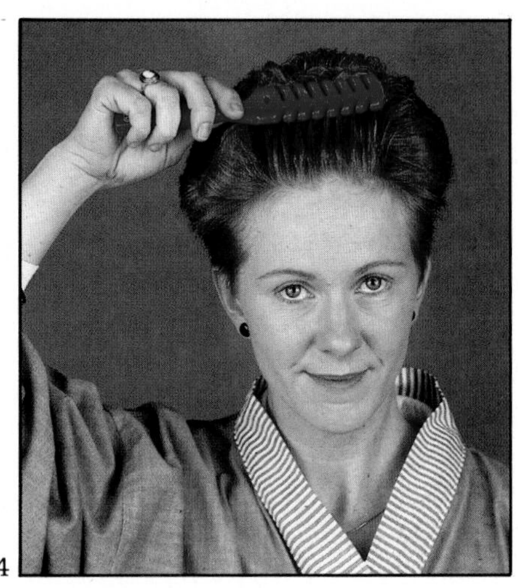

4

3 Hold the styler in position for a few seconds. If using the brush to boost your style between washes, push the button for instant steam and lasting results.
4 Brush through from the crown working forwards. A vent brush is used, the quills of which are widely spaced, penetrating the hair and producing a more casual result.
5 Smart, easy-to-control style accentuating the neat head shape.
6 The perfect style for a busy housewife or career woman who always needs to look her best.

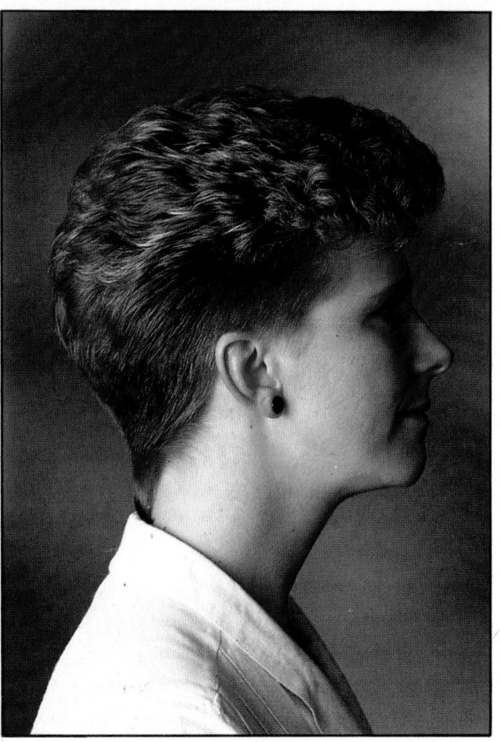

5

6

Stylewise, keep it soft and easy to manage, and avoid tight, curly perms, they are so aging. Teach yourself to blow-dry and use a hot brush. If you prefer to roller set, then follow some of the guidelines illustrated in this chapter. Light fringes hide forehead lines, and swept back sides emphasize the eyes that may now be slightly deeper set.

Looking through some recent press cuttings I came across a photograph of finalists in a glamorous grandmother competition. How different they looked from the average gran of forty years ago: flattering hairstyles with grey hair skilfully coloured, soft layers dressed into full, bouncy shapes framed youthful faces and there were trim figures that would be the envy of many twenty year olds. Who said gran should sit at home knitting? From the look of these ladies they'll be out dancing the night away alongside their daughters.

Right: in her early forties, Mirna is fortunate enough to have superb facial bone structure which allows her to wear her hair in a variety of ways.
Below right: this particular design is a slightly longer, softer design than Eva's, on the previous page. After shampooing, hair mousse was applied for added body. The hair was blow dried using a radial bristle brush, following the lines of the cut.
Facing page: a flattering shape which relies on the all-important cut, which is the foundation for any style, no matter what age you are.

CHAPTER 29

Long and Lustrous

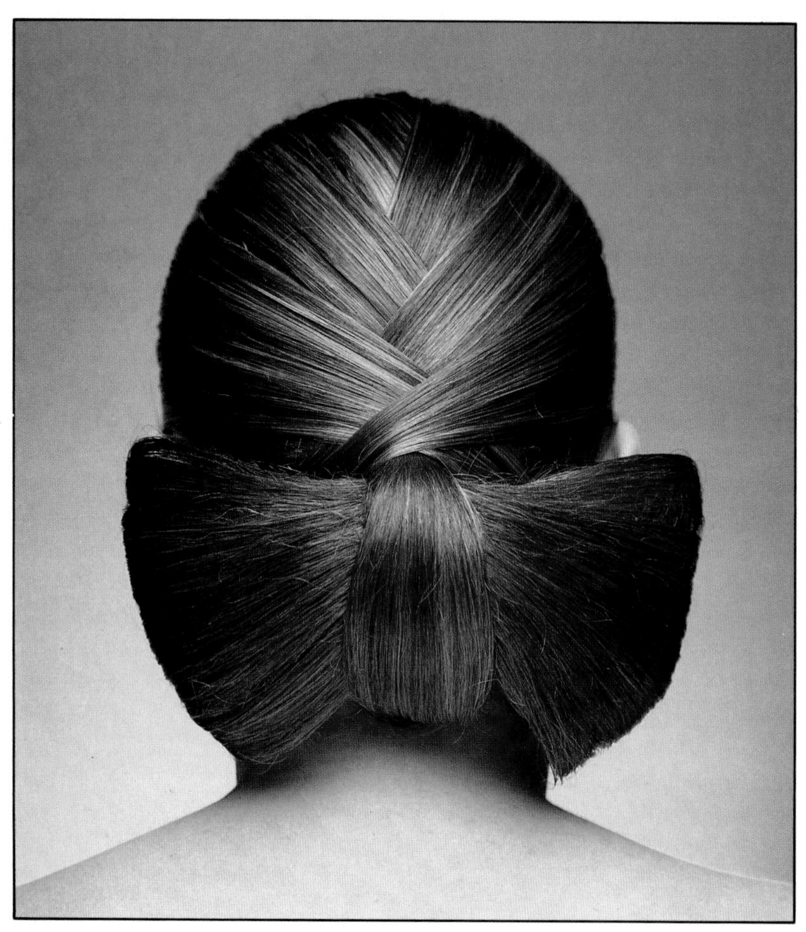

Above: a sleek, sophisticated creation, perfect for that special occasion.
Far right: ornamental combs and pins; the easiest way to enhance the simplest style and cover tell-tale grips and pins.

The popularity of long hair has waxed and waned according to the whims of fashion. But there are those who, regardless of fashion, will always wear their hair long, and this is just the way it should be, providing of course that long, flowing locks suit you.

Now, more than ever, styles for long hair have greater versatility: from simple braids and chignons to complicated and intricate woven designs. Improved permanent waving products and techniques allow for more scope, so that long hair need not be left just to hang, like Alice in Wonderland's, but can be permed and curled, depending on its texture and condition.

For many, long hair epitomises the ultimate in femininity, and this attitude applies to both men and women. Perhaps it is a leftover from our cave dwelling heritage, when stone-age man dragged his mate off to his lair by her hair. Does long hair bring out the beast in a man, and is this why so many of us have to grow our hair at least once in the hopes that a virile 'he man' will suddenly appear? Joking apart, once we are old enough to choose our hair's length and style, we all usually go through a long hair phase before finding the style that complements the image we wish to project. For some people long hair will be retained as a curtain to hide behind, or because the men in their lives refuse to let them have it cut. The last reason is one I have heard time and time again over the years. Men seem to disregard the finer points, such as whether long hair suits you, or if it is of the right type and texture to grow long.

For those of you aspiring to long hair here are a few points you should take into consideration.

a Will it suit me – i.e. my facial characteristics?

b Can I cope with it? Shampooing, condition and drying, take more time; long hair must be kept clean and swingy to look good.

c Can I dress my hair into an upswept style myself should the occasion demand?

d Will it fit in with my lifestyle, clothes, job, leisure, etc?

e Am I prepared to have regular haircuts to keep it in peak condition?

f Have I the right type of hair to grow long?

Let's consider each of those points in more detail.

Suitability requires little explanation and depends entirely on the individual. If you already have long hair or are growing it, correct shampooing and conditioning are

Above: hair ornaments come in an amazing variety of shapes and colours. Some of the materials used are pretty unusual as well, ranging from basic plastic to tortoiseshell or leather and crystal as shown here.
Right: the better the equipment, the easier it is to style your hair. Good quality brushes, combs, dryers and rollers are a boon. Don't forget the fun items like bands, bows and even shock waves and colour flashes to brighten your hair.
Far right: plaited strips of suede make simple but effective headgear, especially when coordinated with your outfit.

vitally important. Follow the guidelines described in the previous chapters. Choose a mild shampoo and always use a conditioner. Invest in a wide-toothed comb and a good hairbrush, either bristle or plastic, making sure each quill is well finished and rounded off. When combing, dry or wet, always start at the nape and work from the points (ends of the hair) towards the scalp. Take small sections at a time until all the hair is combed through; never brush wet hair straight after shampooing, use a comb. If your hair is greasy apply conditioner to middle lengths and ends only, and do not massage into the scalp. Drying: dry naturally whenever possible. If the hair is to be set, then part dry before putting in rollers, protect fragile ends with a small square of tissue. Blowdrying: always remember to direct the air down the hair shaft with the cuticle; never aim the air up from points to roots, if you do you will raise the cuticle, damaging the hair, and the result will be dull, fuzzy, split hair. Never use a very hot dryer close to the hair and always keep the hot air moving.

Naturally, the size roller or brush you use will depend on whether your hair is curly or straight and the degree of curl required: e.g. the smaller the brush or roller the tighter the curl and vice versa. Do bear in mind that the weight of your hair will affect the amount of curl and its holding power. For example, very thick, heavy, straight hair will drop fairly quickly.

The more classical, upswept styles require a good foundation; the roots must move upwards or back, in the direction of the finished style. Therefore, when you are setting try to imagine the final result and place your rollers accordingly. If you're blow drying, lift the hair with your fingers or a brush and dry thoroughly in an upward direction. This is also a good tip if you intend to wear your hair down and want it to look full and bouncy. Always apply a setting

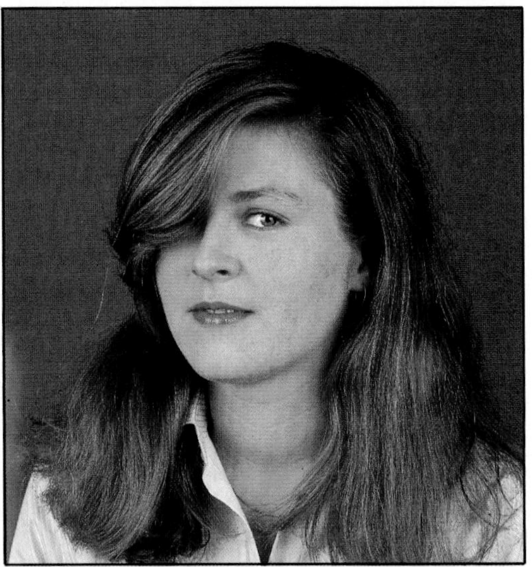

1 Long hair can be a problem on holiday, especially after a day at the beach. Here's a colourful way to pretty up your hair.
2 After shampooing, gather all the wet hair into a high ponytail.

important date it's wise to experiment a little beforehand. Hopefully, the step by step illustrations shown here will help you. It's a good idea to purchase plenty of hairgrips, fine hairpins, hairspray and some covered elastic bands – you could be surprised at how many you will need!

Padded shapes to help support a full hairstyle come in very handy, particularly if you are not very adept at backcombing. These used to be made from hair combings but nowadays synthetic hair is substituted. Pads come in a variety of shapes and sizes: long sausage shapes, ovals rounds and basic colours such as blonde, brown, black and red. Pinned onto the head they add fullness and eliminate the need for excessive backcombing; the hair is simply

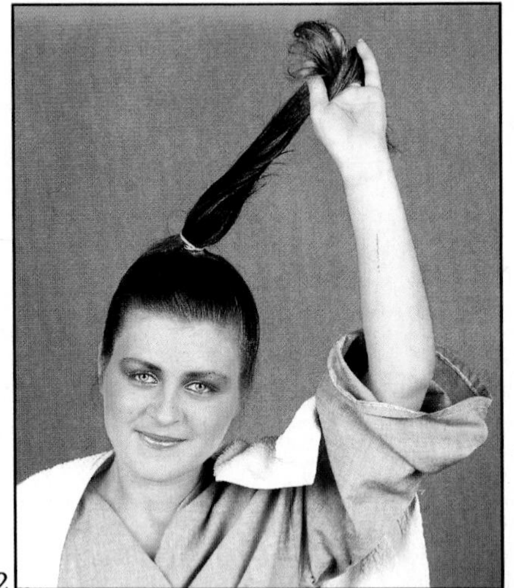

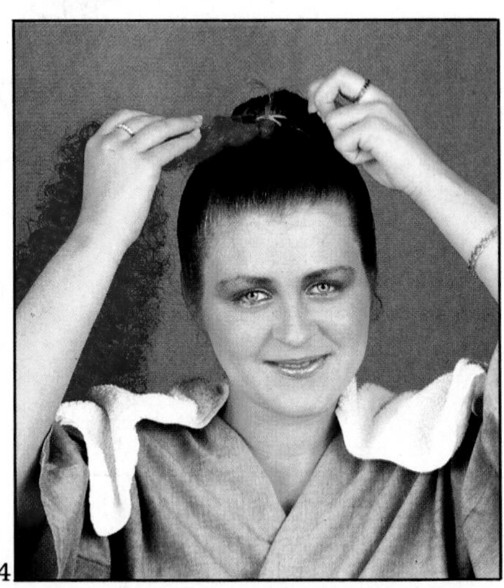

3 Apply gel to the front, sides and nape to keep stray ends in place.
4 Take one very long, brightly coloured switch and pin it firmly in front of the ponytail.
5 Gel ponytail and wrap it around the base of the switch. Secure ends round the bun with hair pins.
6 Cover any visible pins with a ringlet around the base of the bun.
7 A cascade of colour. This is a quick and novel way to brighten up your hair and a definite eye catcher.

lotion of some description prior to drying as this will prevent your hair from going too soft and flyaway.

Dressing your hair into an upswept, classical style will require patience and practice, so if you're preparing for an

1 The following style is great for wavy, layered hair like Ashley's. If your hair is straight, it's a good idea to curl it first.
2 Section the hair from ear to ear over the crown. Divide front into three – top and two sides – part off a small square on the crown and place remaining hair in a ponytail.
3 Smooth square crown section down close to ponytail and grip just above it; use hairspray to control stray ends.
4 Smooth left side back and over to the right side of the ponytail. Grip close to band.
5 Repeat with right side section, gripping close to left side of ponytail.
6 Use an Afro-type comb to fluff out ponytail.

smoothed over the padding and discreetly pinned.

Plain, simple hairstyles are the perfect foil for hair ornaments. It's a good idea to begin a collection of hair accessories such as pretty silk flowers, ribbons, slides and ornamental combs. If you're lucky enough to visit the Far East, watch out for some exquisite hair slides, combs and pins, especially the hand-painted, lacquered variety, as they are usually very resonably priced.

Our lifestyles affect everything we do and wear. If your hair only looks good when it's dressed up, perhaps you should consider a shorter style. But, if you're an aspiring ballet dancer, then long hair is a must as it will have to be worn in a sleek, tight chignon most of the time. These days we have less and less time to pamper ourselves, and if your hair encroaches into your leisure and social life then a style reappraisal is necessary. Long hair obviously takes longer to do than short hair and requires that bit extra care, but for day-to-day styling you should be fairly adept at handling it and not have to spend hours in front of the mirror every morning.

Is your hair of the right type and texture to grow long? There is really only one type of hair that I feel is best worn at a shorter length and this is very fine, thin, fragile hair. If you have this problem hair you have probably already found that it is difficult to grow long. Being so weak it tends to break and split very easily, and the additional length puts more strain on the delicate fibres. Very thick, curly hair has its own problems. There is a tendency for this type of hair to be dry and unruly. As it grows it seems to get wider rather than longer and it is not until it passes the shoulders that there is sufficient weight to keep it down and looking long. However, with perseverance and regular treatments long hair can be yours.

Cutting is vitally important even when you're trying to grow your hair. Six-weekly trims remove unsightly split ends which, left untended, will travel up the hair shaft and require far more drastic cutting than a mere quarter of an inch. It's hard to part with your hair when you're trying to grow it, even the minutest snippet, but remember there is no point in having long hair if it looks like a dried-up haystack.

Hot brushes, curling tongs and heated rollers are a great way to boost any hairstyle, but particularly long hair. Heated rollers add body, curl, and root lift; perfect if you want to put your hair up. Hot brushes and tongs smooth out frizzy hair and create bounce and curl – especially beneficial for those who prefer casual styles. When using any appliance that invloves direct heat being applied to the hair, take care. Bear in mind that your hair may be over six years old at the points and very fragile; protect the ends of your hair with tissue or wind the hair around the rollers or tongs, starting at the roots, so that the ends come into contact with the heat last of all.

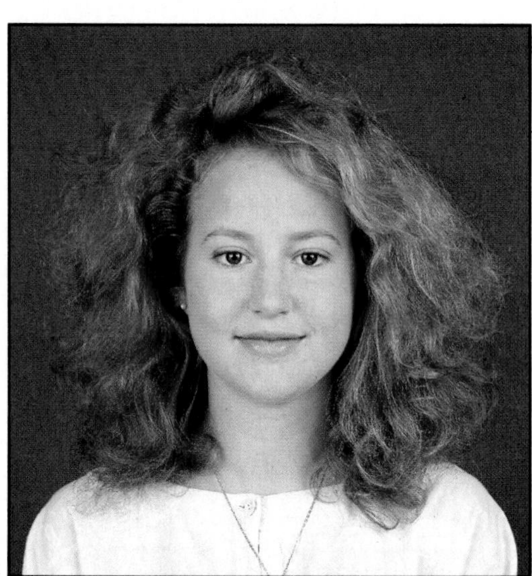
1

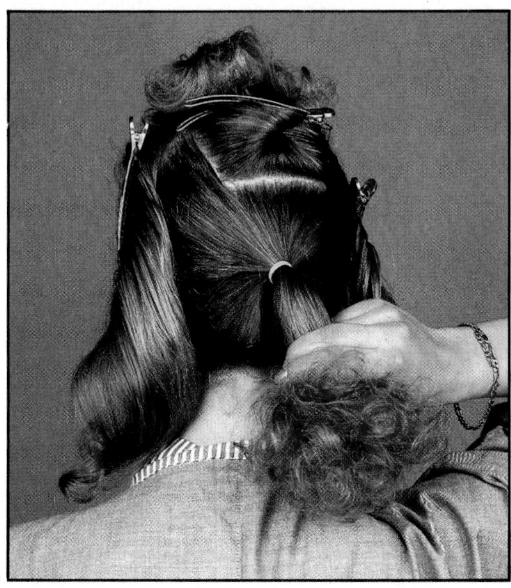
2

Some timely tips: for a really way-out, curly look try setting your hair in rags. Work with small sections of hair on clean, almost dry, hair. The longer you leave them in, the curlier you'll go. If rags don't appeal, invest in a set of special rollers (available from major stores and hairdressers), similar to a long frankfurter, which are very soft and pliable. The hair is twisted and wound around the roller which is then bent over to

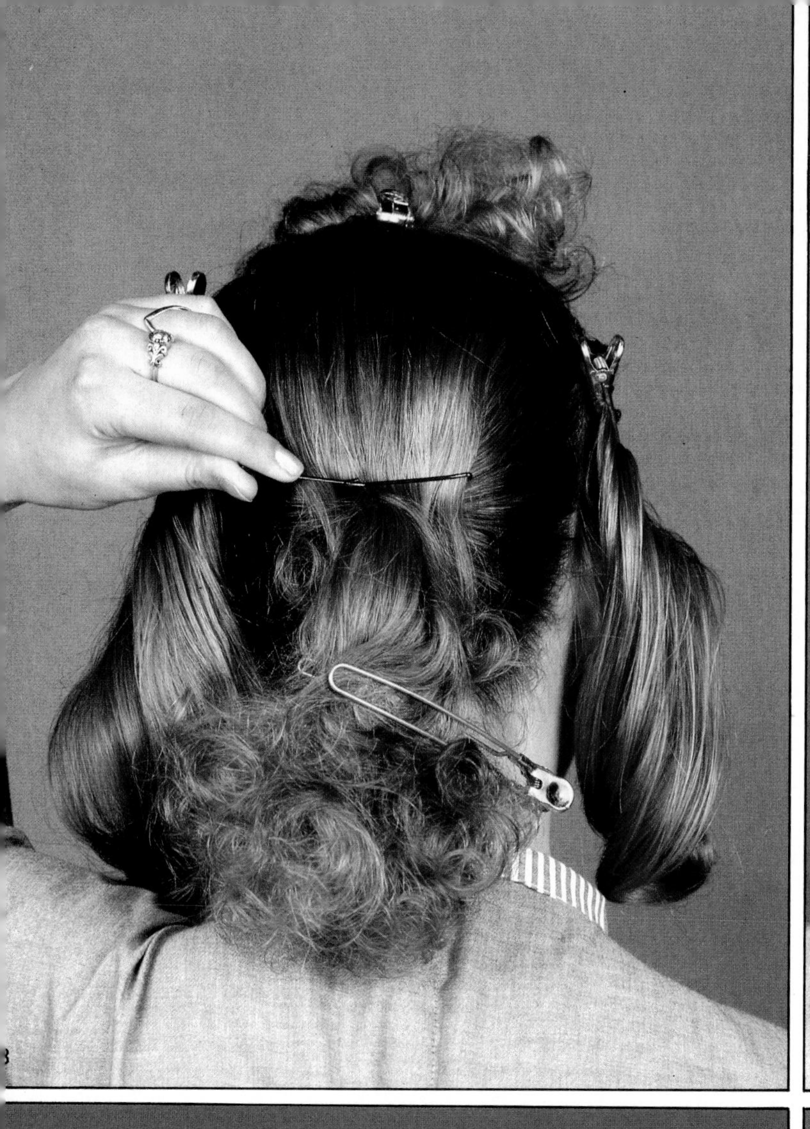
3

4

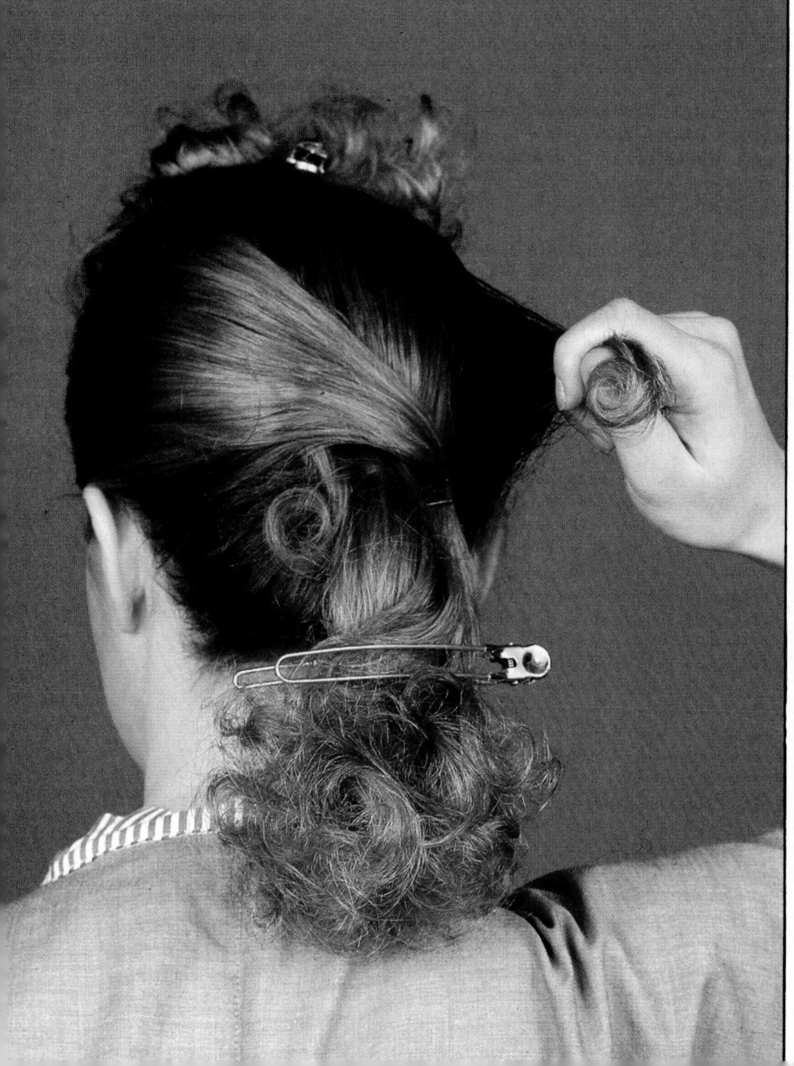

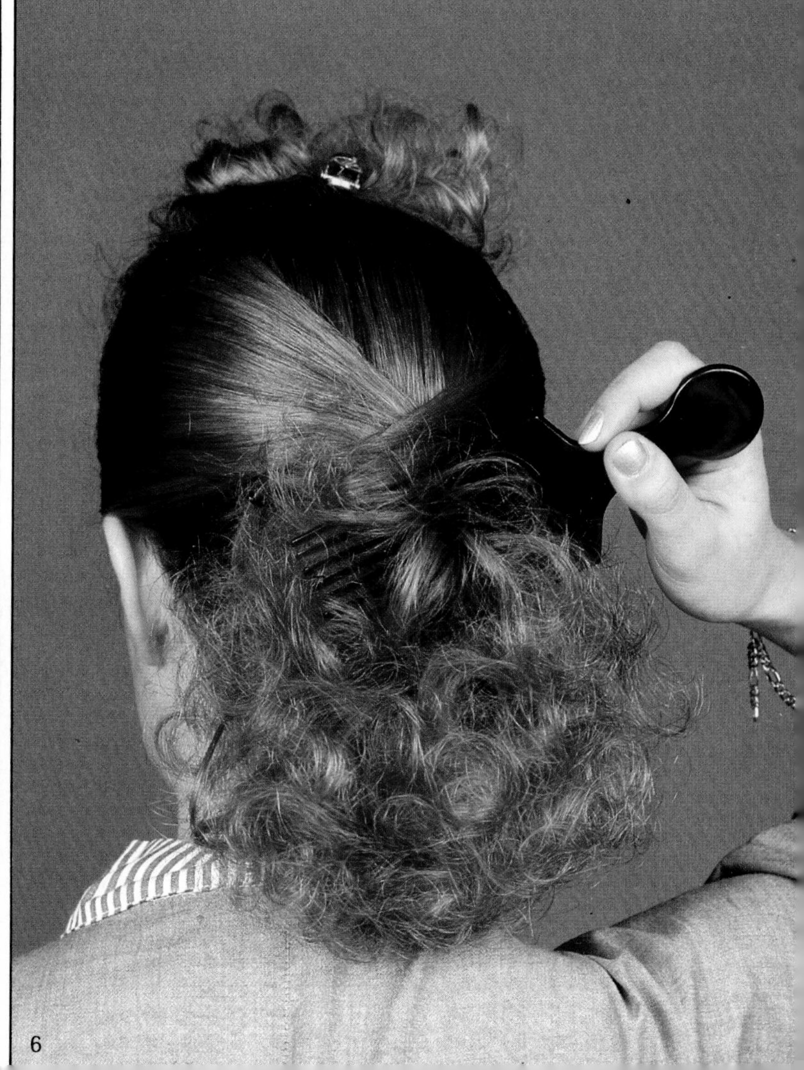
6

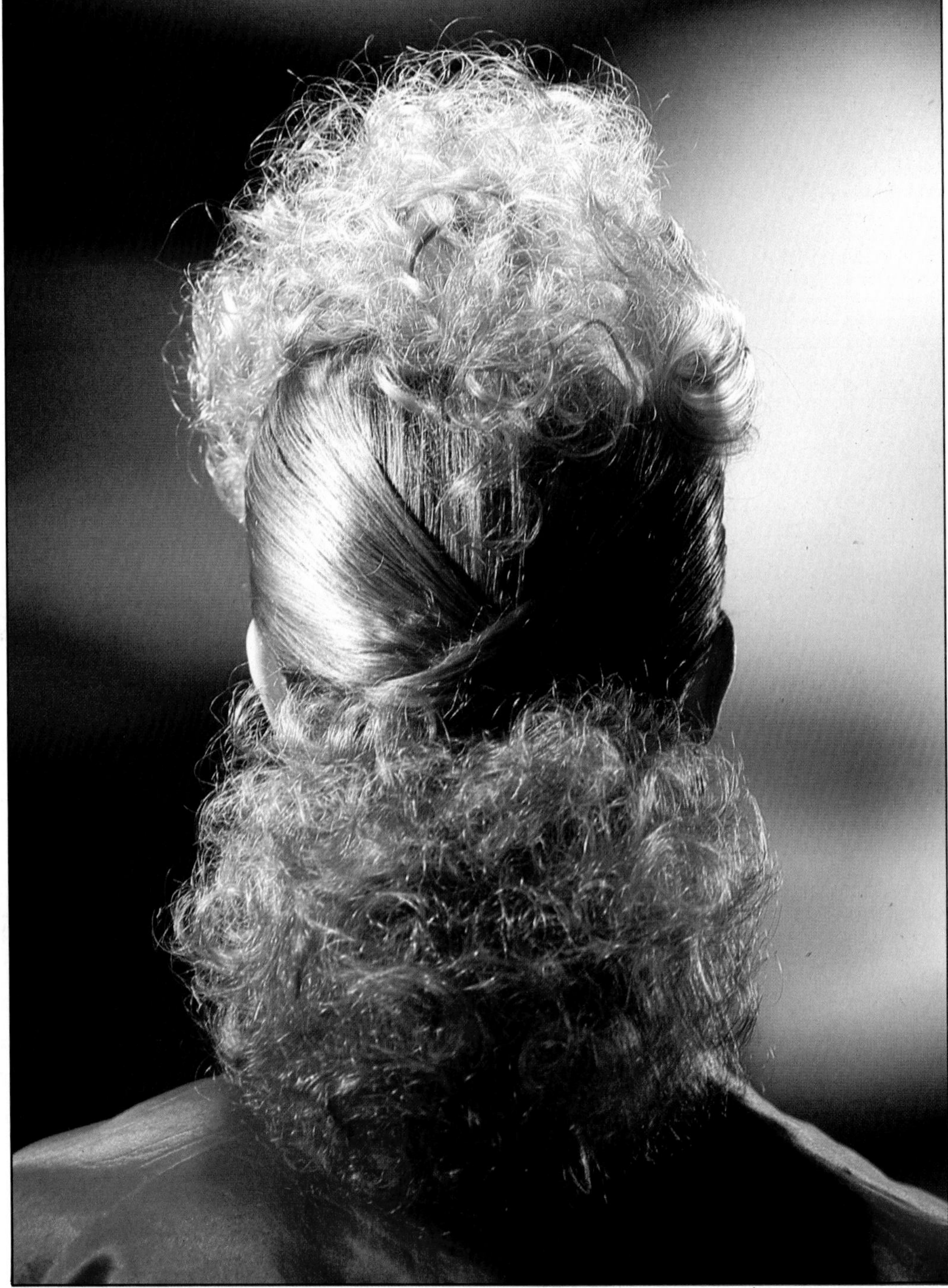

Right: with the ponytail fluffed out, release final top section, fluff out and spray into position as if dressing out shorter hair. This style provides a great contrast in textures ranging from very sleek to a froth of curl.
Facing page: this is an extra, simpler style consisting of just two ponytails, one positioned behind the ear the other at the front, at a diagonal to the first. Backcomb and fluff out both ponytails. Spray and add the finishing touch with two ornamental chop-sticks.

secure it – no pins required. They are great fun to use and less damaging to the hair than small, spiky, plastic rollers.

Permanent waves and colours: long hair should only be permed or coloured by a qualified hairdresser. Never attempt to do it yourself at home. It's worth bearing in mind that if anything goes wrong it can only be cut out, thereby removing many years of growth with one fell swoop of the scissors. If you would like a perm don't expect to get lots of lift and bounce at the roots; this can only be achieved if the hair is cut shorter on top or in layers, blending from short over the top and crown to very long at the back. So, be prepared to part with some of your hair if your heart is set on a long, full, curly look.

Finally, nothing beats a head of long hair that gleams with health and swings as you walk, and we all envy those with such beautiful hair. Who knows, perhaps the modern version of stone-age man is waiting just around the next corner!

CHAPTER 30

The Elegant Fifties

Facing page: looking attractive is not the prerogative of the young. As long as one adapts one's beauty and haircare routine to suit the changes in skin tone and hair texture, good looks can be yours for life.

By far and away the greatest physical changes likely to happen to a woman in her late forties to early fifties are caused by the menopause. Hopefully, along with these changes you will have reached a phase in your life when you have more time to relax, adjust and take stock of yourself. A few women will experience the effects of the menopause as early as forty, but for the majority it will occur around the age of fifty. The physical aspects are now widely discussed in magazines and home medical books, but what of the effects on your hair?

As with the onset of puberty, your hormones will be going through quite a change, affecting your mood and appearance. One effect of the change may result in some hair loss. This can also be due to the stress and tension you are feeling at the time, but there is no reason why the hair loss should be excessive, so do consult your doctor if it is worrying you. Your hair can also feel dryer and the scalp more sensitive, so choose a shampoo for dry hair, and condition regularly. Grey/white hair has a natural tendency to appear dry, more dry in fact than hair that has been coloured. This does not mean that the lady in her fifties with golden blonde hair has not got similar problems; it's just that natural or tinted hair reflects light and therefore seems to be healthier and more shiny. Dry hair will often be accompanied by a dry skin, so plenty of moisturizer for your complexion and regular moisturizing/protein packs for your hair.

The circulation may become sluggish and a good scalp massage will work wonders, helping to relieve tension and stimulating the blood supply to the hair follicle and papilla.

Common problems for many women are night sweats and hot flushes. The sudden rise in body temperature causes excessive sweating and your hair reacts by going limp and flat, sticking untidily to your skin, especially around the hairline. Although distressing and uncomfortable, the last thing you should worry about is your hair; wait until you have cooled down and the sweating has subsided before you attempt to restyle it. During this time it is advisable to keep the hairstyle soft and unfussy, in a shape that can be washed daily and left to dry naturally or quickly blowdried. It is now that a good haircut will pay dividends and be worth every penny. A soft perm if your hair is limp will add body, although it is worth pointing out that perms are not always terribly successful at this time, especially if you are on certain medications. The important thing is to keep your hair and scalp clean.

If you normally go to the salon for a weekly hairdo, then continue, but do not get upset if the style drops more quickly. For your own comfort avoid sitting under a hot dryer for obvious reasons. A visit to the hairdresser at this stage should be looked on as a morale booster and a time to unwind. Save any grandiose ideas about elaborate styles until your body has adjusted.

It must be said that some women go through the menopause fairly smoothly and those on Hormone Replacement Therapy (HRT) seem to suffer very few adverse effects such as hot flushes, etc.

Paradoxically, as the hair on the scalp can thin slightly at this time so the hair on the face, particularly the upper lip, can increase. You may find this distressing but it is a very common problem and one that very dark haired people have to cope with every day of their lives. If your facial hair is fine and downy then a mild bleach is all that's required to lighten and soften the hair (facial bleaches are available from most good chemists). Stronger, coarser hair needs sterner treatment, such as electrolysis, which is the only permanent method of hair removal. If this is a method you would like to try, do ensure that you consult a fully qualified person and don't

From facial hair back to hairstyles. Eventually, the menopause will be behind you, the only children you have to look after will be grandchildren, and your life is now your own. Perhaps you still work or are involved in charity work of some kind. It's a great help to get out and become involved with some outside venture that encourages you to mix with people of all ages, and keeps you looking and feeling young and conscious of your appearance. After all, it does not follow that your hairstyle changes to fingerwaves and a hairnet when you turn fifty.

Choose your hairstyle to suit you and your lifestyle. As we age, softer, face-framing styles are more flattering; hard, flat, scraped-back styles only tend to emphasize lines and wrinkles. Try not to let your hair get untidy; wild looks only look sexy on the young. Age must compensate with confidence and elegance; something that is acquired with maturity.

If you want to try a new style, think carefully: is a twice-weekly shampoo and set better for you than a monthly cut which you have to blow dry? This is not because I doubt anyone's ability to blow dry their own hair, but if you suffer from stiffness, rheumatism or arthritis you may find it difficult to hold a blow dryer above shoulder level for a long period of time. If you have the right quality of hair, the ideal style is a perfect cut and easy blow dry, but,

1

1 Pam has lovely grey hair that she normally blow dries. The soft shape is supported by a body perm.
2 To set, use a styling aid. Pam uses a pearl mousse, which adds a subtle silver tone.
3 Smooth ends over roller and wind down. Secure with plastic pin.
4 Massage mousse through evenly from roots to points.

2

3

5 Comb hair in direction to be set. Part a small mesh of hair the same size as roller.
6 Side hair is set in loose pin curls towards back, top rolled to side, crown back.
7 When dry, brush vigorously to blend roller sections. If set is too tight, relax with the blow dryer.

attempt to do it yourself with some sort of home kit; the result could be permanent scarring. Other methods include shaving, a definite NO to this one, and waxing. Waxing is not really suitable for older skins because of facial lines and lack of elasticity, and the majority of manufacturers advise against it. Depilatory creams are cheaper, if rather smelly; ensure that the one you purchase is suitable for the face and follow the directions to the letter. At the first sign of irritation rinse immediately with cold water.

5

7

Complete the style with the fingers or a tailcomb. The secret when styling grey hair is not to create hard, rigid lines but to keep the movements soft and flowing. That subtle hint of pearly silver complements Pam's hair and skin tone perfectly.

unfortunately, few of us are blessed with such good-tempered hair.

Hair colours should be subtle. Grey/white hair can look very striking, but beware of yellowness caused by cooking, coal fires and smoking. If you style your own hair then always keep a bottle of silver-coloured setting or blow dry lotion handy; it won't turn your hair blue but it will help to neutralise those yellow tones. If your hair is salt and pepper, try a steel-grey or neutralising ash rinse for a deeper blend of light and dark hair.

Semi-permanent colours help to blend in the grey hair or freshen up hair that looks dull and faded. It's fine to blend in white hair, but do avoid going very dark as it's unlikely to enhance your complexion.

Permanent tints last longer and give better coverage of white hair. Do follow manufacturers' directions if you're tinting at home and, once again, not too dark or exotic. Choose soft browns or blondes with gold or warm tones as these will reflect warmth into your skin, rather than very ash tones which, on a mature person, can make the skin look very pale and ill even though they're fighting fit.

Money can be a problem when a pension has to be stretched to cover all the bills. If you're over sixty, keep an eye on your local salon for special offers, reduced rates, and discounts for senior citizens. Usually, these offers are at the beginning of the week, when salons are quieter, and it can mean a great saving on the normal prices.

CHAPTER 31

True or False

1 With the aid of a wig it's all change for Anita.
2 The hair must first be flattened and evenly distributed. Anita divides her hair into small sections.
3 The sections are curled and fixed with grips close to the scalp.

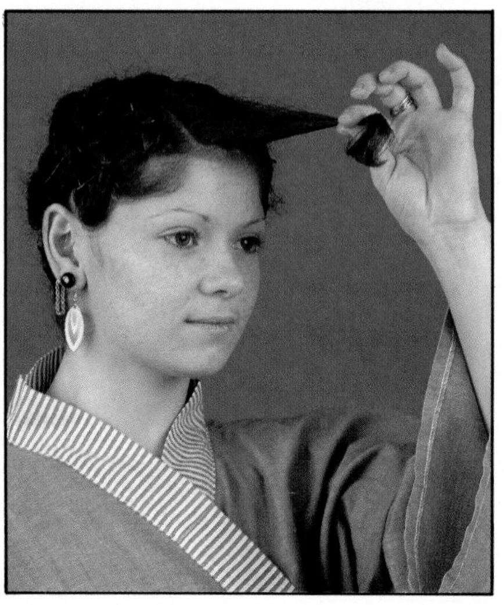

4 Hold the wig at the front by the ear pieces. With the front of the wig low over the forehead, slide it on keeping ear sections level. Hold firmly at front and pull down into the nape. Slide front edge back to the natural hairline and check that the sides are level. Adjust elastic inside wig for a snug fit. Style to frame face.
Facing page: the final effect.

The idea of using hair (other than your own) to adorn your head is not a twentieth century innovation. Look back over the centuries and you will find that both men and women have often worn wigs. In fact, at one point in time the most exotic and glamorous wigs were worn mainly by men. However, modern wigs are a far cry from those heavy, cumbersome and often smelly creations.

Today's wigs really started life in the fifties and sixties, as until then all postiche (correct term for added hair) had to be made by hand. This time-consuming method made them very expensive and put wigs and hairpieces out of the reach of the average person, who simply wanted a temporary change of style for fun or convenience.

During the sixties, machine-made wigs appeared on the scene; made from refined Asian hair (made to feel like European hair) they were cheap and plentiful. Everybody loved them and your wardrobe was not complete without at least one wig. Unfortunately, the international demand for these wigs puts a severe strain on the amount of Asian hair available; after all, it takes a long time to grow hair long enough to be cut off and made into a wig. So what was the solution? It was to develop a synthetic fibre that looks and feels like hair. This was duly accomplished and many new, improved fibres have been created since.

If you haven't looked at a wig for the last ten years you could be in for a surprise, as nowadays the base (foundation) is light and stretchy, allowing the scalp underneath to breathe. Natural-looking partings and breaks eliminate that 'wiggy' look.

Presuming that we have rekindled a spark of interest in false hair, let's take a look at the reasons for owning a wig or hairpiece.

One of the main reasons has got to be fun. You can try different colours and lengths of hair, it can be curly or straight, and your own hair remains intact underneath. For people who never manage to grow their hair it's a chance to have long, flowing locks and, of course, vice versa. Or, maybe your life is very hectic and having a couple of wigs or dressed hairpieces all ready to slip on could save your time and temper.

Another and more serious reason for acquiring a wig is hair loss. This could be due to an accident, illness or certain medical treatments.

From the reasons why, to where to buy. If you're looking for a large, ready-made, ready-to-wear collection to choose from, walk into virtually any major department store and you should find a range of wigs in both synthetic fibres and human hair. If this idea doesn't appeal ask at your hairdressers, although the disadvantage is that many salons no longer stock wigs, so your choice whill have to be made from a catalogue. It will then have to be ordered and, as with mail order clothes, you may not like it when it arrives. The most expensive way to purchase a wig is to have one made to measure. A hand-made wig or hairpiece is costly, but the fit will be superb and the colour mixed to your preference. Your hairdresser may make wigs, if not they should be able to put you in touch with a reputable wig maker.

What type of hair? European hair is beautiful and, of course, very expensive. Asian hair wigs are far cheaper, they can be set, blow dried, backcombed and styled and will resist a degree of rough handling. But if you're completely hopeless at styling hair why not try one of the excellent synthetic wigs? Permanently styled, they are easy to maintain as, after washing the curl just bounces right back. You can put rollers in but it's not advisable to use tongs, heated rollers or blow dryers on made-made fibres.

Choose your wig with care; I know I said they are fun but you don't want to look ridiculous. Try them on in front of a full-length mirror so that you get a good idea of balance and can see everything in proportion. Some wigs can be very overpowering, in fact they can make you look like a mass of hair on legs.

Hairpieces also come in a variety of fibres, sizes and lengths. These are ideal if you want to add extra length or bulk to your hair. They can be dressed into plaits, ringlets, sleek curls or freaky curls and pinned onto your own, slicked-back hair.

Once you have made your purchase take it along to your hairdresser so that they can personalise the wig for you and give you some additional tips on care.

Wearing a wig. If your hair is very short it will easily tuck under the foundation, but if it is medium to long then you must reduce the bulk and length first. Begin by taking fairly large sections of hair and winding each into a large, flat pin curl, and secure every curl with grips. Try to position the curls evenly over the scalp. Now hold the wig at the sides with the front hairline low over your forehead and slide the wig back to your front hairline, checking that the sides are level over the ears. Hold onto the front and pull the wig down towards the nape then, using a tail comb, tuck under any stray, wispy hairs. Dress to frame your face. One trick you can use if your wig and natural hair match in colour is to leave some of your natural hair out around the front hairline and dress this over the edge of the wig. Never style your wig straight back as a hard, artificial hairline will soon give the game away.

Taking care of your new hair. Wigs will stay in shape longer and be easier to style if you always keep them on a wig block. You have probably seen these heads in stores; made of light-weight polystyrene they are relatively inexpensive and will keep your wig neat. Brush and comb gently, taking care not to snag the foundation. With regard to cleaning, real hair wigs may require professional cleaning but always read the manufacturer's directions, and wash and style according to their recommendations.

Recently, there has been a surge of interest in synthetic hairpieces. Long wefts of synthetic hair in natural or vibrant colours are being semi-permanently attached to the hair. This is called hair weaving, derived from long established black hairdressing techniques, which has become a popular way to have instant, long hair. Tiny meshes of natural hair are first braided or woven with thread very tightly to the scalp, the synthetic or real hair wefts are attached by sewing. It is a long, time-consuming business but will last for several weeks before it need be repeated. Single ringlets or plaits (dreadlocks and bobtails) are attached in a similar manner but each

Facing page: another wig, this time in a classic bob design.

Right: as an actress, Janey loved the idea of projecting a different image by wearing a wig (facing page).

lock of hair is attached individually.

Above all, act naturally when you're wearing a wig or hairpiece; try not to keep patting it to see if it's still there or asking people if they can tell; of course they can if you make it so obvious. Wear it with confidence and panache, and enjoy the new you.

At this point it seems appropriate to include a little advice for you to pass on to the man in your life. It's an unfortunate fact of life that some men will inevitably lose their hair. Many will not like it, but a gradual acceptance will prevail. Others rebel against nature's outrageous mistake and, having tried all the lotions and potions around to no avail, resort to more drastic methods. This is where you can help, first and foremost by making sure he visits a reputable trichologist who can check that the scalp is healthy and that the hair loss is normal (male pattern baldness). Now he can decide on which method of adding hair he prefers.

A toupee is the most common way of covering baldness. Hand or machine-made, they can look great but usually look appalling. If this method is contemplated then have one made to measure so that the colour can be matched and it can be fitted and styled properly. One only has to look at some of the presumably comfortably-off personalities on TV and films sporting 'hearth rugs' to have doubts about the benefits of a toupee.

Hair weaving. We have already mentioned this for women and it can look very natural. Unlike a toupee it will not come off, so it's great for sports enthusiasts. Either fine meshes of hair are attached individually to your own hair, or a light-weight, washable toupee is woven or sewn onto a weft made from your own hair. Take it from someone who used to perform this operation: the first few days can be agony as the weave must be tight to start. Every six weeks, as the hair grows, the whole process must be repeated.

Transplants. Punch grafting is a popular technique and seems to be in favour with celebrities. Small grafts or plugs of hair and scalp are transferred from one area of the head to another. It's only possible to do a certain number of grafts in one session, so several sessions may be necessary. Rejection of the donor hairs is always a problem: but many people seem happy with the results once the tufted, lumpy effects of the initial grafts subside.

Scalp reduction is another possible solution. As the name implies, small areas of the bald scalp are surgically removed and the rest of the scalp is drawn gently together to fill in the space. Depending on the degree of baldness it may take one, two or three operations before the hair meets properly.

These techniques involve the use of local anesthetics and require surgical skill, so do ensure that you consult a reputable surgeon who specialises in transplants, etc.

Maybe, like me, you prefer a man to be bald if that is what nature decreed. But please don't let anyone you care for cultivate four hairs to a great length so that they can be carefully spread over a bald pate. Keep hair short and sharp as it's far more stylish. Anyway, I seem to remember reading that a bald head indicates a very sexy man!

CHAPTER 32

The Portfolio

In this, the final chapter, we take a closer look at the more avant-garde side of hairdressing, when all thoughts of practicality are disregarded.

Hair, to a creative hairstylist, is like clay or wood to a sculptor; a medium which can be moulded and shaped into a pleasing form. Or, it can be like an artist's canvas, just waiting for some colour to bring it to life.

Hairdressers always enjoy the challenge and opportunity to let their imaginations run riot. But, unfortunately, creating unusual designs can be a long and time-consuming business which is not compatible with the day-to-day running of a salon.

Weird and wonderful creations are not the perogative of this decade. In centuries past women have been known to sport galleons or even birds in cages entwined in their hair. We no longer resort to such extremes but, thanks to the manufacturers – like Wella – we have products and equipment which allow us to work with the hair as never before.

In recent years we have seen hats made of hair and not artificial hair either; some have been smooth, others have been intricately woven. And in colours that no one would have dreamed of twenty years ago. And now the latest innovation – hair extensions. Walk into a salon with short

Above: Andy is the perfect model for an extravagant hair creation.
Above right: a giant crest peaks over the forehead.
Facing page: green glitter completes this 'Gala' style.

Above: shades of Romeo and Juliet seem to echo through the theme of this hair design, while Melissa (facing page) goes turban-style with a tumble of fake and real curls.

hair and walk out, a few hours later, with long hair. Virtually nothing is impossible and in the world of hairdressing we are continually changing and evolving.

The majority of photographs in this chapter do not show hairstyles that you can try at home or ones that you would wear every day. However, they do give you an indication of what can be achieved if you and your hairdresser have the time.

So, if you feel like causing a sensation one night and think that nothing can be done to your hair – think again – our photographs tell a very different story.

Below: model Jennifer prepares herself for two dramatic changes.
Right: change number one is entitled 'Silver Fox' – pastel blonde hair with black tips.
Facing page: change number two 'Close crop' – a look that's so very striking on blonde hair.

Overleaf: added colour for that vivacious look.

Below: casually-elegant hair design for the girl-about-town.
Right and facing page: black and white hair extensions were added to Sonia's hair; some stand up in plumes while other cascade over the shoulders. Hair, clothes and make-up were all designed to complement one another and create the 'total image'.

Overleaf, left: 'Bird of Paradise' – all the colours of the rainbow flow through the hair as it fans out from the head.

Overleaf, right: 'Blonde on Blonde' – subtle shades of blonde combine for a natural effect. Backcombing exaggerates the shape as it curls over the eye.

Right: 'Ultra Chic' – a short, heavily-texturised style that has that spiky feel and yet still looks feminine as long tendrils of hair feather onto the face.
Facing page: 'Chopped Bob' – the modern version that bears little resemblance to the original bob; short, layered and very casual. Subtle shades of red and gold mingle to emphasise the tousled look.

Overleaf: the sultry, sexy look that epitomises today's approach to long hair by combing short and long lengths to create this voluminous shape which perfectly balances the popular, wide-shouldered fashions. Photograph courtesy of Wella.